The Role of Crises in Shaping Financial Systems

AF766705

The Role of Crises in Shaping Financial Systems: From the Global Financial Crisis to COVID-19 underscores the role of crises as turning points for the financial sector and its interactions with the real economy. It sheds new light on the financial industry through the lens of three recent crises – the global financial crisis, the sovereign debt crisis, and the COVID-19 pandemic. The book provides in-depth insight into the financial systems in European Economic Area countries, accentuating the role of crises in shaping the condition and development of the financial arena. The authors pay special attention to the differences between "old" and "new" Europe, i.e. countries that joined the EU in 2004 or later. It explores the implications of recent turbulences for financial institutions, financial markets, and public finance, and their relationship with the economy. The book examines low or negative interest rates, non-standard monetary policy, fiscal stimulus, dense safety nets, regulatory inflation, weak profitability of the financial sector, and the sovereign-bank nexus. Post-crisis developments are assessed, comprehensively and empirically, from both macro- and microeconomic perspectives to help readers understand the nature of policy measures and their socio-economic implications.

The authors outline their predictions for the future of financial systems, focusing on the structural changes and legacy of the COVID-19 crisis and global financial interlinkages.

The book adopts both theoretical and practical approaches to explore the key issues and, as such, will appeal to academics and students of financial economics and international finance, as well as policymakers and financial regulators.

Małgorzata Iwanicz-Drozdowska is a Full Professor of Economics and Finance and Head of the Financial System Department at SGH Warsaw School of Economics, Poland.

Elżbieta Malinowska-Misiąg is an Assistant Professor at the Financial System Department, SGH Warsaw School of Economics, Poland.

Piotr Mielus is an Associate Professor of Economics and Finance at SGH Warsaw School of Economics, Poland.

Paweł Smaga is an Associate Professor at the Financial System Department, SGH Warsaw School of Economics, Poland.

Bartosz Witkowski is a Full Professor of Economics and Head of the Institute of Econometrics at SGH Warsaw School of Economics, Poland.

Banking, Money and International Finance

26. Global Stock Market Development
Quantitative and Behavioural Analysis
Marcin Kalinowski

27. The Digitalization of Financial Markets
The Socioeconomic Impact of Financial Technologies
Edited by Adam Marszk and Ewa Lechman

28. The Digital Disruption of Financial Services
International Perspectives
Edited by Ewa Lechman and Adam Marszk

29. The Economics and Finance of Commodity Price Shocks
Mikidadu Mohammed

30. Digital Finance and the Future of the Global Financial System
Disruption and Innovation in Financial Services
Edited by Lech Gąsiorkiewicz and Jan Monkiewicz

31. Artificial Intelligence and Big Data for Financial Risk Management
Intelligent Applications
Edited by Noura Metawa, M. Kabir Hassan and Saad Metawa

32. The Role of Crises in Shaping Financial Systems
From the Global Financial Crisis to COVID-19
Małgorzata Iwanicz-Drozdowska, Elżbieta Malinowska-Misiąg, Piotr Mielus, Paweł Smaga, and Bartosz Witkowski

33. Insurance Market Integration in the European Union
Slawomir Ireneusz Bukowski and Marzanna Barbara Lament

For more information about this series, please visit: www.routledge.com/series/BMIF

The Role of Crises in Shaping Financial Systems

From the Global Financial Crisis to COVID-19

Małgorzata Iwanicz-Drozdowska, Elżbieta Malinowska-Misiąg, Piotr Mielus, Paweł Smaga, and Bartosz Witkowski

Routledge
Taylor & Francis Group
LONDON AND NEW YORK

First published 2023
by Routledge
4 Park Square, Milton Park, Abingdon, Oxon OX14 4RN

and by Routledge
605 Third Avenue, New York, NY 10158

Routledge is an imprint of the Taylor & Francis Group, an informa business

© 2023 Małgorzata Iwanicz-Drozdowska, Elżbieta Malinowska-Misiąg,
Piotr Mielus, Paweł Smaga and Bartosz Witkowski

The right of Małgorzata Iwanicz-Drozdowska, Elżbieta Malinowska-Misiąg,
Piotr Mielus, Paweł Smaga and Bartosz Witkowski to be identified as authors
of this work has been asserted in accordance with sections 77 and 78 of the
Copyright, Designs and Patents Act 1988.

All rights reserved. No part of this book may be reprinted or reproduced or utilised
in any form or by any electronic, mechanical, or other means, now known or
hereafter invented, including photocopying and recording, or in any information
storage or retrieval system, without permission in writing from the publishers.

Trademark notice: Product or corporate names may be trademarks or registered trademarks,
and are used only for identification and explanation without intent to infringe.

British Library Cataloguing-in-Publication Data
A catalogue record for this book is available from the British Library

Library of Congress Cataloging-in-Publication Data
LC record available at https://lccn.loc.gov/2022019576

ISBN: 978-1-032-12641-8 (hbk)
ISBN: 978-1-032-12642-5 (pbk)
ISBN: 978-1-003-22553-9 (ebk)

DOI: 10.4324/9781003225539

Typeset in Times New Roman
by Newgen Publishing UK

Contents

1 Introduction

According to the Cambridge Dictionary, a crisis is a time of great disagreement, confusion, and suffering or an extremely difficult point in a situation. Greek etymology indicates that crisis is connected with decisions. In economics, a crisis is turbulence imposing a major structural change. No doubt, in such a period of stress, all agents must take difficult decisions in uncertain circumstances. These decisions are enforced by a new state of disequilibrium that changes the rules of economic play. It is especially visible in the financial market, where turbulences are immediately transferred to market players and traded instruments.

In recent decades, we have witnessed three significant waves of disequilibria. The first is known as the Global Financial Crisis (GFC). It started in August 2007, with some depreciation of the valuation of funds engaged in credit-linked assets. It quickly brought a few minor earthquakes like Bear Sterns and Northern Rock failures, which were followed by the huge outbreak on September 15, 2008 when Lehman Brothers collapsed. The GFC shock originated on the financial and banking markets in the US, which, via a contagion mechanism, caused negative spillovers to the real economy not only in the US but also in Europe in 2008. The contagion was caused by the losses investors and banks suffered from trading "toxic" financial instruments and the burst of the real estate bubble. The key detonators of the GFC are usually described as: (i) a crash on the real estate market connected with subprime borrowers' insolvencies, (ii) leverage on derivatives, especially those linked with credit risk, that materialized in a very acute way, and (iii) mis-selling and mispricing on B2C markets that opened risk that nobody could quantify, while bearers of the risk did not understand its nature. All of this changed the level of risk on the market significantly, and undermined its most valuable asset, i.e., trust. After the initial shock, market liquidity dried up and the confidence crisis undermined the stability of financial markets. The GFC caused a demand-driven recession, where overheated housing and financial market collapse damaged economic demand, consequently depressing growth and employment in the following years. The start of the economic downturn led to credit risk materialization and a systemic banking crisis in the US and many EU countries (Iwanicz-Drozdowska et al. 2016). Thus, the GFC originated in

DOI: 10.4324/9781003225539-1

the financial system (endogenous shock) and contributed to the business cycle decline over time via demand-driven downturn. It took many months or even years for the market to recover, but the "new normal" was definitely different from the old one.

The consequences of the GFC were deep and long term, and included a rise in credit risk, a liquidity squeeze, and a shrinking of market liquidity (Soros 2008; Brunnermeier, Pedersen 2009). Some changes had structural and profound significance: disappearance of interbank term unsecured deposits, a reduction of the banks' bonds market, and increased regulatory control on derivatives and banks' balance sheets. In fact, economies survived due to the strong and fast fiscal reaction of governments and the monetary stimulus of central banks. Markets entered the age of "helicopter money" – cheap cash provided by monetary authorities (Allen, Moessner 2010).

The second destructive wave was less global and more local – it related to the euro area (or eurozone, EA). It is known as the PIIGS crisis and came from the risk of insolvency of peripheral economies of the euro area: Portugal, Italy, Ireland, Greece, and Spain. Markets were fragile after the GFC turmoil, which still created market concerns: in August 2011, the rating of the US was reduced for the first time in history. In comparison with the GFC, the sovereign debt crisis had been brewing for a long time. The first signs were visible at the turn of 2009/2010, while severe liquidity problems on the euro money market occurred in December 2011. The final accord of this turbulence was a restructuring default of Greece in March 2012 (followed by a payment default in June 2015). As a result, the market was flooded by cash coming from the quantitative easing policy of ECB (Cour-Thimann, Winkler 2012).

In contrast, the origins of the COVID-19 recession include mainly non-economic factors (the scale of the infected population and emerging virus variants). Its development was much more rapid than during the GFC. In early 2020, in response to the outbreak of pandemic in China, many countries began to introduce administrative lockdown measures and stay-at-home policies to limit the spread of the virus and the emerging health crisis. This immediately caused a drop in economic supply (and consequently demand as well), disrupted global value chains, and clogged supply lines, which directly contributed to the economic slowdown already underway in 2020 Q1. The abrupt contraction in the private sector cash flow amplified the risk of defaults on loans to consumers and businesses, raising concerns about the health of the financial system. In fact, only the first shocking strike of the COVID-19 pandemic was adverse for financial markets: spring 2020 brought depreciation of assets on capital markets and a sharp rise in risk aversion, causing liquidity problems and damming loan production (Ali et al. 2020; Zhang et al. 2020). However, markets swiftly revived due to the abundant cash assistance of anti-crisis governmental shields (stimulus packages). As there were signs of economic rebound in late 2021, the negative impact of the pandemic on the banking sector only very gradually started to materialize in 2021 and beyond. Hence, as Borio (2020) described in detail, the COVID-19 crisis was caused by an exogenous symmetric, massive shock across the global economy and induced a supply-driven recession. Put plainly, during the GFC the economy was hit by a sudden tornado that required immediate emergency response, while in the COVID-19 pandemic policymakers wished to flatten the curve of the number of infections and consciously put their economies into "medically induced comas". Nonetheless, 2021 brought new challenges: accelerating inflation, an energy crisis, and disruption of supply chains.

Both the GFC and COVID-19 crises were of global dimension. The rise in risk aversion and uncertainty were another key similarity and a factor driving crisis management policies and post-crisis economic development. Increased uncertainty led firms and private households to postpone purchase decisions, resulting in an aggregate demand shock and prolonging economic downturn. In the post-pandemic era, the fundamental uncertainty concerns both the scale and duration of the COVID-19 shock, as well as the new economic equilibrium. Such uncertainty is reflected in the heightened financial market stress, as measured by the composite indicator of systemic stress (CISS[1]) for the euro area and VIX.[2] Both CISS and VIX reached record levels during the subprime and the sovereign debt crises in the euro area (see Figure 1.1). The CISS increased at a lower rate at the outbreak of the COVID-19 pandemic – the pandemic peak was below the levels observed during the GFC.

Financial and economic crises are inherent and cyclical phenomena in market economies. History has shown that it is almost impossible to avert a crisis, so it remains an ongoing challenge to increase resilience to both expected and unexpected shocks. Financial crises often act as "game

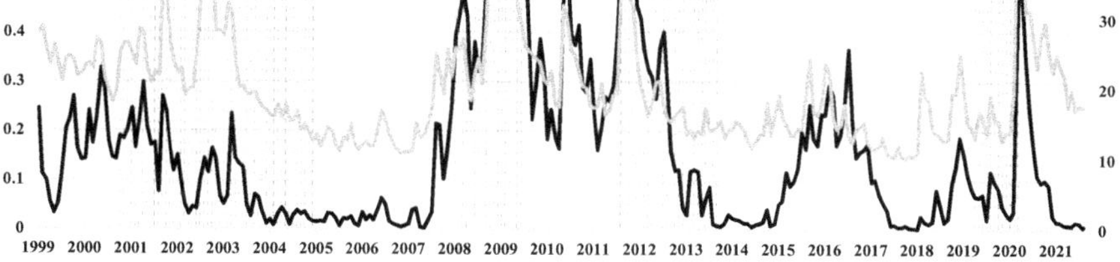

Figure 1.1 The evolution of CISS and VIX around crises in the euro area (1999–2021H1).

Note: the shaded areas represent euro area slowdowns and recessions as defined by the Eurostat Business Cycle Clock; black line – CISS for the euro area (LHS); grey line – VIX (RHS).

Source: own work based on ECB SDW, Chicago Board Options Exchange, and FRED data.

changers", leading to a re-evaluation of previous economic paradigms and to a major redesign of how the economy and financial system should function in the new, post-crisis environment. Therefore, the main goal of this book is to assess the impact of recent crises (the global financial crisis, or GFC; the sovereign debt crisis, or PIIGS; and the COVID-19 pandemic) on the financial system, the stability of the financial system, and the prudential framework in Europe. It provides significant insight into the financial systems in most of the European countries, with special attention to the European Economic Area (EEA). In order to account for differences between countries, we divide them for analytical purposes into "old" (or "developed") European countries, i.e. pre-2004 EU members (including the UK), Norway and Switzerland, and "new" (or "developing" or "emerging") European countries, i.e. the countries that have joined the EU since May 2004.[3] Additionally, where needed, we refer to the euro area due to its uniform monetary policy. As the financial systems in Europe are to a large extent bank-based, we explore the banking industry as a leading financial intermediary in Europe. The timeframe of the data analysis ends in mid-2021. In the following chapters, we explore the implications of recent financial turbulences for financial institutions, public finance, and financial markets, as well as their relationship with the real economy. Assessment of post-crisis developments is comprehensively and empirically demonstrated both from macro- and microeconomic perspectives to understand not only the short- but also the medium-term economic consequences of anti-crisis policy measures and post-crisis reforms. The methods used in this monograph include a critical review of up-to-date literature, case studies, economic analysis of the legal frameworks, and multifaceted data analysis. Each of the following chapters deals with the implications of financial crises for the safety net, monetary, prudential, and fiscal policies, financial markets, and, last but not least, the real economy.

To achieve our goal, we suggest four research hypotheses which are explored in the subsequent chapters:

> **H1**: Given the post-GFC regulatory reforms, the EU banking sector was resilient enough and suffered to a lesser extent from the impact of the COVID-19 pandemic than from GFC shock.
>
> **H2**: Although stimulus packages (including fiscal, monetary, and regulatory components) during the COVID-19 crisis were implemented faster than in the case of the GFC, the countries did not avoid an initial sharp decline in GDP.
>
> **H3**: Outbreak of a crisis creates disequilibria in the financial market, affecting especially emerging markets due to their sensitivity to the changing market sentiment. Central banks' post-crisis expansionary activities and regulatory constraints created stabilizing effects in the financial markets that influenced market prices and their volatility and market liquidity.

H4: The relationship between the financial and the real economy was different, including the direction of causality, during each of the recent turbulences.

Chapter 2 presents the evolving type and strength of the short-term and long-term reactions of safety net institutions to crises. First, we assess the impact and effectiveness of both standard and non-standard monetary responses. Second, we evaluate the response of prudential authorities (micro- and macroprudential) to the crises and their role in maintaining financial stability. Third, we evaluate outcomes of these reforms and the European banking sector's resilience during crises through the lens of key financial ratios and panel data estimations. In this chapter, we test the first hypothesis (H1) and in part the second hypothesis (H2), which is also addressed in the next chapter. While testing the H1 hypothesis, we focused on the largest banks, identified as global (G-SIBs) or domestic (D-SIBs, also named "other systemically important financial institutions", or O-SIIs) systemically important banks (according to the latest available lists) due to the fact that regulators pay much attention to their safety and soundness.

Chapter 3 analyzes the role of the fiscal anti-crisis policy of European countries with regard to the financial and real sectors. We assess the type of government responses to crises, focusing on their speed, scale, and target entities. We begin with policy initiatives at the EU level, including emergency and recovery initiatives, as well as temporary state aid regulations, activities aimed at strengthening the budgetary framework and fiscal surveillance, and finally the facilities to provide assistance to countries in financial distress. Then, we present case studies of government stimulus packages to support the financial institutions during the GFC (Ireland) and sovereign debt crisis (Greece), while as the third example we chose Cyprus – the first to test the large-scale bail-in solution in Europe, before the implementation of the Bank Restructuring and Resolution Directive. Further, there are case studies of government support for the real sector from a euro and non-euro area country (Germany and Poland). The last part of this chapter is devoted to the interlinkages between fiscal and financial stability, and the implications of government support measures for the real economy during the crises. The second hypothesis (H2) is addressed in this chapter.

Chapter 4 focuses on the reactions of financial markets to crises and assesses the long-term impact the crises had on the use of financial instruments. Financial markets are often among the first to react to signs of approaching crises and are prone to contagion. In this chapter, we analyze sentiment indicators to show the evolution of the level of risk aversion in the market. Special attention is paid to Central and Eastern European (CEE) markets that reacted differently to exogenous shocks coming from "old" Europe. This chapter includes a review of the impact of post-crisis monetary authorities' activities and new financial regulations on market pricing, credit risk, and liquidity. The case studies comparing the market reactions to the subsequent turbulences and co-movement of economic indicators and asset prices in various market segments are then presented. The research accounts for the government stringency index to show evidence of the authorities' response to the evolution of the pandemic situation. In this chapter, we address the third hypothesis (H3).

Chapter 5 in turn explores the causality between finance and the real economy in the context of the crises, which is preceded by a brief literature review on the finance-growth nexus. To this end, we combine changes in daily financial market indicators with monthly macroeconomic data to detect differences in the direction of causality among the three analyzed crises. Next, we assess in detail the differences in causality of finance and growth in "old" and "new" European countries. Here, we test the fourth hypothesis (H4).

In the final chapter, we summarize findings and conclusions and outline the predictions of the future of the financial system, including the epilogue, concerning geopolitical events from February to March 2022. Special attention is paid to the structural changes, challenges, and legacy of the COVID-19 crisis and global financial interlinkages.

We would like to extend sincere expressions of gratitude to the Dean of the Collegium of Management and Finance at the Warsaw School of Economics (SGH), Professor Joanna Wielgórska-Leszczyńska for her continued support for the preparation of this monograph. We stress that the opinions expressed herein are solely those of the respective authors and do not reflect those of the associated institutions.

Notes

1 CISS is a composite index of the current level of stress in the euro area as a whole. It includes mainly market-based financial stress measures that are split equally into five categories, namely the financial intermediaries sector, money markets, equity markets, bond markets, and foreign exchange markets.

2 The CBOE Volatility Index (VIX) is a real-time market index representing the market's expectations for volatility over the coming 30 days and is used to measure the level of risk, fear, or stress in the market.

3 Due to strong linkages between emerging markets caused by basket portfolio management, we include some non-EU emerging countries in the FX financial markets analysis (like Turkey, Russia, Mexico, Brazil, and South Africa).

References

Ali, M., Alam, N. & Rizvi, S., 2020, Coronavirus: an epidemic or pandemic for financial markets, *Journal of Behavioral and Experimental Finance*, 100341.

Allen, W., Moessner, R., 2010, Central bank co-operation and international liquidity in the financial crisis of 2008–09, BIS working papers, No. 310.

Borio, C., 2020, Covid-19 economic crisis: dangerously unique. *Business Economics*, 55, 181–190. https://doi.org/10.1057/s11369-020-00184-2.

Brunnermeier, M., Pedersen, L. H., 2009, Market liquidity and funding liquidity, *Review of Financial Studies*, 22(6), pp. 2201–2238.

Cour-Thimann, P., Winkler B., 2012, The ECB's non-standard monetary policy measures: the role of institutional factors and financial structure, *Oxford Review of Economic Policy*, 28(4), pp. 765–803.

Iwanicz-Drozdowska, M., ed., 2016, *European Bank Restructuring During the Global Financial Crisis*. Palgrave Macmillan Studies in Banking and Financial Institutions, Palgrave Macmillan.

Soros, G., 2008, *The New Paradigm for Financial Markets. The Credit Crisis of 2008 and What it Means*, Public Affairs, London.

Zhang, D., Hu, M., & Ji, Q., 2020, Financial markets under the global pandemic of COVID-19, *Finance Research Letters*, 36, 101528.

2 Safety net responses to crises

2.1 Monetary response

The monetary response to the crises requires the application of expansionary tools. The scale of such a response depends on several factors, for instance:

- characteristics of the source of shock – what caused the crisis;
- the degree of available policy space – how much stimulus can be deployed;
- how much monetary support is needed and why;
- types of monetary instruments available – what tools should be used;
- the (side-)effects of monetary easing;

For the GFC (combined with the PIIGS crisis as a kind "prolongation" of the GFC) and the COVID-19 crisis, both similarities and differences in monetary response are identified and will be analyzed along with the abovementioned aspects. The crisis origins are discussed in Chapter 1.

2.1.1 Policy space

Central banks in European countries had much more space to lower interest rates in response to the GFC, as opposed to limited space at the outbreak of the COVID-19 pandemic (see Figure 2.1). In 2008–2009, many central banks in Europe significantly slashed the official interest rates in order to provide accommodative monetary conditions. In the case of Hungary and Romania, this policy space was higher than in the case of the ECB and other central banks in more advanced European countries. The scale of easing of interest rates in response to the GFC was significant and similar among the central banks in Europe. Further, in 2014, some central banks even reduced their main policy rates to below zero (although not always for the same reasons[1]). Thus, given the prevalence of the "zero lower bound" (ZLB) constraint at the onset of the COVID-19 crisis in advanced European countries, monetary policy space was more constrained. As a result, unconventional measures other than interest rate reductions were needed to provide the necessary monetary easing during the COVID-19 pandemic in European countries facing

DOI: 10.4324/9781003225539-2

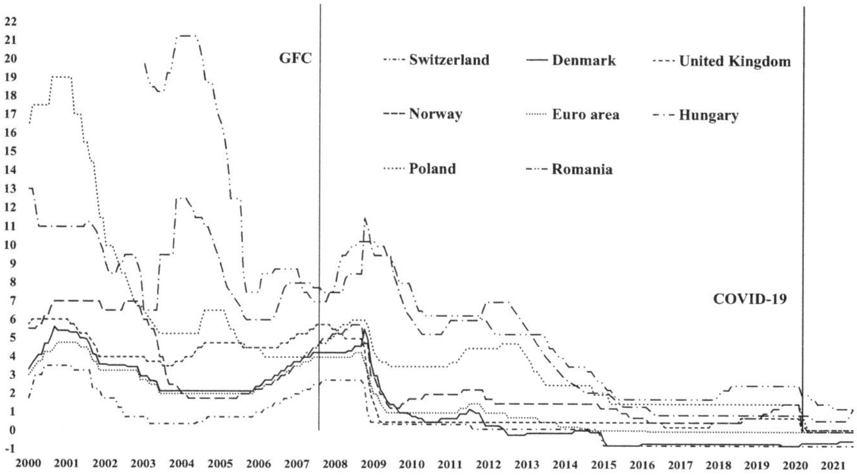

Figure 2.1 Central bank policy rates and financial crises (2000–2021H1).
Source: own work based on BIS policy rate statistics.

ZLB (Yilmazkuday 2022). Nevertheless, in both crises, monetary policies provided massive support.

2.1.2 How much monetary support was needed and why?

The contraction of GDP in the case of the COVID-19 crisis was much more rapid and severe compared to the GFC (see ESRB 2021). According to Verwey et al. (2021), unlike the GFC, which was characterized by a persistent decline in investment, the COVID-19 contraction in GDP was largely driven by a drop in private consumption, with expansive public policies mitigating the negative supply side effects. In line with Mojon et al. (2021), the COVID-19 pandemic prompted a historically deep and globally synchronized recession (across the advanced economies, GDP declined by twice as much in the first half of 2020 as it did in the GFC, which was itself an unusually deep global recession). In 2021, in many EU countries GDP growth remained well below its pre-pandemic levels. Therefore, the required scale and speed of the monetary response was higher in reaction to the outbreak of the COVID-19 pandemic than during the GFC. Further, the sectoral impact of crises was different. During the COVID-19 pandemic, the biggest decline was in the services sector (including travel and tourism), as well as the automotive industry, while in the GFC the losses were mainly borne by the financial sector.

The monetary policy actions taken at the onset of the pandemic were targeted at stabilizing financial markets, preventing liquidity shortages, and limiting the extent to which the health crisis would evolve into a full-blown financial crisis. The experiences of the GFC showed that liquidity squeeze usually preceded more serious market turbulences. Aggressive monetary easing (e.g. asset purchases of government bonds) during the COVID-19 outbreak were aimed at avoiding a sharp across-the-board rise in market interest rates (Barbier-Gauchard et al. 2021), when the pandemic caused strong tightening of financial conditions and higher sovereign yields in the EU countries. Thus, monetary stimulus made it cheaper for governments and private firms to raise funds, thereby alleviating the funding risk and lowering debt-servicing costs. In this way, central banks supported favourable financing conditions for new public debt issuances to pay for high fiscal support packages during the pandemic. This also ensured that large-scale issuance of government bonds would not significantly impair the proper functioning of sovereign bond markets (Cavallino and De Fiore 2020). Overall, the central banks' goal was to alleviate the contraction in real activity by supporting the banking sector and financial markets in continuing to provide credit to the private sector. Thus, central banks performed their traditional crisis role as lenders of last resort to the financial sector, and – indirectly – also to the private and public sectors of the economy, which was especially evident in the case of the pandemic crisis in 2020. The objective of the "positive monetary shock therapy" was to prevent a temporary pandemic shock from generating effects which would persist over time. Therefore, the aims of monetary intervention were similar for both the GFC and COVID-19 crisis.

2.1.3 What tools to use

In reaction to the GFC, central banks around the world first took measures to bolster the liquidity of their banking sectors. Another element of expansive monetary response included interest rate cuts and extensive introduction of various unconventional QE programs, including central bank purchase of government securities, corporate bonds, and commercial papers (Cukierman 2013; BIS 2019). Their reaction was gradual and persisted over the several years since 2007. Contrastingly, in response to the outbreak of the COVID-19 pandemic, central banks in Europe reacted boldly, quickly, and on a massive scale (see Table 2.1) in a relatively short time window. Those central banks which had non-zero interest rates, began the crisis response by cutting them. Interest rate cuts were used as a standard measure of the first line of defence. Next, they focused on liquidity provision and subsequently launched QE programs (like the ECB's pandemic emergency purchase program), as well as provided currency swap lines, similar to the ones offered during the GFC (Niedźwiedzińska 2020; Grasselli 2021). In contrast to the traditional gradual approach to monetary tightening, the crisis-driven loosening of the monetary policy was swift and almost immediate. Initially, during the COVID-19 crisis, central bank measures were aimed at restoring financial market functioning, while subsequent policies targeted facilitating the financing of both public and private sectors as well (Cavallino and De Fiore 2020). This is confirmed

Table 2.1 Central bank monetary measures in selected European countries in response to COVID-19 in 2020+

Tool type	*Measures*	*EA*	*UK*	*CH*	*DK*	*NO*	*SE*	*CZ*	*HU*	*PL*	*RO*
Interest rate	Policy rate cut		X			X	X	X	X	X	X
Lending operations	Liquidity provision	X	X		X	X	X	X	X	X	X
	Targeted lending	X	X	X			X			X	
Asset purchases	Government bonds	X	X				X		X	X	X
	Commercial paper	X	X				X				
	Corporate bonds	X	X				X		X		
	Other private	X					X		X		
Foreign exchange	USD swap line	X	X	X	X	X	X				
	Swaps								X		
	Spot intervention			X				X			
Reserve policy	Remuneration			X							
	Requirement ratio									X	
	Compliance								X		

Source: Cantú et al. (2021) based on central banks' websites. The presented countries cover almost all EEA members and the UK.

by Cantú et al. (2021), who developed an extensive database on monetary policy announcements (from 02.2020 to 04.2021). In European countries, monetary policy actions were concentrated in March and April 2020, but a "long tail" partly reflects additional fine-tuning of the policy responses over the course of 2020, as policymakers learned from each other and from the markets' reactions to their initial policies. According to Arena et al. (2021), after the initial turbulence in early 2020, the objectives of asset purchase programs were partly tilted more toward supporting monetary policy transmission over a longer period.

Overall, the monetary toolkit used in reaction to the pandemic was similar to the one used during the GFC. Policies implemented in 2020+ involved mainly extending measures already in place (e.g. as a legacy of the GFC or PIIGS crises), depending on the available policy space, with limited use of reserve requirement. This is in contrast to the GFC, which saw the origins of modern quantitative easing, rarely evidenced in the previous crises. However, the experiences gained with unconventional monetary measures during the GFC proved useful and made it possible to re-deploy them quickly and effectively in response to the health crisis. As a result, the monetary response was much faster in the case of COVID-19 than in the case of the GFC. Examples include either prolongation of previous QE programs, or creation of new ones, almost all of which had short (one-year) maturities. During COVID-19 crisis, central banks were purchasing mainly national government bonds. Additionally, the interest rate cuts were often complemented with communication policy in the form of forward guidance, signaling that rates would stay low for an extended period of time. The types of tools used were in general similar among the "old" and "new" European countries, although there were some differences in the scope of eligible securities under asset purchase programs and the use of USD swap line (mainly by advanced European countries).

2.1.4 The (side) effects of monetary easing

In general, monetary stimulus both in the case of the GFC and pandemic crisis in 2020 may be deemed effective, as post-GFC it fostered economic recovery, while post-COVID-19 it helped avert prolonged economic meltdown. Nevertheless, there is less consensus about the extent of negative side effects in the medium and long term of expansive monetary policy in response to crises.

Using a sample of 62 past banking distress episodes from 1980–2016, Adler and Boissay (2020) argue that overall swifter and broader-ranging policy actions mitigate the impact of banking distress on economic activity. Specifically, central bank lending schemes are more effective in restoring output growth when set up in the first year of distress. Thus, the provision of central bank liquidity is more effective (impaired asset facilities are more successful when used in the second year). Moreover, the ECB's long-term refinancing operations post-GFC and asset purchases managed to reduce long-term interest rates, ameliorate the credit channel, and avoid a credit crunch by mitigating liquidity and funding risks in the euro area banking system. This ultimately contributed to relaxation of bank lending standards and supported bank lending and thus the financing of the economy, without undue rise in credit risk (Evgenidis and Salachas 2019; Boeckx et al. 2020; Gibson et al. 2020). Also during the sovereign debt crisis, ECB interventions (asset purchases) managed to reduce liquidity risk premia, bond yield volatility (including spreads), default risk and market segmentation (Gibson et al. 2016; Markmann and Zietz 2017). Further, the ECB monetary policy expansion caused positive spillover effects to non-euro area countries from Central, Eastern and Southeastern Europe (CESEE), with the strength of effects depending on trade openness and financial integration (Kucharčuková et al. 2016; Potjagailo 2017).

Similarly, when assessing the post-COVID-19 data, Borio (2020) argues that the monetary response to the pandemic crisis was effective as well. The financial markets stabilized relatively quickly in the wake of the central banks' response in April 2020 (equity prices rebounded, credit spreads narrowed, money market tensions dissipated, and market liquidity improved) and thus immediate financial meltdown was averted. Boissay et al. (2020) found that central banks' response to the COVID-19 crisis supported the economy, including by pre-emptively staving off banking distress, which allowed banks to remain resilient and finance economic sectors affected adversely by the pandemic crisis. Moreover, Aguilar et al. (2020) and Hutchinson and Mee (2020) empirically found the positive impact of the ECB's monetary response in 2020 on the main stock market indices in the euro area, sovereign yields and on the GDP growth. The credit growth in most European countries likewise rebounded in 2020 and thus credit crunch was avoided, while Europe suffered a post-GFC credit crunch (Borio 2020). Asset purchase programs in developed European countries during the COVID-19 crisis were effective, restored investor confidence, stabilized government bond markets and boosted equity prices, without creating significant exchange rate pressures (Sever et al. 2020; Arena et al. 2021). If not for the pandemic response measures, persistent impairment in access to market-based funding, coupled with the substantial surge in loan demand for emergency liquidity needs, would have seriously undermined banks' intermediation capacity. The cumulative impact on loan growth of the non-standard monetary policy measures deployed was sizeable (Altavilla et al. 2020). Yet, the transmission of the ECB's monetary easing in reaction to the COVID-19 crisis might also have been hampered by buoyant housing cycles in many EU countries (Apergis 2021). It will be difficult to disentangle the effectiveness of monetary policy post-COVID-19, as it was accompanied by massive fiscal (see Chapter 3) and prudential stimuli (see Section 2.2).

Unconventional monetary actions carried out by the ECB in response to the GFC caused side effects. The expected benefits included contributing to achieving the inflation target (when inflation was below the target) and supporting economic recovery in the short and medium term. However, the harmful impact of expansive monetary policy is more difficult to quantify. It may also undermine financial stability in the medium to long term, leading to accumulation of systemic risks in the EU financial system post-GFC. The main source of such systemic risks included ultra-low interest rates (low interest rate environment – LIRE). This is not an entirely new phenomenon and is caused simultaneously by many factors. The long-term trend of gradual decrease of interest rates is visible in both emerging and advanced economies. According to the ESRB (2016) report, the decline started in the mid-80s, but accelerated after the GFC and the European sovereign debt crisis.[2] The COVID-19 pandemic required even more aggressive monetary easing to support the mitigation of economic shocks. Along with the heightened uncertainty regarding the future dynamics of the pandemic, this increased the associated systemic risks in the following years even further.

The negative effects of LIRE are numerous, and it impacts not only implementation of monetary policy but also the stability of the financial system. Lowering interest rates close to or below zero makes central banks face the "zero lower bound" (ZLB) constraint, which causes uncertainty concerning the transmission mechanisms of negative rates and limits further monetary easing using interest rates. In this case, a central bank will have to rely on unconventional tools like QE to a larger extent, which, via purchasing bonds and other securities, makes it more exposed to market and interest rate risks. LIRE contributes to an increasing share of government bonds with negative yields on the market, and induces a broad-based search for yield behaviour which increases the risk and leverage incurred by financial institutions (ESRB 2021a). It also increases financial system sensitivity to market shocks and systemic liquidity risks. LIRE additionally puts pressure on profitability of banks and financial institutions having long-term liabilities with guaranteed returns, i.e. pension funds and life insurers (ESRB 2016). Among direct costs for banks, they face a costly negative deposit facility rate charged on excess liquidity deposited with the ECB (Claeys 2021). Further, in LIRE, banks interest margins are squeezed – as the interest income is reduced, banks have less flexibility to offer negative rates on deposits, due to legal, economic (risk of deposit outflow) and psychological impediments. Thus, the transmission mechanism of LIRE to the real economy is hindered.

What is more, LIRE fosters excessive indebtedness, increasing the vulnerability of both private and public sector debt to interest rate risk in case of future interest rate hikes. An increase in credit demand encouraged by lower rates may become unsustainable and lead to accumulation of cyclical imbalances (credit bubble, real estate bubble, as exemplified in the real estate market vulnerabilities in recent years in many European countries). Further, the provision of "cheap" bank credit causes a risk of funds being channeled to non-viable ("zombie") companies and their existence being sustained, ultimately leading to inefficiencies in the economy. Massive public support for corporates during the COVID-19 pandemic only strengthened this effect. At the same time, on the positive side, in the short term, LIRE improves the debt-servicing capacity of bank debtors, lowering their credit risk, and enables cheaper market financing for banks. Still, the timeframe in which these negative effects materialize remains unclear – so far, the search for yield and pressures on profitability have already been visible for several years in financial institutions in Europe.

There is no silver bullet to mitigate the negative side effects of LIRE. Reducing policy rates to below zero is a challenge for central banks also due to external communication. Central banks which applied negative interest rate policy (e.g. the ECB) try to reduce the scale of adverse impact of their policy on banks by introducing tiering[3] mechanisms. Limiting financial stability risks goes beyond central banks' monetary policy remit and requires, apart from regular monitoring, also changes in prudential regulations (e.g. more stringent treatment of interest rate risk in banks, higher countercyclical capital buffer and systemic risk buffer, borrower-based measures) and increased monitoring of debt-servicing capacity, credit and liquidity risks. Unfortunately, most of the proposed solutions tackle the effects but not the causes of LIRE. Further, it remains unclear to what extent such measures will be introduced or effective in the near future. Nevertheless, the upsurge in global inflation after the pandemic (resulting mainly from disrupted value chains, increases in energy prices, and rising costs of climate transition as well as from the war in Ukraine) points to additional uncertainty in the future interest rate paths of central banks. Thus, in the coming years the interest rates in the EU "won't be low any longer".

Furthermore, post-crisis asset purchase programs lead to significant increases in balance sheets of central banks. The increase was equal to or higher during the COVID-19 crisis than the response to the GFC. Thus, the exit from monetary stimulus (gradual unwinding of asset purchases) without distorting market liquidity and financial stability remains a key challenge going forward. Overall, it is too early to comprehensively evaluate the long-term effectiveness of lockdown measures and the effects of expansionary monetary response to the ongoing COVID-19 pandemic. Still, the macroeconomic projections of the European Commission and ECB in 2022 were optimistic, and the trend of output was projected to return to its pre-COVID-19 trajectory in 2022. This indicates that the pandemic shock would have caused only a temporary ("V-shaped") EEA recession, in contrast to the longer-lasting economic damage triggered by the GFC.

2.2 Prudential response

The monetary response was followed by a prudential response, which will be explained from a regulatory perspective and practice of macroprudential policy implemented after the outbreak of the GFC and COVID-19. As presented in Chapter 1, the origins of shocks differed significantly between the two core crises (the GFC and COVID-19). Thus, the tendency after the outbreak of the GFC was to tighten regulations, especially for the banking industry and capital markets, while the COVID-19 pandemic reversed this trend, and this was reflected in the easing or postponing of the introduction of certain regulations and enabling flexible interpretation of some of them. In the case of the euro area sovereign debt crisis, the regulatory response was not so evident, as there was only some fine-tuning of risk weights. Later in this chapter (Section 2.3), we will comment on the financial situation in the banking sector, showing implications of new rules.

2.2.1 Regulatory measures

The outbreak of the GFC, like previous crises, started a wave of regulatory adjustments aimed at reduction of the risk which accumulated and then materialized in the financial industry. This time, however, the situation was different due to the implementation of Basel 2 rules developed by the Basel Committee on Banking Supervision (translated in the EU into CRD III) from the beginning of 2008. From its inception, Basel 2 was supposed to make banks' capital adequacy more transparent and improve banks' risk management. Soon after its implementation, it transpired that the "emperor had no clothes." The GFC prompted policymakers (at the G-20 summits in Washington in 2008, London and Pittsburgh in 2009, and Toronto in 2010) to take a number of steps to clarify "division of labour" within the financial safety net and strengthen prudential regulations to fill identified gaps. The most significant post-GFC changes included the strengthening of bank capital and introduction of liquidity requirements, a resolution mechanism and the identification of global systemically important financial institutions (G-SIFIs). At the EU level, an important role was played by the de Larosière Group report published in February 2009, which, in addition to diagnosing the causes of the GFC, provided proposals for reforms. Additionally, the need for more transparency and better valuation of financial instruments, especially more sophisticated ones, appeared to be crucial for the whole financial industry. The origin of this problem was linked to the US subprime market and the features of financial instruments based on securitization of mortgage loans of poor quality.

The EU report (The de Larosière Group 2009) identified the following most important weaknesses in the pre-crisis financial safety net:

- unsatisfactory quality and quantity of bank equity capital;
- no liquidity regulations for banks;
- underestimation of risk by models implemented in banks, especially in the case of market risk;
- procyclicality of the regulatory framework;
- weak internal controls and risk management;
- improper model of credit rating agencies;
- insufficient transparency of the valuation of financial instruments;
- regulation of the insurance sector lagging behind;
- lack of standardization of over-the-counter derivatives;
- lack of well-capitalized central clearing houses;
- lack of a regulatory level playing field due to national exceptions;
- bank remuneration policy increasing risk appetite;
- lack of a coherent EU framework for crisis management;
- non-harmonized legal framework for deposit guarantee schemes in the EU;
- lack of macroprudential supervision;
- insufficient coordination and harmonization of supervisory practices.

To alleviate these weaknesses in the EU, many new or adjusted regulations were introduced and new pan-European institutional settings for effective supervision were established. As these are collectively called "regulatory tsunami," in this chapter we will analyze the most important measures which shaped the situation in the banking industry. Therefore, in the following paragraphs, we present Basel 3.0 (reflected in the EU as CRD IV/CRR and later versions) and International Financial Reporting Standard 9 (IFRS 9) as regulations aimed at increasing financial system resilience, as well as the Directive on Deposit Guarantee Schemes (DGS) and the Bank Resolution and Restructuring Directive (BRRD) as regulations strengthening the crisis management framework. Similar solutions have been adopted in countries outside the EU (Switzerland, Norway and currently the UK). Additionally, we present institutional changes shaping supervisory structures in the EU and the creation of new macroprudential bodies. As Basel 3 rules are linked to the identification of G-SIFIs, we also refer to this new regulation.

Importantly, the regulations mentioned above apply mostly to the banking sector. However, this sector is not the only one facing new regulatory requirements. IFRS 9 is an important game changer in the financial industry overall and it required all institutions to adjust their accounting rules. CRD/CRR packages apply also to investment firms, not solely to banks. Additionally, EU authorities introduced the Solvency II package, which uses a similar philosophy to regulate insurance companies (2009/138/EC). Moreover, specific capital market regulations were introduced, especially the European Market Infrastructure Regulation (EMIR), which aimed at increasing the safety and transparency of OTC trading, and Markets in Financial Instruments II (MiFID II, 2014/65/EC), aimed at improving investors' protection by reducing the potential of mis-selling and asymmetry of information especially regarding the risk profile of offered instruments. These game changers for financial markets and instruments will be discussed later in Chapter 4.

2.2.2 Capital and liquidity regulations

The fine-tuning of Basel 2 took place in 2009 in order to reduce the most significant drawbacks of market risk treatment (Basel 2.5). In 2010, far-reaching improvements in the Basel framework were proposed (Basel 3), which fully entered into force in 2019. These measures addressed mostly the first four weaknesses identified by the de Larosière Group as described above. An important change was a more restrictive approach to defining own funds (Tier 1 – going concern capital and Tier 2 – gone concern capital) and maintaining a higher solvency ratio by introducing capital buffers. Certain instruments were (with a phase-out period) excluded from Tier 1 capital since they did not allow losses to be absorbed when it was necessary. Additionally, from that moment on, Tier 1 capital was required to be at least 75% of the overall capital, which was more restrictive than under Basel 2. In order to significantly improve the quality of bank capital, a new category emerged within Tier 1, which was common equity Tier 1 (CET1), composed of ordinary shares, accumulated profits, and share premiums. As CET1 is regarded as the best at absorbing losses, CET1 must be at least 75% of Tier 1. Moreover, to deleverage banks, the Basel Committee proposed the implementation of a leverage ratio (defined as the ratio of Tier 1 to total exposure, i.e. assets and off-balance-sheet items; its test level was 3%). The leverage ratio is a kind of "plain vanilla" capital ratio with no possibility for window dressing. At a later stage, the Basel Committee and the European Commission decided to take steps towards reducing the possibility of such window dressing.

Capital buffers – as an addition to the regular capital adequacy ratio (or total capital ratio, TCR with its 8% minimum threshold) – were introduced to strengthen bank solvency and the ability to absorb losses. Regulators implemented five new buffers (covered by CET1), which are:

- capital conservation buffer – 2.5% of risk exposure to assure that in the case of losses it would allow TCR to stay above the 8% minimum threshold;
- countercyclical buffer – set between 0 and 2.5% following a decision by the macroprudential authority in order to reduce the procyclicality in the financial system;
- buffer for systemically important banks (SIBs) – between 1% and 3.5% for Global-SIBs and up to 2% for Domestic-SIBs (also called "other systemically important institutions" – O-SII) to make big banks more resilient to crisis (these are two buffers);
- systemic risk buffer – from 1% to address the non-cyclical risk in the banking sector or in a sub-sector in a given country.

These new regulations forced banks to increase capital levels and/or shrink their total exposures to meet new capital regulations. The concept of identifying the largest banks is not new, since for a very long time there was a discussion on banks labelled "too big to fail." However, this problem had been underscored on the political agenda. "No special treatment" for such institutions existed. The outbreak of the GFC and its consequences put pressure on policymakers to address this problem. The Basel Committee on Banking Supervision (BCBS) developed an initial methodology to identify G-SIBs (BCBS 2011), which was applied by the Financial Stability Board (FSB) to determine the list of systemically important banks. Such a list was published for the first time in November 2011. This methodology was subsequently refined. BCBS methodology is based on 12 ratios that are divided into five groups to which the same weights have been applied. The BCBS methodology uses accounting and supervisory data as proxies of five main characteristics (size, interconnectedness, substitutability of services, complexity, and cross-jurisdictional activity), which can be theoretically related to systemic importance.

In the initial phase of the global financial crisis (the subprime phase in the US), the following problems became apparent: the lack in some banks of sufficient quality of liquid assets to maintain liquidity in an emergency, and the lack of structural matching of funding sources to the asset structure. Before the GFC, many banks financed long-term loans using the interbank market. In order to address these two problems, the Basel Committee proposed in the Basel 3 package two liquidity measures with 100% thresholds:

- liquidity coverage ratio (LCR) – relating to current liquidity (up to 30 days);
- net stable funding ratio (NSFR) – relating to structural liquidity.

The regulation of liquidity was a necessary step to strengthen the banking sector's resilience to liquidity shocks and improve banks' funding structures.

Basel 3 extended the requirements for the trading book and the components that can qualify for it, and also the approach of Value-at-Risk (VaR) estimation by requiring the estimation of stressed VaR (sVaR), i.e. VaR under conditions of significant changes in market prices. This was intended to address the issue of drawback of risk underestimation for the trading book. As the GFC analysis showed, many institutions classified as trading book instruments financial products which were not actually tradeable on the market. Therefore, liquidity of the instruments is a key feature for classification as a trading book component.

Following the experience of the global financial crisis and the euro area sovereign debt crisis, stricter rules were introduced for the risk weights of the EU countries (CRD IV/CRR package), abandoning the "automatic" assignment of zero-risk weights, albeit not for exposures to the ECB (0%), as well as for exposures to governments of the member states and central banks, denominated and funded in the currency of that member state (0%).

The introduction of Basel 3 forced banks to improve the quantity and quality of their capital and liquidity as well as to build their resilience to shocks. As banks' profits dropped during the crisis, they needed to restructure their balance sheets to adjust to new requirements, including the CET1 increase, and bear additional costs of funding to meet liquidity requirements. Although the post-crisis tightening of regulations was welcomed by various stakeholders, after a few years another reform was prepared, which in turn was supposed to simplify the approach to regulating banks and limit the flexibility of regulations (*Basel 4*). This reform is mostly aimed at reducing the potential for window dressing, i.e. introduction of an output floor, abandoning methods reducing capital requirements in operational risk, and the use of conditional VaR (called "expected shortfall," or ES, see for example Chang et al. 2019), focused on the tail of the risk distribution, instead of stressed VaR in market risk. All of these measures are expected to further improve capital adequacy. These changes were supposed to enter into force in 2022, but due to the COVID-19 pandemic implementation has been postponed by one year in order to ease the burden on banks.

2.2.2.1 IFRS 9

Another significant change in the regulatory framework was reflected in IFRS 9, which entered into force in 2018. This change focused on clarification of the use of fair value (in most cases it is the equivalent of the market price) and caused a fundamental change in loan provisioning. The financial assets which the bank intends to sell, or the intention to do so is not clearly stated, are measured at fair value. The other assets are presented at the amortized cost, which is, in general, more stable than the fair value. In order to classify financial assets properly, two tests are needed. The first is the solely payment of principal and interest test (SPPI) and the second is the business model test. SPPI is designed to check whether cash flows are solely attributable to payments of principal and interest. The business model test checks whether the instrument will be kept on the balance sheet (called "hold") or whether the bank has no clear view on it: (1) "hold or sell" or (2) "neither hold nor hold or sell." Only if SPPI is successful and the business model identified as "hold" is the instrument presented at amortized cost; the fair value is used otherwise (through either the profit and loss account or bank capital). This change addresses the problem identified for the pre-GFC period regarding transparency of financial instrument valuation (e.g. the use of amortized cost for loans that were not supposed to be held on the bank's balance sheet) and the "originate and sell" problem, which was specific for subprime market loans.

Another problem identified in the accounting rules was provisioning and write-downs based for a long time on incurred losses. The outcome of this approach was a high level of provisions during the economic downturn, which caused bank profits to plummet. Therefore, economists (e.g. Saurina 2009; Balla and McKenna 2009) suggested applying dynamic provisioning, i.e. preparing for the economic downturn in good times. This approach assumes provisioning throughout the life of the financial asset with an increase in the level of write-down when the situation of the borrower deteriorates and it is based on the expected losses concept.[4] The key issue is to assess the significant increase in credit risk (SICR, see for example Chawla et al. 2016) based on the deterioration of the internal rating and on forward-looking information (FLI, e.g. macroeconomic forecasts). In the case of materialization of SICR, a lender has to apply the PD lifetime and thus estimate the write-downs until the instrument's maturity. This kind of approach should smoothen the level of provisions through the economic cycle.

However, the outbreak of the SARS-CoV-2 pandemic has shown that reliance on such assumptions, and in particular on FLI, could lead to a significant spike in write-downs which would affect the entire banking sector. Forecasts are used to create scenarios on the basis of which write-downs are estimated. The outbreak of the pandemic worsened, among others, the macroeconomic scenarios, and this was reflected in the level of provisions. Soon after the outbreak of the pandemic, at the end of March 2020, the European Banking Authority (EBA) issued a position paper indicating that there should be no automatism in the assessment of the SICR and that the situation of borrowers should be assessed taking into account, on the one hand, the impact of pandemic-related restrictions and, on the other hand, government support packages targeted at many industries. In the case of pandemic moratoria, the duration of the moratoria should not be counted as a repayment delay. The flexibility of IFRS 9 itself and of supervisors helped avoid the need for large-scale write-downs.

2.2.2.2 Deposit guarantee schemes and resolution

The collapse of Lehman Brothers in mid-September 2008 and the accompanying panic among market participants prompted the EU authorities to surge the deposit guarantee level to EUR 50,000 (October 2008) and then to EUR 100,000 (from 1 January 2011) in order to rebuild depositors' trust in the banking sector. These and other key changes were reflected in the revision of the Deposit Guarantee Schemes Directive of March 2009 (2009/14/EC), however further changes, aimed at strengthening the financial capacity of deposit guarantee schemes, were implemented later. Finally, in 2014, the Directive of the European Parliament and of the Council of 16 April 2014 on deposit guarantee schemes (2014/49/EU) was adopted. It was agreed that deposit guarantee institutions were to be funded *ex ante*. The target level of accumulated funds was set at 0.8% of guaranteed deposits (10-year period to accumulate funds). As in many countries, deposit guarantee schemes were funded on an *ex-post* basis. This change increased the burden on the banking sector.

The resolution mechanism was implemented in order to improve crisis management tools and avoid a bailout. The resolution was first used in the US in the 1980s during the Savings and Loans Association crisis. Thus, at that time, it did not apply to large entities, but to small ones. The resolution was also used during the GFC for banks of various sizes, but not for the largest banks (except in Cyprus, for example see for more details Iwanicz-Drozdowska 2016). This was before the implementation of the Bank Restructuring and Resolution Directive (2014/59/EU, BRRD) into EU legislation. In order to solve the problem of a bank in financial difficulties, which is too big or too important to be declared bankrupt (i.e. it has some critical functions and it is not in the public interest to declare it bankrupt), resolution tools may be used. They help avoiding significant market disruptions. The basic principle behind the resolution is that creditors should not pay more than they would in a standard insolvency procedure (NCWO – no creditor worse off). The capital, and to a certain extent the creditors' funds, are used to cover losses. To this end, banks are requested to keep a certain level of "eligible liabilities," which are reflected in the level of the minimum requirement for own funds and eligible liabilities (MREL)[5] in the EU. The higher the losses incurred by the bank, the greater the scale of bail-in (write-down and conversion), which is a basic tool in this process. After cleaning the bank of losses, the next steps are taken, namely the sale of the business to a new investor or bridge bank,[6] if at the time of resolution, no investor is interested in a business purchase. Additionally, these tools may be supplemented by asset separation, i.e. transfer for example of bad assets to the asset management company (AMC), which is also called a "bad bank." As the resolution process has to be financed by banks' contributions, it has increased the burden on the banking sector as banks had to build resolution funds from the scratch.

2.2.2.3 Institutional setup

Before the outbreak of the GFC, very rarely was the distinction between micro- and macroprudential supervision used in policymaking. In order to make financial systems more resilient, macroprudential supervision was introduced and in addition the central banks were assigned explicit responsibility for financial stability. Due to the novelty and importance of macroprudential policy, we present this in detail in 2.2.3.

Based on the findings of the de Larosière report, the EU complemented the European financial safety net, made up of institutions operating at the national level, with pan-European sectoral micro- and macroprudential supervision. The framework became operational at the beginning of 2011. Macroprudential supervision on the EU level is assigned to the European Systemic Risk Board, supported by the European Central Bank. It has no "hard" tools but can issue on an "act-or-explain" basis, warnings and non-binding recommendations (e.g. to national authorities) aimed at reducing the risks of the financial industry (e.g. limiting foreign currency lending or accumulation of real estate risks).

Micropudential policy in Europe is in turn assigned to three bodies:

- the European Banking Authority (EBA);
- the European Insurance and Occupational Pensions Authority (EIOPA);
- the European Securities and Markets Authority (ESMA).

These pan-European authorities fulfil mainly a coordination role and ensure appropriate cooperation between the supervisors from EU countries (with direct supervisory powers remaining within the remit of national competent authorities and the ECB). One of their most important activities is the development of technical standards to ensure uniform application of regulations. Together with national supervisors, these agencies constitute the European System of Financial Supervision.

The goal of the implementation of the above institutional setting was to coordinate and cooperate. However, it was evaluated at the political level as insufficient for the euro area with a common monetary policy. In order to ensure a unified approach to the supervision of banks from euro area countries, the concept of the banking union was implemented in November 2014, which may be treated as an extension of the Economic and Monetary Union. The aim of the banking union is to improve resilience of the euro area banking sector. The idea of a banking union originated in Germany and the impetus for it was the need to supervise banks more prudently than before, in order to avoid the risk of cross-border spillovers and mutualization of losses – the need for other member states to pay for the mistakes of local (national) supervisors. It was mostly stimulated by the financial difficulties of Spanish banks. A non-euro area country can "opt-in" to the banking union on a voluntary basis by requesting the establishment of close cooperation between the ECB and its national competent authority, but so far only Bulgaria and Croatia (in October 2020) have taken up this option, as a transitory step towards euro adoption.

The implementation of a banking union started with the introduction of the Single Supervisory Mechanism (SSM) – "Pillar I." Euro area banks became supervised jointly by the European Central Bank, which cooperates with national supervisors. The ECB directly supervises the largest banks in the euro area, while other banks are supervised indirectly, i.e. the ECB supervises the work of national supervisors and sets the necessary common guidelines. The next stages were the introduction of regulations concerning the Single Resolution Mechanism (SRM), "Pillar II," and the Single Deposit Insurance Scheme (EDIS), "Pillar III," which is at an early stage of development. The EDIS faces to a large extent the problem of the lack of political consensus on its funding mechanisms. Building adequate financial potential of the EDIS would cost the European banking sector a lot of its revenues. Taking into account many other burdens the banking industry has to meet, this one may be excessive and therefore is being postponed, especially given the recent legacy of the COVID-19 pandemic.

All in all, the GFC triggered many changes in the existing prudential framework and sparked the implementation of new tools to strengthen the financial industry and its resilience to crisis. These new tools and regulatory adjustments were aimed at filling the identified gaps in the safety net which evidently showed that "the emperor had no clothes." Meeting this goal required banks to restructure their balance sheets and adjust business models, and burdened them financially (e.g. tightened capital ratios, costs of premiums paid to DGSs and resolution funds). However, banks and other financial institutions were the sources of the GFC, so they had to bear the costs of its aftermath since the taxpayers also bore significant costs of the crisis. The outbreak of the COVID-19 pandemic tested these solutions in a real-life stress test (for more see section 2.3). At this time, no major regulatory reforms have been implemented as a direct response to the pandemic, but the financial safety net in early 2020 had space for easing some requirements (e.g. capital buffers, MREL requirement, SICR interpretation), which would not have been possible without post-GFC reforms.

2.2.3 Lessons learned? Impact of regulatory and institutional overhaul

The significant regulatory measures were announced in 2010, however, they had been implemented gradually. For example, the leverage ratio and NSFR entered into force in the EU in mid-2021, and thus a long time after the outbreak of the crisis and initial detection of the problems with structural liquidity and excessive leverage. The reason for such a long implementation process was the need to allow banks (and the economy) to adjust to new regulatory requirements without significant side effects, such as the reduction of banks' credit supply. Capital buffers and tightened structure and quality of bank capital were the earliest implemented regulatory measures.

As noticed by Herring (2018), each round of reforms results in "increasingly complex regulations" and this regulatory framework is "remarkably opaque, costly to monitor and enforce, and imposes heavy compliance costs on the regulated entities." The post-GFC package of reforms also fits this evaluation. Although it has introduced new solutions, it has mostly correctly filled significant regulatory gaps detected at the outbreak of the GFC (quality of bank capital, deleveraging, liquidity regulation).

There are a few theoretical and empirical studies aimed at evaluating post-GFC regulatory reforms and practices, but accurate evaluation requires long-term data series, which until now have been scarce. In the case of theoretical studies, Ahnert et al. (2021) focused on the sensitivity of bank capital, indicating that regulators should impose risk-sensitive capital requirements if the risk of bank's assets could be measured in a sufficiently precise way. This conclusion, although based on theoretical models, shows that further fine-tuning of regulations under "Basel 4" meets this postulate. A theoretical study by Wei et al. (2017) shows that in the case of *ex ante* evaluation of NSFR, banks tend to reduce short-term financing and in this way increase probability of survival and profits. From the *ex-post* perspective, the situation differs and NSFR reduces banks' profits. While drafting regulations, standard setters should pay attention to these two perspectives, however, the *ex ante* one seems to be more important in policymaking.

Empirical studies focused on short-term liquidity and capital ratios. First, Petrella and Resti (2017) concluded that the stress on the markets is greater for low-rated and long-term bonds issued in small amounts. Therefore, there should be certain thresholds to treat domestic T-Bonds as highly liquid assets. They are not in use however, probably due to the fact that banks keep significant parts of their balance sheets in T-Bonds and introducing such a factor would reduce demand for certain types of government securities. For the period from 2000 to 2015, Hogan et al. (2018) indicated that simple capital ratios are better at predicting bank risk than more complex capital ratios (e.g. TCR), so the implementation of the leverage ratio as a simple measure would help to detect banks' capital adequacy problems in advance.

Although amended regulations filled gaps revealed by the GFC, they are not ideal, and still have certain weaknesses. As mentioned by Herring (2018), they are too complex and even after the implementation of "Basel 4," they will remain complex. Therefore, in parallel to the existing regulatory framework, policymakers should make an effort to establish new, less complex regulations which will not generate significant compliance costs. This is especially important for small and medium-sized banks, since the proportionality principle is not sufficiently applied in EU bank regulation. In other words, it is sometimes better to build a new house and to move into it than to repair a crumbling one. Furthermore, the current regulatory framework does not fully capture the "new" emerging risks from climate change, crypto-assets and decentralized finance, nor the cyber risk.

As the COVID-19 pandemic was actually the first real-time stress test for the financial sector, it made it possible to verify banking sector resilience under significant pressure from the real economy and operational risks. In Section 2.3, we present the situation in the European banking sector to evaluate its financial standing and determinants under these stress test conditions. We will show that especially capital strength, including capital buffers, played a significant role in dealing with this crisis situation. It is however too early to declare victory of the new regulatory framework, since many other stress tests should be taken into account, e.g., liquidity squeezes and shortages, including government bonds from low-rated countries or the sovereign debt (overindebtedness) crisis. Additionally, a return to higher interest rates would create another stress test for the financial sector and the real economy.

2.2.4 First experiences with macroprudential policy in the EU

Macroprudential policy is responsible for maintaining financial stability by limiting the accumulation of systemic risks and increasing financial system resilience to shocks. Before the GFC, the macroprudential framework was a blind spot in financial system regulation, as responsibility for financial stability was diluted among safety net institutions (Galati and Moessner 2013; Kahou and Lehar 2017). Formally non-existent, this policy was implemented in practice mainly by the microprudential supervisor and the central bank in a non-coordinated manner, often being a "side effect" of fulfilling primary goals of those institutions. Along with other deficiencies in the safety net, this led to a severe underestimation of systemic risks, accumulation of which contributed to the large scale of the GFC. Since then, as the main lesson from the GFC, the macroprudential pillar of prudential policy has been significantly strengthened in terms of banking regulations and institutional and analytical frameworks. It became a key, indispensable tool in safeguarding the stability of financial systems around the world. In the EU, national authorities are primarily responsible for macroprudential policy, with the European Systemic Risk Board playing a coordinating role on the EU level and additional support provided by the ECB in the banking union. Also in Norway, Switzerland and the UK, macroprudential policy competences of national central banks were strengthened, along with establishing cooperation mechanisms with ministries of finance and microprudential supervisors.

In post-GFC Europe, there has been increasingly active and restrictive use of newly available and legally binding macroprudential instruments (mainly on the basis of the CRDIV/CRR framework) for the banking sector, including introduction for instance of capital buffers, borrower-based measures, liquidity caps, and sectoral risk weights (Budnik and Kleibl 2018). The restrictive macroprudential stance in EU countries was a reasonable response to cyclical risks, including accumulation of vulnerabilities on real estate markets, excessive credit growth, household indebtedness, consumer lending, external risks, and risks stemming from FX loans as well as from systemically important institutions (ESRB 2020). This pre-COVID-19 approach to macroprudential policy was comparable (see Figure 2.2) in both the "old" and "new" European countries (partly due to similar systemic risks and harmonized prudential regulations). The majority of tightening macroprudential actions took place after 2015, which was driven by the newly

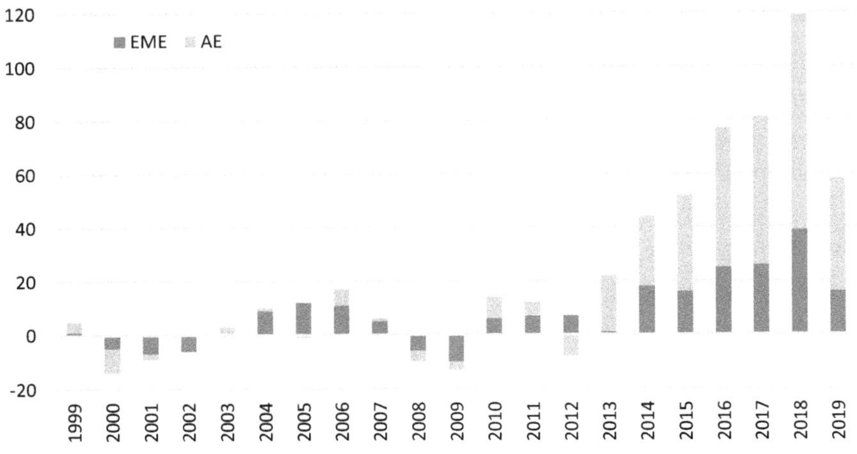

Figure 2.2 Macroprudential policy index (net tightenings) in Europe (1999–2019).

Note: the bars indicate the cumulative sum of the net number of tightening actions of any macroprudential policy instruments over the current year; European emerging economies (EME) include: BG, CZ, HR, HU, LT, LV, PL, RO, SI, SK; European advanced economies (AE) include: AT, BE, CH, CY, DE, DK, EE, ES, FI, FR, IE, IS, IT, LU, MT, NL, NO, PT, SE, UK.

Source: own work based on the IMF's integrated Macroprudential Policy (iMaPP) Database, originally constructed by Alam et al. (2019).

available prudential framework of the CRDIV/CRR, as well as closing credit gaps and an expanding credit cycle, which necessitated adopting a restrictive macroprudential stance to stem the rising cyclical vulnerabilities. As a result, at the end of 2019 some European macroprudential authorities had policy space to use for loosening in case of unexpected shocks. There was, however, a lot of heterogeneity in this regard among EU countries (ESRB 2021b). This policy space, to a larger extent, consisted of structural buffers (i.e. systemic risk and O-SII buffers), rather than buffers releasable by design (like the countercyclical capital buffer). Schnabel (2021) argues that pre-pandemic macroprudential instruments were often activated too slowly or hesitantly. In many European countries, macroprudential policies remain partly under the control of governments, making the implementation of politically sensitive instruments, such as borrower-based measures, more difficult.

Many studies point to the effectiveness of implemented macroprudential measures in curbing leverage, credit and real estate price growth (Akinci and Olmstead-Rumsey 2018; Carreras et al. 2018; Poghosyan 2019; Meuleman and Vander Vennet 2020; Olszak and Kowalska 2022) during the period between the GFC and the COVID-19 crisis. Nevertheless, efficiency of some European macroprudential measures was limited by their late introduction, non-binding nature (e.g. recommendations), and deficient institutional framework, as well as by intersectoral and international spillovers (Franch et al. 2021) or "waterbed effects"[7] e.g. between home and host countries (Ongena et al. 2013). As for CESEEs, results by Eller et al. (2020) and Eller et al. (2021a) suggest that (pre-pandemic) tighter macroprudential measures (like borrower-based measures and capital buffers) curbed not only private sector credit growth and house price growth, but also gross capital inflows in most of the analyzed countries, and the effects of those measures were generally greater in a low interest rate environment. Unfortunately, the vast majority of reviewed studies assess the efficiency of macroprudential policy only with an overly simplistic binary measure (0 or 1) and in a booming phase of the financial cycle, providing limited directions for the loosening of prudential measures in case of economic downturn. In this respect, the sudden major pandemic shock in early 2020 was the first practical test for nascent macroprudential policy and learning-by-doing experience in loosening prudential measures.

The outbreak of the COVID-19 pandemic in 2020 was unexpected and resulted in the first, prompt, simultaneous and significant loosening of macroprudential measures in history (concentrated in March 2020) by national authorities in the EEA and UK. Thus, the macroprudential policy stance shifted from restrictive to expansive (i.e. significantly less restrictive) with the aim of averting a credit crunch (excessive procyclical deleveraging) and releasing funds to allow banks to absorb losses and continue providing financing to the real economy. This direction of change was common among all EEA countries and the UK. The objective of this shift was to alleviate the original pandemic shock, which would be amplified through adverse feedbacks between the real economy and the financial sector (e.g. via emerging weaknesses in corporate and household balance sheets). To the extent allowed by the pre-pandemic macroprudential policy space, almost all European countries released countercyclical capital buffers, and lowered, revoked or delayed introduction of previously announced other macroprudential measures (see Table 2.2). The releases of systemic risk buffers were less common. However, as only a fraction of capital buffers had been explicitly releasable, this somewhat limited the stabilization function of macroprudential loosening. As opposed to a gradual macroprudential tightening post-GFC, the post-pandemic release was immediate and most often to the largest possible extent i.e. lowering buffer requirements to zero. EEA countries with limited policy space lowered for example structural buffers like O-SII, even if the systemic risk contributions of those institutions did not change. Similarly, on the residential real estate market, despite growing cyclical vulnerabilities, macroprudential measures (like borrower-based measures) were sometimes lessened as well.

In the case of CESEEs, Eller et al. (2021b) argue that they also responded quickly to the outbreak of the crisis, mainly by relaxing capital buffer and liquidity requirements, or at least refrained from previously planned tightening. At the same time, borrower-based measures, minimum reserve requirements and risk weights were only rarely relaxed. Eller et al. (2021b)

Table 2.2 Loosening of macroprudential measures in 2020 in selected European countries

Member state	*Countercyclical capital buffer*	*Systemic risk buffer*	*SII buffer*	*Real estate instruments*
Austria	→	→	→	→
Belgium	↓	n/a	→	→
Bulgaria	↓	→	→	n/a
Croatia	→	↓	→	→
Cyprus	→	n/a	↓	→
Czech Republic	↓	→	→	↓
Denmark	↓	→	→	→
Estonia	→	↓	→	→
Finland	→	↓	↓	↓
France	↓	n/a	→	→
Germany	↓	n/a	↓	→
Greece	→	n/a	↓	n/a
Hungary	→	↓	↓	→
Iceland	↓	→	→	→
Ireland	↓	→	→	→
Italy	→	n/a	→	n/a
Latvia	→	n/a	→	→
Liechtenstein	→	→	→	→
Lithuania	↓	n/a	↓	→
Luxembourg	↑	n/a	→	↑
Malta	→	n/a	↓	↓
Netherlands	→	↓	↑↓	→
Norway	↓	↑↓	→	↑↓
Poland	→	↓	→	↓
Portugal	→	n/a	↓	→
Romania	→	→	→	→
Slovakia	↓	→	→	→
Slovenia	→	n/a	→	↓
Spain	→	n/a	→	n/a
Sweden	↓	→	↓	→
Switzerland	↓	→	→	→
United Kingdom	↓	↓	↑	→

Source: own work based on ESRB (2021b).

Notes: ↑ refers to a tightening; ↓ refers to a loosening; → refers to no change; n/a stands for non-applicable. The latter denotes that no related measure has been notified to the ESRB. "Real estate instruments" include any instrument (borrower-based or capital-based) dedicated to the residential or commercial real estate sectors. Tightening/loosening refers to the policy situation compared with the situation before the adoption of the measure. More detailed notes are available in ESRB (2021b).

further found that CESEE-11 countries that entered the crisis with better capitalized and more profitable banking systems tended to implement less pronounced macroprudential easing. Overall, banking sectors in EU countries in which capital buffers were released in 2020 had on average a 1 pp. higher CET1 ratio (end 2019) than those which did not. Thus, such unprecedented prudential easing in response to the pandemic was possible, because banks had substantially strengthened their capitals in the post-GFC period, largely as a result of the international regulatory reforms. Additionally, banks were allowed to flexibly and temporarily operate below the level of capital defined by Pillar 2 guidance and the combined buffer requirement, as well as below liquidity requirements.[8] Pandemic prudential easing was rightfully accompanied by the recommended ban (among others by the ESRB and SSM) on bank dividend payments and share buy-backs to ensure that the newly released bank capital would not lead to investor pay-outs, instead of being used for lending, as intended. Dautovic et al. (2021) found that those recommendations appear to have mitigated the procyclical behaviour of euro area banks closer to the threshold for automatic restrictions on distributions and were successful in conserving capital and helping the banking system support the real economy and facilitate the recognition of future losses.

The assessment of effectiveness of macroprudential loosening during the pandemic is hindered by the need for longer data series (in line with the medium-term perspective of macroprudential policy) and the fact that it was accompanied by complimentary and very strong monetary and fiscal expansions. Therefore, disentangling the effects of prudential support measures will be challenging in the future. So far, after more than two years since the outbreak, a major banking crisis in the European countries has been avoided. Banking sector resilience has been maintained and no significant credit deleveraging has been observed, thus post-pandemic macroprudential policy easing can be assessed as effective. Altavilla et al. (2020) argue that euro area post-pandemic micro- and macroprudential measures effectively reduced capital requirements, thus complementing monetary policy action by providing ample space for banks to support the economy (with an estimated contribution to loan growth of around 2 p. p.). At the same time, liquidity provisioning measures along with microprudential and macroprudential interventions have been able to mitigate the adverse impact of the escalating diffusion of the COVID-19 crisis on banks' intermediation capacity as well. Similarly, Avezum (et al. 2021) find empirical evidence that the pandemic buffers releases in EU countries contributed to, on average, mitigating the procyclicality of credit provision and led to higher credit growth to households, specifically for house purchase and for small businesses purposes. On a world-wide sample, simulations of Lewrick et al. (2020) show that – despite the build-up of capital over the past years – usable buffers alone may not be enough to bolster lending should the pandemic crisis deepen to a scale comparable to that of the GFC. However, given the increasing vaccination rates and healthy banking sector in the EU, the impact of subsequent "COVID waves" is likely not to be as severe as the initial ones.

Still, the experiences with the first "field test" of expansive macroprudential policy in the EU point to several drawbacks and inefficiencies of the current framework in practice. Banks turned out to be reluctant to use the released capital and lower their capital ratios. Banks' unwillingness was driven by several factors: (i) a desire to avoid market stigma and negative stock market reactions from investors and rating agencies; (ii) keeping some distance from the threshold of automatic restrictions on distributions; (iii) uncertainty among banks about coping with future losses and unknown post-crisis speed of buffer replenishment required by supervisors (Villeroy de Galhau 2021). Regulatory interactions and overlaps between capital buffers, leverage and MREL requirements also limited the usability and effective releasability of capital buffers. As a result, banks might opt to deleverage instead of using the buffers, (ESRB 2021c). This points to the need to rethink the overall complexity of the macroprudential framework, improve buffer usability, and fill the existing gap in the macroprudential framework for the non-bank financial sector.

Further, the need for rapid decision-making at the onset of the pandemic strengthens the arguments in favour of allocating the micro- and the macroprudential functions to a single agency (e.g. a central bank), to reduce the tensions and time needed to take swift, coordinated decisions on prudential easing (Restoy 2020). Moreover, it is reasonable to maintain a non-zero (i.e. a neutral) level of capital buffers at all times, for prudential and pre-emptive reasons to ensure sufficient policy space in case of unexpected shocks (de Guindos 2021). This logic is in line with the approach pursued already in pre-pandemic times for example by the United Kingdom and the Czech Republic. Having higher capital buffers at the onset of the pandemic would have led to significantly improved bank lending and reduced the fall in GDP in the euro area in 2020 (Darracq et al. 2020). ECB (2021) points out that banks with a capital adequacy level closer to their combined buffer requirement were found to de-risk their balance sheet, thus curtailing their lending to non-financial corporations more than other banks.

Additionally, identification of an imbalance between cyclical and structural buffers during the pandemic suggests that capital buffers have to be designed to be releasable to a larger extent and allow for more flexibility in macroprudential policy (e.g. make the capital conservation buffer releasable). Thus, policymakers should be able to build up more "releasable macroprudential space" for periods of unexpected stress – further research is needed. Macroprudential regulations, which so far focused on tightening procedures, should also specify the details of loosening particular instruments. This should be accompanied by clear supervisory guidance on how and when the released buffers will need to be fulfilled again in the future. This is what was deficient in macroprudential communication after the pandemic loosening. Thus, as a result of the pandemic, the evolution of the macroprudential framework can be expected.

2.3 In the eye of the storm – crises and banking sector financial standing

2.3.1 Pre- and post-crisis trends in the European banking sector condition

This chapter briefly presents the most important trends in the condition of the European banking sector between 2005 and 2021 (given the availability of long data series).[9] The analysis focuses on a comparative assessment of trends before and after the GFC and the COVID-19 pandemic. Where possible, differences and similarities between the "old" and "new" European countries are indicated as well. The focal point of this analysis is banks' resilience to crisis shocks.

In line with the analysis of Iwanicz-Drozdowska et al. (2016), the GFC hampered the growth of the size of banking systems in the EU, which stalled during the next several years after the GFC. Given the major economic slump after the GFC and the high scale of losses due to a full-blown financial crisis, the dynamic growth of the banking sector has stopped (this was especially visible in EU "periphery" Western countries). Additionally, for the rescued banks in the EU, reducing the scale of their operations was frequently a prerequisite for receiving state aid. Contrastingly, so far, the COVID-19 pandemic has not led to a drop in asset volumes in EU banks, which in turn experienced modest growth (cash balances were the main contributor to this increase). As underlined by the EBA (2021), the continued implementation of accommodative monetary policies and the incentives given to banks to use QE programs have driven this rise. Apart from that, when faced with increasing market turmoil in 2020, banks increased their holdings of sovereign bonds, among others to strengthen their stock of safe assets. Still, the overall asset composition of banks has remained roughly stable post-COVID.

As for the lending growth, it decreased significantly after the GFC, despite the abovementioned support measures implemented on a massive scale. While pre-GFC the credit dynamics (both for households and corporates) was much higher in Eastern than in Western European countries (for instance due to catching-up effects), the pace of post-GFC credit revival was in turn equally modest in both groups of countries. During both crises, credit growth was driven on one hand by reduced demand for corporate credit amid macroeconomic uncertainty, and on the other hand by reduced risk appetite of deleveraging banks. The pre-GFC credit booms in many EU countries ended in collapse thereafter. However, the credit cycle started to slowly recover in the pre-pandemic period. In 2020 and beyond, given the continuation of accumulation of imbalances on residential real estate markets, high mortgage lending growth was observed, especially in Central European countries, which may signal overheating and creation of real estate price bubbles.

As a result, the deterioration of bank profitability was significant post-GFC and – in a low interest rate environment – remained a weak structural issue in the European banking sector (in the EEA and in the UK). Nevertheless, profitability slightly rebounded in the period between the two crises, especially in Eastern Europe. Since the pandemic outbreak, so far, bank profitability has not decreased in Western or Eastern European countries as dramatically as it did in reaction to the GFC shock. According to the EBA (2021), many banks indicated that their return on equity remained below the cost of equity also in the post-pandemic period. Still, at end 2021 profitability of European banks has on average returned to pre-pandemic levels.

Bank profitability post-GFC was significantly burdened by a major rise in NPL ratio several years thereafter. This upsurge was higher in Eastern than in Western Europe, and peaked in 2013–2014, after which it started to decline steadily (see Figure 2.3). As a result, the NPL ratios in both groups of countries at the onset of the pandemic were as low as in the pre-GFC period. This post-GFC improvement in asset quality was driven, apart from better macroeconomic conditions, also, among others, by strict supervisory guidance, requiring banks to prepare NPL reduction strategies, improvements in loan provisioning and NPL transparency, as well as the development of secondary markets for NPL. In turn, in the post-pandemic period, asset quality continued to improve even further, as the immediate risk of deterioration of debt-servicing capacity of the private sector was mitigated by the monetary, fiscal and prudential support (e.g. in form of loan moratoria). Nevertheless, as

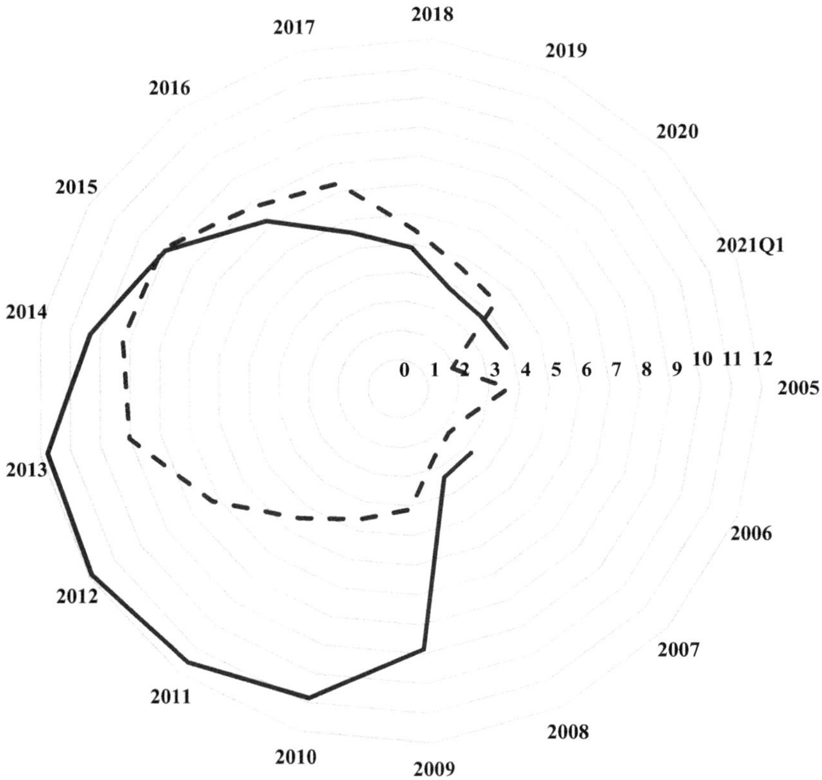

Figure 2.3 Developments in asset quality in the European banking sector in 2005–2021 (NPL ratio, in %).

Note: dashed line – West Europe; solid line – East Europe.

Source: own work based on IMF data (Financial Soundness Indicators).

economic activity has not yet returned to pre-pandemic levels and uncertainty is still elevated, asset quality needs to be monitored closely in the coming years. As for liquidity, it was at an insufficient level pre-GFC. However, given the significant strengthening of liquidity requirements post-GFC, as well as continued access to buoyant funding conditions, supported by central banks' accommodative monetary policy, European banks have faced limited liquidity risk over the recent years. The pandemic did not change that trend and liquidity ratios remain comfortably above regulatory minima.

The resilience (proxied by capital adequacy) of European banks was unsatisfactory in the pre-GFC period (see Figure 2.4) as well. This resulted in low loss-absorbing capacity when faced with GFC-induced shocks, undermining financial stability. Post-GFC capital requirements were made more stringent and enhanced. As a result of increased capital requirements, stricter supervision and inception of macroprudential capital buffers, EU banks significantly improved their capital ratios post-GFC. The gradual growth in the capital adequacy ratio since 2008 resulted primarily from a stronger capital base and less as a result of decreased risk-weighted assets, which overall is beneficial for systemic risk resilience. Thus, the banking sectors' capital position at the onset of the pandemic was much better than pre-GFC, both in Western and Eastern European countries. This is also confirmed by the bank-level data (Figure 2.5), as over time the distribution of TCR shifted to buckets with much higher values.

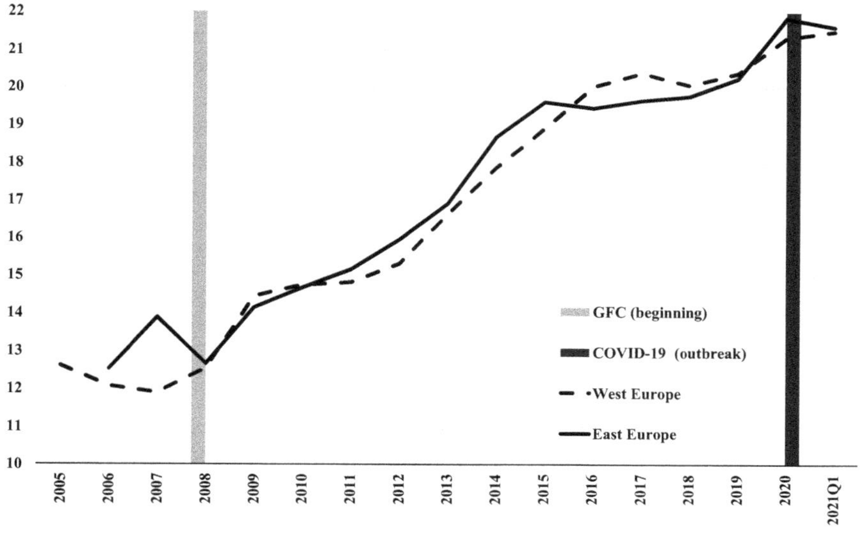

Figure 2.4 Regulatory Capital to Risk-Weighted Assets in the European banking sector in 2005–2021 (in %).

Source: own work based on IMF data (Financial Soundness Indicators).

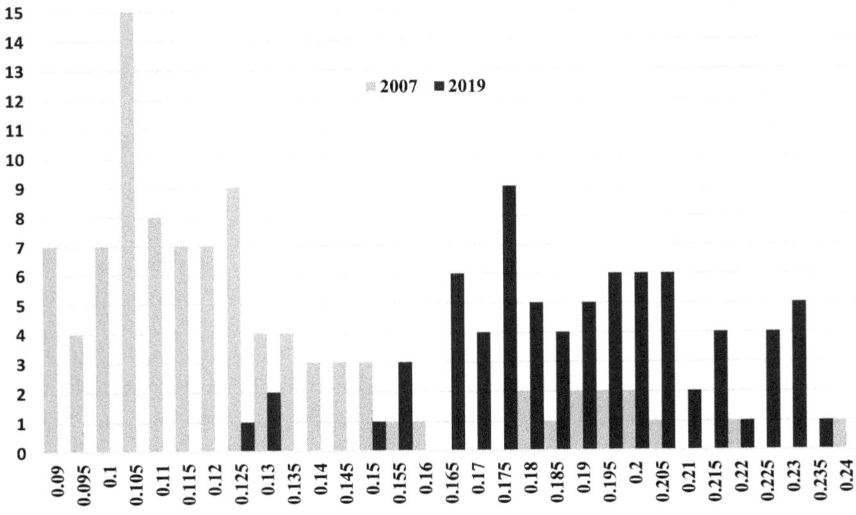

Figure 2.5 Distribution of Total Capital Ratio in 2007 vs 2019.

Note: number of banks in a given bucket of TCR ratio (in %) from the sample of systemically important banks in European countries.

Source: own work based on the Orbis database.

After the pandemic outbreak, capital ratios continued their increasing trend thanks to the recovery of profitability (after the initial pandemic shock), as well as recommendations by the ESRB, ECB and EBA on the restriction of distributions and dividend payments, encouraging the accumulation of retained earnings. Banks' capital positions have been indirectly supported by pandemic public support programs for households and corporates, which reduced the credit risk accumulation, by partially shifting this risk to the government that offered public guarantee schemes for new lending. Therefore, bank capital ratios in EU countries continued to remain above the regulatory minima even during the pandemic. The EU banking sector's resilience to shocks was additionally confirmed by the 2021 stress test results of the ECB and EBA.

2.3.2 Determinants of bank soundness during crises

In previous subsections, we explained the significant role capital adequacy plays in bank regulation and in maintaining its stability. Therefore, our empirical analysis embraces two capital ratios, namely the proxy of leverage, defined as equity to total assets and TCR. As banks' asset quality and provisioning are procyclical (e.g. Skała 2015), i.e. in the case of an economic downturn asset quality deteriorates resulting in increased provisions, we also pay attention to provisioning as a measure of evaluating asset deterioration. The increase in provisions may be treated as a result of a bank's previous credit policy.

2.3.2.1 Data and methodology

The list of dependent and independent variables is presented in Table 2.3. The control variables we selected were bank-level and macroeconomic variables, which are frequently used in various studies (e.g., Allen et al. 2017, Olszak et al. 2018, Skała 2020).

We cover in this analysis the period from 2001 to 2020 to identify determinants of banks' safety in the long term. Data were extracted from Orbis databases for the largest banks in the analyzed countries (i.e. D-SIBs or O-SIIs). This resulted in about 2,000 bank-year observations (the exact number of observations varies due to missing data). Due to the fact that we only examined the largest banks in European countries, we do not use the bank size as a control variable. Additionally, we provide results for the 2005–2020 period, which covers 2–3 years before the outbreak of the crisis, the crisis period and the post-crisis period, except the COVID-19 pandemic period. This allows confirming the stability of the results.

The data constitute a panel of banks observed in the 2001–2020 period. A one-way linear static model is used to describe the considered relations. Given the sample size, a random effects specification is used as a baseline and the fixed effects approach is used mostly in the form of a robustness check. The dependent variables represent changes of the respective measure which

Table 2.3 Variables

Variables	*Notation*	*Definition*
Dependent variables		
Equity to total assets (change)	ΔEQ_to_TA	$EQ\_to\_TA_{t} - EQ\_to\_TA_{t-1}$
Total Capital Ratio (change)	ΔTCR	$TCR_{t} - TCR_{t-1}$
Loan loss reserves to gross loans (change)	ΔLLR_to_G_loans	$LLR\_to\_G\_loans_{t} - LLR\_to\_G\_loans_{t-1}$
Independent variables		
Loan growth (change; current or lagged)	ΔLoans or ΔLoans (-1)	$(Loans_{t} - Loans_{t-1}) / Loans_{t}$
ROA (lagged)	ROA(-1)	ROA_{t-1}
NIM (lagged)	NIM(-1)	NIM_{t-1}
NPL (change)	ΔNPL	NPL=non-performing loans to gross loans; $NPL_t - NPL_{t-1}$
GDP growth	ΔGDP	GDP (in current prices, change)
Inflation	HICP	$HICP_t$
Unemployment	UNEMP	$UNEMP_t$

prevents spurious regressions resulting from nonstationarity. Also, the risk of endogeneity is eliminated by lagging adequate regressors.

There is a high risk of a change in the modelled relations during the crisis periods and it is likely that a specification that neglects this fact would be misleading. In order to allow for the parameter heterogeneity over time, we introduce two additional specifications which include crises dummies. First, we introduce interactions of a crisis dummy (similar for example to Allen et al. 2017) for periods marked as crisis periods, i.e. dummy crisis=1 for 2008–2012 and 2020 (marked as "crisis" 0 otherwise (marked as "non-crisis"). Second, we further develop this approach by dividing the 2001–2020 period into three sub-periods, namely: crisis (2008–2012 and 2020, marked as "crisis"), pre-crisis (2005–2007, 2017–2019, marked as "pre-crisis"), and a "regular" period with no spectacular crisis-trigger events (2001–2004, 2013–2016, marked as "regular"). The respective dummies are then introduced and interacted with other regressors. This approach means capturing not only the parallel change in the value of the dependent variable (as in the case of a simple dummy variable) but also the change of the underlying relationship between the regressors and the dependent variable which is reflected by the regression parameters (slopes).

2.3.2.2 Results and discussion

Tables 2.4–2.6 present the results of the estimations for capital ratios and loan loss reserves. In the discussion, whenever the concept of the significance of a variable is used, a 5% level is assumed for brevity. We treat the results of random effects equations as baseline models, while the results of fixed effects are given for robustness check purposes.

In the case of leverage proxy, i.e. the equity to total assets ratio (models 1.3–1.4, 1.3A–1.4A), our results confirm that in the improvement of the capital ratio certain regressors play a statistically significant role. Capital ratio increases under favourable economic growth conditions supported by the increasing inflation rate (HICP), which helps avoid stagnation in the economy. In the analyzed period in Europe, inflation rates were stable around low levels. Lagged ROA decreases together with the capital ratio, underlying that higher profitability is capital-consuming, as banks may increase in size, keeping equity capital at a stable level. This is a common way to improve profitability. These results have been confirmed by fixed effect models (1.1–1.2, 1.1A–1.2A). At this stage, there are no differences between 2001–2020 and 2005–2020, so we believe that these results are stable over time.

TCR as a capital ratio (models 2.3–2.4, 2.3A–2.4A) is more risk-sensitive, i.e. some types of assets are more capital-consuming than others. One of the most capital-consuming assets is loans, which is reflected in the role of loan growth (ΔLoans). As the results confirm, the growth of loans coincides with the decrease of the TCR. The role of lagged ROA is the same as in equations for leverage ratio. The GDP growth shows however the opposite as it decreases

Table 2.4 ΔEquity-to-assets equations

	Fixed effects				*Random effects*			
	(1.1)	*(1.2)*	*(1.1.A)*	*(1.2.A)*	*(1.3)*	*(1.4)*	*(1.3.A)*	*(1.4.A)*
	All	*All*	*2005+*	*2005+*	*All*	*All*	*2005+*	*2005+*
ΔLoans	−0.0019	−0.0010	−0.0018	−0.0008	−0.00153	−0.000947	−0.00123	−0.000595
	(–1.18)	(–0.62)	(–1.02)	(–0.45)	(–1.05)	(–0.65)	(−0.78)	(−0.38)
ROA(-1)	−0.2490***	–0.1960***	–0.2440***	–0.1840***	–0.198***	–0.172***	−0.199***	−0.167***
	(−6.66)	(−5.00)	(−5.98)	(−4.29)	(−6.10)	(−5.12)	(−5.70)	(−4.63)
NIM(-1)	−0.2320***	−0.2190**	−0.2840**	−0.2520**	−0.0432	−0.0408	–0.0486	–0.0444
	(−3.36)	(−3.19)	(−3.09)	(−2.76)	(−1.34)	(−1.24)	(–1.34)	(–1.21)
ΔGDP	0.0380**	0.0420**	0.0389**	0.0435**	0.0372**	0.0414***	0.0397**	0.0446***
	(2.97)	(3.29)	(2.82)	(3.15)	(3.17)	(3.52)	(3.15)	(3.52)
HICP	0.0797**		0.0956***		0.0588**		0.0712**	
	(3.26)		(3.39)		(2.64)		(2.81)	
ΔNPL	0.0197	0.0222	0.0199	0.0232	0.0200	0.0229	0.0215	0.0257*
	(1.58)	(1.79)	(1.44)	(1.69)	(1.67)	(1.93)	(1.64)	(1.97)
UNEMP		0.0429**		0.0510**		0.0161		0.0176
		(2.93)		(2.88)		(1.68)		(1.60)
constant	0.0060***	0.00325	0.0070***	0.0033	0.00166*	0.00112	0.00171	0.00113
	(3.70)	(1.64)	(3.30)	(1.27)	(1.98)	(1.07)	(1.82)	(0.94)
N	2008	2008	1761	1761	2008	2008	1761	1761

Notes: *t* statistics in parentheses.

* $p < 0.05$, ** $p < 0.01$, *** $p < 0.001$.

Table 2.5 ΔTotal capital ratio equations

	Fixed effects				*Random effects*			
	(2.1)	*(2.2)*	*(2.1.A)*	*(2.2.A)*	*(2.3)*	*(2.4)*	*(2.3.A)*	*(2.4.A)*
	All	*All*	*2005+*	*2005+*	*All*	*All*	*2005+*	*2005+*
ΔLoans	–0.0085** (–3.17)	–0.0080** (–3.01)	–0.0087** (–3.03)	–0.0078** (–2.74)	–0.00840*** (–3.34)	–0.00806** (–3.22)	–0.00846** (–3.17)	–0.00786** (–2.96)
ROA(–1)	–0.4080*** (–6.38)	–0.4280*** (–6.42)	–0.4370*** (–6.40)	–0.4370*** (–6.11)	–0.295*** (–5.29)	–0.311*** (–5.43)	–0.312*** (–5.31)	–0.319*** (–5.27)
NIM(1)	–0.2650* (–2.14)	–0.2210 (–1.80)	–0.2860 (–1.80)	–0.2200 (–1.39)	–0.0959 (–1.70)	–0.0431 (–0.75)	–0.0883 (–1.44)	–0.0264 (–0.42)
ΔGDP	–0.0875*** (–4.02)	–0.0859*** (–3.96)	–0.0890*** (–3.86)	–0.0855*** (–3.71)	–0.0753*** (–3.75)	–0.0767*** (–3.81)	–0.0732*** (–3.45)	–0.0742*** (–3.48)
HICP	0.0849* (2.04)		0.1350** (2.87)		0.0735 (1.94)		0.123** (2.90)	
ΔNPL	–0.0294 (–1.37)	–0.0190 (–0.90)	–0.0433 (–1.89)	–0.0288 (–1.26)	–0.0282 (–1.36)	–0.0199 (–0.97)	–0.0412 (–1.87)	–0.0277 (–1.27)
UNEMP		–0.0478 (–1.80)		–0.0366 (–1.23)		–0.0346* (–2.02)		–0.0372* (–1.99)
constant	0.0143*** (4.93)	0.0188*** (5.19)	0.0146*** (4.00)	0.0184*** (4.15)	0.00961*** (6.64)	0.0127*** (6.90)	0.00930*** (5.89)	0.0131*** (6.46)
N	1879	1879	1679	1679	1879	1879	1679	1679

Notes: t statistics in parentheses.

* $p < 0.05$, ** $p < 0.01$, *** $p < 0.001$.

Table 2.6 ΔLoan loss reserves to gross loans equations

	Fixed effects				*Random effects*			
	(3.1)	*(3.2)*	*(3.1.A)*	*(3.2.A)*	*(3.3)*	*(3.4)*	*(3.3.A)*	*(3.4.A)*
	All	*All*	*2005+*	*2005+*	*All*	*All*	*2005+*	*2005+*
ΔLoans(-1)	0.00210*	0.00261**	0.00127	0.00215*	0.00232**	0.00277**	0.00161	0.00235**
	(2.24)	(2.80)	(1.33)	(2.28)	(2.66)	(3.18)	(1.84)	(2.69)
ROA(-1)	−0.256***	−0.186***	−0.304***	−0.192***	−0.216***	−0.180***	−0.236***	−0.180***
	(−7.44)	(−5.09)	(−8.66)	(−5.16)	(−6.98)	(−5.58)	(−7.72)	(−5.62)
NIM(-1)	0.0253	0.0654	0.164*	0.214***	0.0487	0.0746*	0.0975***	0.122***
	(0.47)	(1.27)	(2.45)	(3.30)	(1.64)	(2.56)	(3.32)	(4.12)
ΔGDP	−0.176***	−0.170***	−0.177***	−0.167***	−0.168***	−0.162***	−0.163***	−0.155***
	(−16.35)	(−15.73)	(−16.12)	(−15.22)	(−16.31)	(−15.67)	(−15.90)	(−14.86)
HICP	0.0887***		0.133***		0.0812***		0.125***	
	(4.29)		(5.70)		(4.31)		(5.93)	
UNEMP		0.0568***		0.0972***		0.0240*		0.0313**
		(4.30)		(6.61)		(2.50)		(3.24)
constant	0.00155	−0.00299	−0.00190	−0.00953***	0.000642	−0.000725	−0.000888	−0.00225*
	(1.22)	(−1.85)	(−1.24)	(−4.96)	(0.84)	(−0.70)	(−1.18)	(−2.18)
N	2107	2107	1845	1845	2107	2107	1845	1845

Notes: t statistics in parentheses.

* $p < 0.05$, ** $p < 0.01$, *** $p < 0.001$.

TCRs. This may be explained by the fact that banks search for more profitable and more risky assets when the economy is booming, and these assets consume more capital to secure their risk. These results have been confirmed by robustness checks (models 2.1–2.2 and 2.1A–2.2A). Again, at this stage, there are no differences between 2001–2020 and 2005–2020, so these relations seem stable over time as well.

As already mentioned, loan loss provisioning is procyclical, so the changes in our dependent variable, i.e. loan loss reserves to gross loans ratio (models 3.3–3.4 and 3.3A–3.4A) were expected to coincide with macroeconomic factors. The role of the GDP growth and the role of the unemployment and inflation rates are confirmed by the baseline estimations and by robustness check. GDP growth decreases provisioning, while the rising unemployment rate and inflation (due to decreasing income in real terms) seem to increase it, which is in line with our expectations and intuition. Bank-level statistically significant variables are the following: lagged growth of loans (with a positive sign), lagged ROA (with a negative sign), which was expected. First, the growth of loans in the previous period increased provisioning. The plausible explanation for this is that, especially in recent years, provisioning has been dynamic, and granting each loan results in new provisions estimated for a 1-year horizon. Moreover, the smaller (or the larger) portion of loans may default, which causes an increase in provisions. Second, lagged ROA may represent the outcome of the profit management policy (or income smoothing, e.g. Skała 2015), which, in general, reduces the need for provisioning in bad times as banks attempt to build a kind of "airbag" in good times. Unlike in previous models, for the period 2005+ the role of NIM, which reflects the pricing policy, has been confirmed. The higher the lagged NIM, the higher the provisioning, which may be interpreted as meaning that banks granted loans to more risky customers (reflected in higher NIM) in previous periods, resulting in higher provisions due to more frequent defaults.

All in all, the differences between periods are visible only in provisioning via the pricing channel. No other differences have been confirmed. Therefore, we found that the capital ratios of the largest European banks are not directly impacted by the credit policy, including pricing, while provisioning is impacted directly, especially in periods around crises.

As discussed earlier, the results might be misleading if the described relations were different in the crisis vs the non-crisis periods. To clarify this, Tables 2.7 and 2.8 present results accounting for crisis periods. In Table 2.7 the results are divided into two parts: crisis vs non-crisis, while in Table 2.8 there are three sub-periods, namely crisis, pre-crisis and regular.

Our results confirm that during crisis periods (models 1.5–1.6 and 3.5–3.6) equity to total assets and provisioning are lower than during a non-crisis period. Although the first finding is in line with expectations and intuition, the second one is counterintuitive, i.e. one may expect provisioning to be higher during a crisis. We speculate that this is because of dynamic provisioning and the policy of banks to "save for rainy days." This may be a sign that large

Table 2.7 Equations with crisis interactions

	(1.5) *fixed* *ΔEQ_to_TA*	(1.6) *random* *ΔEQ_to_TA*	(2.5) *fixed* *ΔTCR*	(2.6) *random* *ΔTCR*	(3.5) *fixed* *ΔLLR_to_G_loans*	(3.6) *random* *ΔLLR_to_G_loans*
non-crisis	Reference category					
crisis	−0.00466*	−0.00446*	−0.00450	−0.00406	−0.00498**	−0.00381*
	(−2.46)	(−2.47)	(−1.39)	(−1.31)	(−3.07)	(−2.42)
ΔLoans	−0.00866***	−0.00744***	−0.0196***	−0.0172***	0.00268**	0.00292**
	(−3.59)	(−3.39)	(−4.69)	(−4.54)	(2.77)	(3.24)
ROA(-1)	−0.302***	−0.241***	−0.336***	−0.215**	−0.182***	−0.141***
	(−6.46)	(−5.86)	(−4.17)	(−3.04)	(−4.25)	(−3.65)
NIM(-1)	−0.189*	−0.0465	−0.206	−0.124	0.0201	−0.00243
	(−2.57)	(−1.15)	(−1.55)	(−1.72)	(0.35)	(−0.07)
ΔGDP	0.0324	0.0410	−0.000890	0.0119	−0.213***	−0.181***
	(1.24)	(1.81)	(−0.02)	(0.30)	(−9.67)	(−9.12)
HICP	0.0264	0.000866	−0.0764	−0.0926	0.0492	0.0415
	(0.76)	(0.03)	(−1.27)	(−1.69)	(1.84)	(1.73)
ΔNPL	0.0550***	0.0553***	0.0345	0.0276		
	(3.30)	(3.51)	(1.18)	(0.99)		
non-crisis#ΔLoans	Reference category					
crisis#ΔLoans	0.0136***	0.0124***	0.0209***	0.0176***	−0.00516	−0.00586
	(4.40)	(4.24)	(3.84)	(3.48)	(−1.52)	(−1.83)
non-crisis#ROA(-1)	Reference category					
crisis#ROA(-1)	0.160*	0.130	−0.193	−0.235*	−0.135*	−0.170**
	(2.26)	(1.94)	(−1.59)	(−2.05)	(−2.06)	(−2.68)

(continued)

Table 2.7 Cont.

	(1.5) *fixed* *ΔEQ_to_TA*	*(1.6)* *random* *ΔEQ_to_TA*	*(2.5)* *fixed* *ΔTCR*	*(2.6)* *random* *ΔTCR*	*(3.5)* *fixed* *ΔLLR_to_G_loans*	*(3.6)* *random* *ΔLLR_to_G_loans*
non-crisis#NIM(-1)	Reference category					
crisis#NIM(-1)	0.0652	0.0820	0.104	0.128	0.243***	0.242***
	(0.92)	(1.21)	(0.84)	(1.08)	(3.99)	(4.08)
non-crisis#ΔGDP	Reference category					
crisis#ΔGDP	0.0111	0.00659	−0.114*	−0.110*	0.0863**	0.0602*
	(0.36)	(0.23)	(−2.14)	(−2.24)	(3.17)	(2.36)
non-crisis#HICP	Reference category					
crisis#HICP	0.0991*	0.111*	0.323***	0.329***	0.0564	0.0692
	(1.98)	(2.36)	(3.78)	(4.12)	(1.32)	(1.69)
non-crisis#ΔNPL	Reference category					
crisis#ΔNPL	−0.0911***	−0.0897***	−0.162***	−0.147***		
	(−3.48)	(−3.70)	(−3.56)	(−3.50)		
constant	0.00709***	0.00337**	0.0132***	0.0101***	0.00253	0.00187*
	(3.96)	(3.07)	(4.13)	(5.30)	(1.80)	(2.02)
N	2008	2008	1879	1879	2107	2107

Notes: t statistics in parentheses.

* $p < 0.05$, ** $p < 0.01$, *** $p < 0.001$.

Table 2.8 Equations with crisis interactions for 3 sub-periods

	(1.7) fixed	*(1.8) random*	*(2.7) fixed*	*(2.8) random*	*(3.7) fixed*	*(3.8) random*
	ΔEQ_to_TA		*ΔTCR*		*ΔLLR_to_G_loans*	
ΔLoans	0.00489*	0.00498**	0.00128	0.000472	−0.00288	−0.00295
	(2.42)	(2.58)	(0.37)	(0.14)	(−0.91)	(−0.99)
ROA(-1)	−0.144*	−0.111*	−0.537***	−0.451***	−0.305***	−0.311***
	(−2.54)	(−2.10)	(−5.55)	(−4.98)	(−5.86)	(−6.31)
NIM(-1)	−0.143	0.0355	−0.115	0.00343	0.294***	0.237***
	(−1.70)	(0.65)	(−0.78)	(0.04)	(4.24)	(4.95)
ΔGDP	0.0432*	0.0476**	−0.117***	−0.0981***	−0.126***	−0.121***
	(2.35)	(2.75)	(−3.75)	(−3.35)	(−7.77)	(−7.73)
HICP	0.129***	0.112**	0.251***	0.237***	0.115***	0.111***
	(3.45)	(3.22)	(3.99)	(4.06)	(3.38)	(3.44)
ΔNPL	−0.0361	−0.0343	−0.128***	−0.120***		
	(−1.84)	(−1.87)	(−3.81)	(−3.78)		
crisis	Reference category					
pre-crisis	0.00441	0.00454*	0.00175	0.00148	−0.00129	−0.00261
	(1.82)	(1.97)	(0.43)	(0.38)	(−0.66)	(−1.38)
regular	0.00387	0.00378	0.00503	0.00456	0.00703***	0.00596***
	(1.83)	(1.87)	(1.38)	(1.30)	(4.01)	(3.48)
crisis#ΔLoans	Reference category					
pre-crisis#ΔLoans	−0.0150***	−0.0132***	−0.0215***	−0.0177**	0.00984*	0.00859*
	(−4.31)	(−4.04)	(−3.55)	(−3.17)	(2.45)	(2.29)
regular#ΔLoans	−0.0107*	−0.0108*	−0.0213*	−0.0199*	0.00429	0.00491
	(−2.23)	(−2.38)	(−2.43)	(−2.40)	(1.28)	(1.57)

(continued)

Table 2.8 Cont.

	(1.7) fixed	(1.8) random	(2.7) fixed	(2.8) random	(3.7) fixed	(3.8) random
	ΔEQ_to_TA		ΔTCR		$\Delta LLR\_to\_G\_loans$	
crisis#ROA(-1)	Reference category					
pre-crisis#ROA(-1)	−0.233	−0.0926	−0.103	0.219	0.617***	0.673***
	(−1.60)	(−0.68)	(−0.42)	(0.95)	(4.94)	(5.77)
regular#ROA(-1)	−0.147*	−0.132	0.244	0.254*	0.0910	0.116
	(−2.01)	(−1.91)	(1.94)	(2.14)	(1.38)	(1.83)
crisis#NIM(-1)	Reference category					
pre-crisis#NIM(-1)	−0.181	−0.222*	−0.132	−0.282	−0.559***	−0.550***
	(−1.82)	(−2.37)	(−0.77)	(−1.75)	(−7.27)	(−7.41)
regular#NIM(-1)	−0.0134	−0.0254	−0.0866	−0.0782	−0.154*	−0.163*
	(−0.17)	(−0.34)	(−0.63)	(−0.59)	(−2.32)	(−2.52)
crisis#ΔGDP	Reference category					
pre-crisis#ΔGDP	−0.00101	−0.000327	0.150	0.139	0.0319	0.0469
	(−0.02)	(−0.01)	(1.79)	(1.79)	(0.80)	(1.25)
regular#ΔGDP	−0.00267	-0.00578	0.121	0.104	−0.167***	−0.132***
	(−0.07)	(−−0.17)	(1.96)	(1.80)	(−5.46)	(−4.57)
crisis#HICP	Reference category					
pre-crisis#HICP	0.0308	−0.0119	−0.146	−0.145	0.0934	0.0897
	(0.40)	(−0.17)	(−1.13)	(−1.20)	(1.52)	(1.53)
regular#HICP	−0.128*	−0.136**	−0.359***	−0.372***	−0.139**	−0.135**
	(−2.27)	(−2.63)	(−3.69)	(−4.16)	(−3.07)	(−3.17)

crisis#ΔNPL	Reference category					
pre-crisis#ΔNPL	0.0828*	0.0962**	0.132*	0.137*		
	(2.19)	(2.73)	(2.07)	(2.29)		
regular#ΔNPL	0.0919**	0.0817**	0.172***	0.137**		
	(3.20)	(3.09)	(3.39)	(2.94)		
constant	0.00283	−0.00109	0.00888*	0.00604*	−0.00344	−0.00188
	(1.36)	(−0.76)	(2.47)	(2.48)	(−1.95)	(−1.48)
N	2008	2008	1879	1879	2107	2107

Notes: t statistics in parentheses.

* $p < 0.05$, ** $p < 0.01$, *** $p < 0.001$.

banks are active in income smoothing. For the non-crisis period, lagged ROA decreases all dependent variables confirming that higher profitability is capital-consuming, but on the other hand it gives more space for profit management. The growth of loans in a non-crisis period reduces capital ratios and increases provisioning as expected. The growth of GDP helps reduce provisioning, confirming its procyclical nature. Increasing NPLs require the equity capital increase to maintain banks' safety. Bearing in mind that the largest banks, especially in the post-GFC period, were forced to deleverage, we find that this process was probably more intensive in the case of growing NPLs.

Against this background, when we look at differences during the crisis, we find that the growth of loans increased banks' capital ratios during times of crisis (i.e. the sum of "crisis#ΔLoans" and "ΔLoans" is positive in Table 2.7 where the crisis vs non-crisis periods are considered). One may assume however that as a matter of fact, the growth of loans was possible if banks were adequately capitalized. Undercapitalized banks were not able to grant new loans. The differences between periods are most visible in the case of provisioning (models 3.4–3.6) and for the role of NPLs (models 1.5–1.6). In a time of crisis, lagged ROA decreased provisioning to a larger extent, which underlines the role of profit management. Additionally, high lagged NIM coincided with the increased provisioning being a probable sign of excessive risk-taking in pre-crisis time. Although the growth of GDP still decreases provisioning, it is to a lesser degree. In the non-crisis period, the growing NPL increased equity to total assets, while in times of crisis this has changed – NPLs decreased capital ratios as banks had to absorb losses. Moreover, in times of crisis, the rate of inflation coincides with the increase of capital ratios (which is likely to mean that it helps it to increase faster).

We further consider the three-period disaggregation allowing for the differences across the pre-crises and regular periods. In the corresponding set of equations, the reference category is a crisis period. The obtained estimates confirm the previous conclusions regarding the role of the lagged ROA, GDP growth and inflation for capital ratios and provisioning. The most visible differences among periods relate to provisioning, which is higher in regular times than in times of an actual crisis. Although this finding seems to be counterintuitive, this may be due to income smoothing and dynamic provisioning. Additionally, if a crisis emerges in the financial sphere, bank debtors from the real sphere may suffer with some delay.

Looking at differences in the equity-to-assets ratio (models 1.7 and 1.8), in pre-crisis and regular periods the loan growth decreases capital ratio, while in times of crisis it increases. This opposite role should be linked to overall capital management policy. In non-crisis times, banks try to maximize the return on equity and therefore consume capital via loan growth. In times of crisis, however, the growth of loans is possible for well-capitalized banks and banks that while deleveraging, switched the structure of their assets towards loans. In comparison with the crisis period in a regular period, the role of the inflation rate is reduced, but still with a positive sign.

In the case of the TCR equation (models 2.7 and 2.8) the growth of NPL changes its sign from the negative during the crisis to positive for pre-crisis and regular periods. As noted, banks have to absorb losses from NPLs, which is clearly visible in the crisis period. This difference may be explained by the fact that even if NPLs grow, this growth is not necessarily considerable and/or does not require initially high coverage in allowances.

Provisioning (models 3.7 and 3.8) shows the specific situation in the pre-crisis period in terms of risk pricing. That is, in the pre-crisis period higher lagged ROA increases provisioning, while higher lagged NIM reduces it. We found that although the risk pricing seems to be adequate the overall risk of a bank is probably excessive. Moreover, GDP growth and inflation rate reduce provisioning to a larger extent.

All in all, we identified certain differences between crisis and the other periods (pre-crisis, regular or just non-crisis) with a clear indication that the most sensitive aspects are provisioning and pricing. The role of pricing is especially visible in the pre-crisis period, when banks seemed to take excessive risk, but priced it adequately. We found that the largest banks in Europe actively manage their profits applying income smoothing and adjust their capital policy to the situation in the economy.

Notes

1 For instance, the ECB explained it as easing of monetary policy, improving the transmission mechanism and some unconventional instruments, in order to anchor inflation expectations. At the same time, the DNB and SNB tried to stem excessive capital inflows, while Riksbank aimed at reducing the appreciation pressure on krona.

2 Two explanations for LIRE are empirically presented (ESRB 2016, 2021a) i.e. monetary policy was historically more and more expansive after the financial crises and subsequent recessions (cyclical reasons), implying the temporary nature of LIRE. This implies that monetary policy (reacting to recessions and dampened inflation outlook over the recent decades) of central banks had a significant impact on the creation of LIRE. Additionally, LIRE is fueled by demographic developments (ageing of society), lower productivity growth in a secular stagnation and global savings glut (structural reasons), suggesting that those factors are more permanent and protracted. This is reflected in the decline in the natural rate of interest over the decades to currently historically low levels.

3 A two-tier system for reserve remuneration was introduced by the ECB in late 2019. This system exempts some credit institutions' excess liquidity holdings (i.e. reserve holdings in excess of minimum reserve requirements) from negative remuneration at the rate applicable on the deposit facility. This decision aims to support the bank-based transmission of monetary policy, while preserving the positive contribution of negative rates to the accommodative stance of monetary policy.

4 Expected losses (EL) are defined as PD x LGD. Probability of default (PD) represents the risk of the borrower, while loss given default (LGD) reflects the potential loss on a given type of exposure. PD is estimated for one year and for a lifetime, i.e. for the whole period of the transaction (PD lifetime).

5 Its equivalent for G-SIBs is total loss absorbency capacity (TLAC).
6 This bank is administered by the resolution authority in a given country.
7 Waterbed effects are created in response to macroprudential tightening – less regulated institutions/countries increase credit provision in response to lower credit provision by a more regulated sector.
8 Microprudential supervisors also provided guidance on loan forbearance and encouraged bank flexibility in creation of loan loss provisions and debt restructuring for reasons related to pandemic.
9 Analysis is mostly based on IMF data (Financial Soundness Indicators). European countries cover the EEA and UK and were divided into two groups – average values in West European countries (AT, BE, CH, CY, DE, DK, EE, ES, FI, FR, GR, IE, IT, LU, MT, NL, NO, PT, SE, UK,) and in Eastern European countries (BG, CZ, HR, HU, LV, LT, PL, RO, SI, SK).

References

Adler, K., & Boissay, F., 2020. Dealing with bank distress: Insights from a comprehensive database. BIS Working Papers, No. 909, BIS.

Aguilar, P., Arce, Ó., Hurtado, A., Martínez-Martín, J., Nuño, G. & Thomas, C., 2020. The ECB monetary policy. Response to the COVID-19 crisis 2020. *Documentos Ocasionales*, No. 2026, Banco de España.

Ahnert, T., Chapman, J., & Wilkins, C., 2021. Should bank capital regulation be risk sensitive? *Journal of Financial Intermediation*, Vol. 46, 100870, https://doi.org/10.1016/j.jfi.2020.100870.

Akinci, O., & Olmstead-Rumsey J., 2018. How effective are macroprudential policies? An empirical investigation. *Journal of Financial Intermediation*, Vol. 33, 33–57. DOI: 10.1016/j.jfi.2017.04.001.

Alam, Z., Alter, A., Eiseman, J., Gelos, G., Kang, H., Narita, M., Nier, E. & Wang N., 2019. Digging deeper – evidence on the effects of macroprudential policies from a new database. IMF Working Paper, No. 19/66.

Allen, F., Jackowicz, K., Kowalewski, O., & Kozłowski Ł., 2017. Bank lending, crises, and changing ownership structure in Central and Eastern European countries. *Journal of Corporate Finance*, Vol. 42, 494–515, https://doi.org/10.1016/j.jcorpfin.2015.05.001.

Altavilla, C., Barbiero, F., Boucinha, M., Burlon, L., 2020. The great lockdown: pandemic response policies and bank lending conditions. ECB Working Paper, No. 2465, ECB.

Apergis, N., 2021. The role of housing market in the effectiveness of monetary policy over the Covid-19 era. *Economics Letters*, Vol. 200, 109749, https://doi.org/10.1016/j.econlet.2021.109749.

Arena, M., Bems, R., Ilahi, N., Lee, J., Lindquist, W. & Lybek T., 2021. *Asset Purchase Programs in European Emerging Markets*. IMF Departmental Paper Series, DP/2021/021.

Avezum, L., Oliveira, V. & Serra, D., 2021. Assessment of the effectiveness of the macroprudential measures implemented in the context of the Covid-19 pandemic. Banco de Portugal Working Papers, No. 07, Lisboa.

Balla E. & McKenna A., 2009. Dynamic provisioning: a countercyclical tool for loan loss reserves, *Economic Quarterly*, Federal Reserve Bank of Richmond, Vol. 95(Fall), 383–418; https://ideas.repec.org/a/fip/fedreq/y2009ifallp383-418nv.95no.4.html

Barbier-Gauchard, A., Dai, M., Mainguy, C., Saadaoui, J., Sidiropoulos, M., Terraz, I. & Trabelsi, J., 2021. Towards a more resilient European Union after the COVID-19 crisis. *Eurasian Economic Review*, Vol. 11, 321–348. https://doi.org/10.1007/s40822-021-00167-4.

Basel Committee on Banking Supervision, 2011. *Global Systemically Important Banks: Assessment Methodology and The Additional Loss Absorbency Requirement.* Bank for International Settlements, Basel.

BIS. 2019. Unconventional monetary policy tools: a cross-country analysis. CGFS Papers, CGFS Papers, Number 63.

Boeckx, J., de Sola Perea, M. & Peersman, G., 2020. The transmission mechanism of credit support policies in the euro area. *European Economic Review*, Vol. 124, 103403, https://doi.org/10.1016/j.euroecorev.2020.103403.

Boissay, F., Claessens, S. & Villegas, A. 2020. Tools for managing banking distress: historical experience and lessons for today. *BIS Quarterly Review*, December.

Borio, C., 2020. Covid-19 economic crisis: dangerously unique. *Business Economics*, Vol. 55, 181–190. https://doi.org/10.1057/s11369-020-00184-2.

Budnik, K. & Kleibl J., 2018. Macroprudential regulation in the European union in 1995–2014: Introducing a new data set on policy actions of a macroprudential nature. ECB Working Paper, No. 2123, ECB.

Cantú, C., Cavallino, P., De Fiore, F. & Yetman, J., 2021. *A global database on central banks' monetary responses to Covid-19.* BIS Working Papers, No 934, BIS 2021.

Carreras, O., Davis, E. P. & Piggott, R. 2018. Assessing macroprudential tools in OECD countries within a cointegration framework. *Journal of Financial Stability*, Vol. 37, 112–130. DOI: 10.1016/j.jfs.2018.04.004.

Cavallino, P., De Fiore, F., 2020. Central banks' response to Covid-19 in advanced economies. *BIS Bulletin*, No. 21, BIS.

Chang, C., Jimenez-Martin, J.-A., Maasoumi, E., McAleer, M., & Perez-Amaral, T., 2019. *Choosing Expected Shortfall Over VaR in Basel III Using*, Vol. 60, 95–113, https://doi.org/10.1016/j.iref.2018.12.016.

Chawla, G., Forest, L., & Aguais, S., 2016. Some options for evaluating significant deterioration under IFRS 9. *Journal of Risk Model Validation*, Vol. 10(3), 69–89, DOI: 10.21314/JRMV.2016.158.

Claeys, G., 2021. *What Are the Effects of the ECB's Negative Interest Rate Policy?* Publication for the committee on Economic and Monetary Affairs, Policy Department for Economic, Scientific and Quality of Life Policies, European Parliament, Luxembourg.

Cukierman, A., 2013. Monetary policy and institutions before, during, and after the global financial crisis. *Journal of Financial Stability*, Vol. 9(3), 373–384, https://doi.org/10.1016/j.jfs.2013.02.002.

Darracq, M., Kok, C. & Rottner, M., 2020. *Enhancing Macroprudential Space When Interest Rates Are Low for Long.* Macroprudential Bulletin, ECB.

Dautovic, E., Marques, A. P., Reghezza, A., Rodriguez d'Acri, C., Vila Martín, D. & Wildmann, N. 2021. Evaluating the benefits of euro area dividend distribution recommendations on lending and provisioning. *ECB Macroprudential Bulletin*, No. 13, ECB.

de Guindos, L., 2021. *Macroprudential policy after the COVID-19 pandemic.* Panel contribution at the Banque de France / Sciences Po Financial Stability Review Conference 2021 "Is macroprudential policy resilient to the pandemic?", 1 March 2021.

EBA, 2021. *Risk Assessment of the European Banking System*, Luxembourg, December.

ECB, 2021. *Financial Stability Review*, November, Frankfurt.

Eller, M., Hauzenberger, N., Huber, F., Schuberth, H. & Vashold, L. 2021a. The impact of macroprudential policies on capital flows in CESEE. *Journal of International Money and Finance*. Vol. 119, 102495, https://doi.org/10.1016/j.jimonfin.2021.102495.

Eller, M., Martin, R. & Vashold, L., 2021b. CESEE's macroprudential policy response in the wake of the COVID-19 crisis. *Focus on European Economic Integration*, Issue Q1/21. Oesterreichische Nationalbank.

Eller, M., Reiner, M., Schuberth, H. & Vashold, L. 2020. Macroprudential policies in CESEE – an intensity-adjusted approach. *Focus on European Economic Integration*, Issue Q2/20, Oesterreichische Nationalbank.

ESRB, 2016. *Macroprudential Policy Issues Arising from Low Interest Rates and Structural Changes in the EU Financial System*, Frankfurt.

ESRB, 2020. *A Review of Macroprudential Policy in the EU in 2019*, Frankfurt.

ESRB, 2021a. *Lower for Longer – Macroprudential Policy Issues Arising from the Low Interest Rate Environment*, Frankfurt.

ESRB, 2021b. *A Review of Macroprudential Policy in the EU in 2020*, Frankfurt.

ESRB, 2021c. *Report of the Analytical Task Force on the Overlap Between Capital Buffers and Minimum Requirements*, Frankfurt.

European Commission, 2021. *European Economic Forecast – Summer 2021*, Institutional Paper 156, DG ECFIN.

Evgenidis, A. & Salachas E., 2019. Unconventional monetary policy and the credit channel in the euro area. *Economics Letters*, Vol. 185, 108695, https://doi.org/10.1016/j.econlet.2019.108695.

Franch, F., Nocciola, L. & Żochowski, D., 2021. Cross-border effects of prudential regulation: Evidence from the euro area. *Journal of Financial Stability*, Vol. 53, 100820,https://doi.org/10.1016/j.jfs.2020.100820.

Galati, G. & Moessner, R., 2013. Macroprudential policy – a literature review. *Journal of Economic Surveys*, Vol. 27, No. 5, https://doi.org/10.1111/j.1467-6419.2012.00729.x.

Gibson, H. D., Hall, S. G., Petroulas, P. & Tavlas, G. S., 2020. On the effects of the ECB's funding policies on bank lending. *Journal of International Money and Finance*, Vol. 102, 102112, https://doi.org/10.1016/j.jimonfin.2019.102112.

Gibson, H. D., Hall, S.G. &. Tavlas, G. S., 2016. The effectiveness of the ECB's asset purchase programs of 2009 to 2012. *Journal of Macroeconomics*, Vol. 47, Part A, https://doi.org/10.1016/j.jmacro.2015.09.006.

Grasselli, M. R. 2021. Monetary policy responses to COVID-19: A comparison with the 2008 crisis and implications for the future of central banking. *Review of Political Economy*, 420–445. DOI: 10.1080/09538259.2021.1908778.

Herring, R. J., 2018. The evolving complexity of capital regulation. *Journal of Financial Services Research*, Vol. 53, 183–205, https://doi.org/10.1007/s10693-018-0295-8.

Hogan, T. L., Meredith, N. R., & Harry, X., 2018. Evaluating risk-based capital regulation. *Review of Financial Economics*, Vol. 36, 83–96. https://doi.org/10.1016/j.rfe.2017.10.003.

Hutchinson, J. & Mee, S., 2020. The impact of the ECB's monetary policy measures taken in response to the COVID-19 crisis. *ECB Economic Bulletin*, Issue 5/2020, ECB.

Iwanicz-Drozdowska, M. ed., 2016. *European Bank Restructuring During the Global Financial Crisis*. Palgrave Macmillan Studies in Banking and Financial Institutions, Palgrave Macmillan.

Kahou M. E., Lehar A., 2017. Macroprudential policy: A review. *Journal of Financial Stability*, Vol. 29, 92–105. DOI: 10.1016/j.jfs.2016.12.005.
Kucharčuková, O. B., Claeys, P. & Vašíček, B. 2016. Spillover of the ECB's monetary policy outside the euro area: How different is conventional from unconventional policy? *Journal of Policy Modeling*, Vol. 38(2), 199–225. https://doi.org/10.1016/j.jpolmod.2016.02.002.
Lewrick, U., Schmieder, Ch., Sobrun J. & Takáts E., 2020. *Releasing bank buffers to cushion the crisis – a quantitative assessment. BIS Bulletin*, No. 11, BIS.
Markmann, H. & Zietz, J., 2017. Determining the effectiveness of the Eurosystem's Covered Bond Purchase Programs on secondary markets. *The Quarterly Review of Economics and Finance*, Vol. 66, 314–327. https://doi.org/10.1016/j.qref.2017.04.005.
Meuleman E. & Vander Vennet R., 2020. Macroprudential policy and bank systemic risk. *Journal of Financial Stability*, Vol. 47, 100724, DOI: 10.1016/j.jfs.2020.100724.
Mojon, B., Rees, D. & Schmieder, Ch., 2021. How much stress could Covid put on corporate credit? Evidence using sectoral data. *BIS Quarterly Review*, March, BIS.
Niedźwiedzińska, J. 2020. Initial monetary policy response to the COVID-19 pandemic in inflation targeting economies. NBP Working Paper, No. 335, NBP.
Olszak, M. & Kowalska, I., 2022. Does bank competition matter for the effects of macroprudential policy on the procyclicality of lending? *Journal of International Financial Markets, Institutions and Money*, Vol. 76, 101484, https://doi.org/10.1016/j.intfin.2021.101484.
Olszak, M., Chodnicka-Jaworska, P., Kowalska, I. and Świtała, F. 2018. Bank-type specific determinants of sensitivity of loan-loss provisions to business cycle. *European Journal of Finance*, Vol. 24 (17), 1672–1698. https://doi.org/10.1080/1351847X.2018.1501401
Ongena, S., Popov, A., Udell, G. F., 2013. When the cat's away the mice will play: Does regulation at home affect bank risk taking abroad? *Journal of Financial Economics*, Vol. 108 (3), 727–750. DOI: 10.1016/j.jfineco.2013.01.006.
Petrella, G., & Resti, A., 2017. What drives the liquidity of sovereign bonds when markets are under stress? An assessment of the new Basel 3 rules on bank liquid assets. *Journal of Financial Stability*, Vol. 33, 297–310. https://doi.org/10.1016/j.jfs.2016.07.018
Poghosyan, T., 2019. How effective is macroprudential policy? Evidence from lending restriction measures in EU countries. IMF Working Paper, No. 19/45, IMF.
Potjagailo, G., 2017. Spillover effects from Euro area monetary policy across Europe: A factor-augmented VAR approach. *Journal of International Money and Finance*, Vol. 72, 127–147. https://doi.org/10.1016/j.jimonfin.2017.01.003.
Restoy, F., 2020. Central banks and financial stability: A reflection after the Covid-19 outbreak, FSI Occasional Paper, No. 16, BIS.
Saurina, J., 2009. Dynamic Provisioning, *World Bank Publications – Reports*, No. 10241, The World Bank Group; https://ideas.repec.org/p/wbk/wboper/10241.html
Schnabel, I. 2021. Monetary policy and financial stability. Speech at the fifth annual conference of the European Systemic Risk Board, Frankfurt, 8 December 2021.
Sever, C., Goel, R., Drakopoulos, D. & Papageorgiou, E. 2020. Effects of Emerging Market Asset Purchase Program Announcements on Financial Markets During the COVID-19 Pandemic. IMF Working Paper, WP/20/292, IMF.
Skała, D. 2015. Saving on a Rainy Day? Income Smoothing and Procyclicality of Loan-Loss Provisions in Central European Banks. *International Finance*, Vol. 18, 25–46. https://doi.org/10.1111/1468-2362.12058.

Skała, D. 2020. Shareholder shocks and loan loss provisions in Central European. *Journal of International Financial Markets, Institutions & Money*, Vol. 69 . https://doi.org/10.1016/j.intfin.2020.101244.

The de Larosière Group, The High-Level Group on Financial Supervision in Europe, *Report*, Brussels, 25 February, 2009.

Verwey, M., Licchetta, M. & Zeana, A., 2021. Beyond the pandemic: From life support to structural change, Voxeu, 08 July 2021, https://voxeu.org/article/beyond-pandemic-life-support-structural-change.

Villeroy de Galhau, F., 2021. Financial stability at the nexus of monetary and macroprudential policies, Financial Stability Review, Banque de France, March.

Wei, X., Gong, Y., & Wu, H., 2017. The impacts of Net Stable Funding Ratio requirement on Banks ' choices of debt maturity. *Journal of Banking and Finance*, Vol. 82, 229–243, https://doi.org/10.1016/j.jbankfin.2017.02.006.

Yilmazkuday, H., 2022. COVID-19 and monetary policy with zero bounds: A cross-country investigation. *Finance Research Letters*, Vol. 44, 2022, 102103, https://doi.org/10.1016/j.frl.2021.102103.

3 Fiscal policy reaction to crises

3.1 Policy response – towards strengthening European integration

Fiscal policy response to financial turmoil can be arranged by various measures, which are provided by different channels. Typically, a distinction is made between direct and indirect channels, and each of them is related to some form of fiscal costs (Amaglobeli et al., 2015; Bellia et al., 2019). Direct government interventions most often involve direct fiscal costs, such as capital injections and asset purchases, although their impact on public finances is not always clear-cut, as presented in Section 3.4. Indirect costs reflect the impact of financial crises on the real economy, increasing in particular risk premiums and distorting the supply of credit, which reduces consumption and investment (more in Chapter 5). As a result, public revenues are decreasing and there is pressure on government expenditure, which has a negative impact on the budget balance and increases debt.

In the case of the GFC, as with previous banking crises, the policy response was broadly similar. It started with liquidity support, then other instruments such as asset purchases and capital injections were used, however, according to Laeven and Valencia (2010) all the measures were introduced faster than in the past. The effects of the financial crisis of 2007+ were concentrated primarily in advanced economies, thus liquidity shortages experienced by systemically important financial institutions resulted in large-scale government intervention, and it was also possible to use more diverse assistance measures, including non-standard monetary policy tools. The magnitude of fiscal costs related to banking crises (direct and undirect) depends primarily on the characteristics of the banking sector, especially its size, international relations, and the structure of financing, but at the same time fiscal risk can be mitigated by an appropriate regulatory and supervisory framework (Amaglobeli et al, 2015).

Both the GFC and, to a much greater extent, the COVID-19 pandemic crisis, prompted government interventions to support the real economy. Generally, such support consists of automatic fiscal stabilizers and discretionary measures. Automatic stabilizers are triggered by the fluctuations in economic activity and do not require any government intervention. They

DOI: 10.4324/9781003225539-3

are built-in in the government revenue and expenditure system, and in the case of economic downturn they contribute to stimulate demand, through, for example, increased payments of unemployment benefits. Automatic fiscal stabilizers help to alleviate the impact of the crisis, but they may be insufficient to fully absorb economic shocks in severe downturn (Mohl et al., 2019; Bouabdallah et al., 2020). Government discretionary measures in response to the crises can be classified according to various criteria. We can distinguish direct fiscal measures or financial measures, measures focused on different objectives or recipients, and measures affecting public revenues or expenditures. The impact of these measures on public finances is also diverse. One of the most frequently used measures is short-time work schemes, which are direct government expenditure aimed at employment support or relief for enterprises. These measures affect the budget balance – when total revenue is lower than expenditure, they increase deficit and debt, otherwise they decrease budget surplus. Revenue measures include taxes and social security reductions which, by lowering budget revenues, may lead to an increase in the deficit (if there is no surplus) and in debt. It is worth paying attention to state guarantees. When granted, they lead to improvement in the budget balance, as guarantee fees increase budget revenues. Nevertheless, they constitute contingent liabilities, and if the guarantee is called upon, expenditures must be incurred.

Unlike the GFC, the pandemic crisis hit all economies, although the scale of this impact largely depended on the implemented anti-crisis policy (including lockdowns) and decisions (and possibilities) to what extent these effects would be compensated for. The World Bank reported (2021) that emerging markets and developing economies were affected more severely than advanced economies, however their response was limited due to insufficient fiscal space. Due to the cause of the crisis, additional funds were allocated to health care. In 2020, advanced economies pledged to increase spending on health by 0.5% of GDP, while emerging markets and middle-income economies planned an additional 0.2% of GDP (IMF, 2020, p. 7).

According to the European Commission, joint actions were to provide a more effective and credible response to crisis challenges, also reducing the risk of undesirable side effects that could result from uncoordinated actions of individual countries (European Commission, 2008a). Hence, at the EU level, many measures were taken to both counteract the negative consequences of the financial crisis and prevent such situations from happening in the future, including EU emergence actions and recovery initiatives (Section 3.1.1). As presented in Chapter 2, they were accompanied by monetary and regulatory measures, which contributed to decreasing sovereign risk and ensuring financial stability.

The magnitude of the aid vital for financial institutions and the real economy to alleviate the effects of the crises prompted the European Commission to issue temporary rules for state aid. Such rules were adopted both in the case of the GFC and the pandemic crisis. An analysis of these regulations, and especially of the introduced amendments, proves that the EU strove to adapt to the current requirements and challenges faced by the EU countries, so as to adjust the rules to the implemented or advisable *ad hoc* measures (see Section 3.1.2).

The GFC, and in particular – the sovereign debt crisis, demonstrated the necessity of strengthening fiscal surveillance coordination. It was decided to reform the Stability and Growth Pact (SGP), in particular by adopting legal acts under the "six-pack" (2011) and "two-pack" (2013). The changes concerned both the preventive arm of the SGP, by for example adding a new expenditure benchmark to complement the medium-term budgetary objectives, and the corrective arm, especially in relation to the Excessive Deficit Procedure (EDP) which is triggered when the general government deficit exceeds 3% of GDP and/or debt exceeds 60% of GDP. In February 2012, the Fiscal Pact (the Treaty on Stability, Coordination and Governance in the Economic and Monetary Union) was signed, aimed at increasing budgetary discipline, strengthening the coordination of economic policies and improving governance in the euro area (more on this topic in Section 3.1.3).

Some EU facilities, under which countries facing financial distress could apply for international assistance, were also introduced (Section 3.1.4). Such facilities were considered as advantageous also after the outbreak of the pandemic crisis, and although the earlier established instruments were not used, a new one was created (SURE). It is worth noting that the principles of granting international aid to individual countries often conflicted with the national interests of both donors (as individual countries) and beneficiaries. Such protectionist practices became particularly visible in the case of successive bailouts for Greece.

3.1.1 EU emergency and recovery initiatives

In response to the GFC, in November 2008, the European Economic Recovery Plan (Recovery Plan) was adopted. It was based on two pillars: increasing the purchasing power of the EU, and reinforcing the competitiveness of the European economy in the long term. The strategic objectives of the Recovery Plan included swift demand stimulation and boosting of consumer confidence, reducing the social costs of the crisis, helping to prepare for actions in the event of economic recovery (including structural reforms and supporting innovation) and accelerating the transition towards a low-carbon economy. The real economy was to be strengthened by monetary policy, stabilizing the banking system, actions in the four priority areas of the Lisbon Strategy, involvement of the European Investment Bank (EIB) and the European Bank for Reconstruction and Development (EBRD), and the budget stimulus packages. The Recovery Plan assumed financing at the level of EUR 200 billion (1.5% of EU GDP), of which EUR 170 billion was to come from the budgets of the member states, and EUR 30 billion from EU funding. According to the Recovery Plan, short- and long-term budgetary stimulus should be complemented by structural reforms to stimulate demand

and support the resilience of the economy, all within the framework of the Stability and Growth Pact.

The Recovery Plan was supplemented and reinforced by many other EU initiatives and programs, such as for example the Cohesion Policy of December 2008, extension of the European Globalization Adjustment Fund's activities of June 2009, or later (2010) – the Europe 2020 Strategy.

Measures to counteract the negative effects of the COVID-19 crisis were introduced much faster and on a much larger scale. Soon after the outbreak of the pandemic, in March and April 2020, the Commission decided on several actions in response to the pandemic crisis. In March, the Commission proposed to mobilize EU cohesion policy funding, still unallocated within the 2014–2020 programs – about EUR 8 billion of immediate liquidity to accelerate up to EUR 37 billion of public investment. This initiative, called the Coronavirus Response Investment Initiative (CRII), was later followed by the Coronavirus Response Investment Initiative Plus (CRII+), which complemented the first measures, by introducing additional flexibility at the closure of programs to ensure that available resources were out to full use. Both proposals were swiftly adopted by the European Parliament and the Council of the EU. Other decisions included using the European Support Instrument as for the COVID-19 response. These measures were complemented by the support aimed at providing liquidity to companies, especially small and medium-sized ones, served by the European Investment Fund, being a part of the European Investment Bank Group.

It soon transpired that the EU institutions needed to become much more involved in efforts to rebuild the European economy after the crisis caused by the COVID-19 pandemic and to strengthen the resilience of the economy to crises. In July 2020, the economic recovery package called NextGenerationEU (abbreviated to NextGenEU) was adopted, which, together with the Multiannual Financial Framework 2021–2027 (including flexibility mechanisms), was to be a response to both the pandemic and future challenges. A provisional agreement on the Recovery and Resilience Facility (RRF) – the key financial instrument for the NextGenEU – was reached in December 2020, followed by Parliament approval in February 2021.

The NextGenEU budget, to be financed through bond issuance, is EUR 806.9 billion (EUR 750 billion in 2018 prices), of which EUR 723.8 billion was for the RRF and the rest for contribution to other programs, for example EUR 50.6 billion for REACT-EU (Recovery Assistance for Cohesion and the Territories of Europe). The support provided by the RRF is divided into two parts: EUR 338.0 billion as non-repayable assistance (grants) and EUR 385.8 billion as loans on favourable conditions. The majority of RRF funds (EUR 776.5 billion) should be allocated to "Cohesion, resilience and values."

The maximum allocation for grants is calculated on the basis of the population, the inverse of the GDP per capita, the relative unemployment rate, and the changes in real GDP. As a result, the amounts of grants that can be used by individual countries range from EUR 0.1 billion (Luxembourg) to almost

EUR 70 billion (Italy and Spain). Countries interested in non-returnable RRF support were required to provide recovery and resilience plans, specifying in particular the goals and scope of planned activities. At least 37 % of the recovery and resilience plan's total allocation should contribute to the green transition, including biodiversity, and comply with the principle "do no significant harm,"[1] while a further 20% should be for digital measures. The allocation of funds for a given country follows the approval by the European Commission of the submitted plan. The loans may be granted upon request from an EU country until the end of 2023. The maximum volume may not exceed 6.8% of the state's 2019 GNI in current prices.

3.1.2 Tailoring the state aid framework

The effect of the US subprime mortgage collapse and ongoing turbulence in the world's financial markets became very soon visible also in Europe. As soon as in 2007, the first British bank and two German banks received state aid due to severe liquidity difficulties. This aid was granted under the general rescue and restructuring state aid rules, but it was quickly recognized that a new, more tailored solution was needed (Lowe, 2009).

The increasing deterioration of the condition of financial institutions prompted the Economic and Financial Affairs Council (ECOFIN) to take steps aimed at improving soundness and stability of the financial system. In October 2008, the European Commission issued the first so-called Banking Communication (for detailed titles of all Banking Communications, see Box 3.1) setting out EU-wide principles and conditions for state intervention, including the rules for granting aid in the form of guarantees for bank liabilities and recapitalization. The subsequent communications clarified and supplemented the forms of support for banks or extended the deadline for their application, while the last one (from 2013) replaced the first banking communication and adapted the later ones. The European Commission concluded that due to the serious fiscal instability of the EU countries, which might result in the risk of serious economic disturbances, it was justified to maintain the possibility of supporting financial institutions from public funds. However, it was emphasized that the general principles of state aid control do not cease to apply, even in a time of crisis. The moral hazard and distortions of competition should be limited by reducing the aid to the minimum necessary with the highest possible own contribution of the banks and their capital owners (in line with BRRD, see Section 3.2). The principle was established that recapitalization and impaired asset measures would only be allowed after approval of the bank's restructuring plan, and guarantees would only be available to banks without capital shortages.

The negative impact of the financial crisis was also visible in the real economy. The problems of the banking sector may translate into lower lending, and thus reduce the access to financing for enterprises, especially in the case of small and medium-sized enterprises. Thus, temporary additional

Box 3.1 Banking Communications

1. Communication on the application of State aid rules to measures taken in relation to financial institutions in the context of the current global financial crisis, OJ C 270, 25.10.2008, p. 8.
2. Communication on the recapitalization of financial institutions in the current financial crisis: limitation of aid to the minimum necessary and safeguards against undue distortions of competition ("Recapitalization Communication"), OJ C 10, 15.01.2009, p. 2.
3. Communication from the Commission on the treatment of impaired assets in the Community financial sector ("Impaired Assets Communication"), OJ C 72, 26.3.2009, p. 1.
4. Communication on the return to viability and the assessment of restructuring measures in the financial sector in the current crisis under the State aid rules ("Restructuring Communication"), OJ C. 195, 19.8.2009, p. 9.
5. Communication from the Commission on the application, from 1 January 2011, of State aid rules to support measures in favour of financial institutions in the context of the financial crisis ("2010 Prolongation Communication"), OJ C 329, 7.12.2010. p. 7.
6. Communication from the Commission on the application, from 1 January 2012, of State aid rules to support measures in favour of financial institutions in the context of the financial crisis ("2011 Prolongation Communication"), OJ C 365, 6.12.2011, p. 7.
7. Communication from the Commission on the application, from 1 August 2013, of State aid rules to support measures in favour of banks in the context of the financial crisis ("Banking Communication"), OJ C 216, 30.7.2013, p. 1.

measures of January 2009 (see Box 3.2) were intended to ensure uninterrupted access to finance for businesses and to encourage investment, particularly in sustainable growth. Such measures include a compatible limited amount of aid, not exceeding EUR 500,000 (the higher *de minimis* limit), awarded in the form of aid programs. Guarantees, a subsidized interest rate, and aid for the production of "green" products were also considered as appropriate and well-targeted aid measures. The 2009 communication also introduced temporary derogations or simplified regulations for other previously applied aid measures, namely risk capital measures and short-term export credit insurance. The regulations regarding temporary aid measures were later changed and adjusted to the current requirements. Due to high volatility of financial markets and uncertainty about the economic outlook, the European Commission considered it justified to extend some of the measures provided for in the communication of 2009. However, stricter conditions for these measures were introduced.

Box 3.2 Temporary Community framework for State aid measures during the GFC

1. Communication from the Commission – Temporary Community framework for State aid measures to support access to finance in the current financial and economic crisis, OJ C. 16, 21.1.2009, p. 1.
2. Communication of the Commission – Temporary Union framework for State aid measures to support access to finance in the current financial and economic crisis, OJ C 6, 11.1.2011, p. 5–15.

In 2020, in response to the economic shock caused by the COVID-19 pandemic, the European Commission decided on close coordination of national aid measures. EU control was to support the effectiveness of national measures while ensuring a level playing field and market coherence. As the pandemic exposed enterprises to reduction or even lack of liquidity, which consequently affect the labour market and households' well-being, EU countries have at their disposal various forms of support. Some of them (for example wage subsidies, suspension of CIT payments) do not require the involvement of the Commission, and other forms can be notified directly under EU regulations. On 19 March 2020, the catalogue of these options was supplemented by additional, temporary (applicable until the end of 2020) aid measures set out in the Commission communication. Such measures include direct grants, repayable advances or tax benefits, guarantees on loans, subsidized interest rates for loans, guarantees and loans channelled through credit institutions or other financial institutions, and short-term export credit insurance.

These measures could have been a better response to a pandemic crisis due to rapid approval after notification by a EU country. Successive waves of COVID-19 and the related further limitations, as well as ongoing monitoring of introduced solutions, resulted in numerous modifications and extension of the scope of forms in which assistance was provided. By December 2021, the communication of 19 March 2020 had been changed six times (see Box 3.3).

As part of the first amendment, adopted in April 2020, modifications were made to the established forms of support, and new forms were added, for example aimed directly at development of coronavirus-relevant products. According to the Commission, one of the most important challenges was to preserve employment, which was to be achieved for instance by deferrals of payment of taxes and social security contributions. It was decided that if such deferrals applied to the economy as a whole, they would not constitute state aid, but if applied selectively (to sectors most exposed to the negative effects of the pandemic), they would constitute state aid. Subsidies for costs of wages were treated in a similar way.

In May 2020, a new form of support was established – recapitalization measures, to be granted by the end of June 2021 at the latest. The introduction of the new aid measure was justified by the situation of non-financial

Box 3.3 Temporary Framework for State aid measures to support the economy in the COVID-19 outbreak

Communication from the Commission, Temporary Framework for State aid measures to support the economy in the current COVID-19 outbreak, C(2020)1863, OJ C 91 I, 20.3.2020, p. 1.

Amendments:

1. Communication from the Commission, Amendment to the Temporary Framework for State aid measures to support the economy in the current COVID-19 outbreak, C(2020)2215, OJ C 112 I, 4.4.2020, p. 1.
2. Communication from the Commission, Amendment to the Temporary Framework for State aid measures to support the economy in the current COVID-19 outbreak, C(2020)2215, OJ C 112 I, 4.4.2020, p. 1.
3. Communication from the Commission. Amendment to the Temporary Framework for State aid measures to support the economy in the current COVID-19 outbreak, C(2020)3156, OJ C 164, 13.5.2020, p. 3.
4. Communication from the Commission Third amendment to the Temporary Framework for State aid measures to support the economy in the current COVID-19 outbreak, C(2020)4509, OJ C 218, 2.7.2020, p. 3.
5. Communication from the Commission of 4th Amendment to the Temporary Framework for State aid measures to support the economy in the current COVID-19 outbreak and amendment to the Annex to the Communication from the Commission to the Member States on the application of Articles 107 and 108 of the Treaty on the Functioning of the European Union to short-term export-credit insurance, C(2020)7127, OJ C 340 I, 13.10.2020, p. 1.
6. Communication from the Commission Fifth Amendment to the Temporary Framework for State aid measures to support the economy in the current COVID-19 outbreak and amendment to the Annex to the Communication from the Commission to the Member States on the application of Articles 107 and 108 of the Treaty on the Functioning of the European Union to short-term export-credit insurance, C(2021)564, OJ C 34, 1.2.2021, p. 6.

enterprises which, due to the COVID-19 pandemic, reduced or suspended production or services, resulting in a decrease in undertakings' equity and negatively affected enterprises' creditworthiness. Later, additional measures were introduced (aid in the form of support for uncovered fixed costs, investment support towards a sustainable recovery and solvency support), and the timeframe was extended finally to the end of June 2022.

3.1.3 Strengthening the fiscal framework

The severe deterioration of EU public finances due to the outbreak of the GFC, which in several euro area countries turned into a sovereign debt crisis, revealed the necessity of strengthening budgetary framework. The instruments to ensure fiscal sustainability were provided in Council Directive 2011/85/EU of 8 November 2011, being part of the "six-pack." It underlined the importance of availability of up-to-date, reliable budgetary data, as well as their transparency, for the proper functioning of budgetary surveillance. Transparency was also found to be indispensable in macroeconomic forecasting, which is intended, in particular, to ensure the possibility of regular, unbiased and comprehensive control of the adopted assumptions. This should contribute to the improvement of the quality of the prepared budget forecasts. The European Fiscal Board (an advisory body to the European Commission) has also been operating since 2016 to assess how the EU budgetary framework is implemented.

Fiscal rules have been assigned significant importance. Different rules (budget balance, debt, expenditure and revenue rules) serve to achieve different economic goals, so they need to be chosen according to the implemented economic policy and established fiscal objectives. Where the priority is to achieve public debt sustainability, the most effective rule is the debt rule and the budget balance rule (nominal and cyclically adjusted) (IMF, 2009, p. 6).

In line with the Directive's recommendations, EU countries should have numerical fiscal rules to support, in particular, compliance with the EU deficit and debt limits and the adoption of a multiannual budget planning perspective. The target and scope of these rules should be defined and the effective and timely monitoring of compliance with them should be established, as well as the consequences of non-compliance. The numerical fiscal rules should be taken into account in the annual budget procedure.

The effectiveness of fiscal rules is heavily related to their strength, which, according to the methodology of the European Commission, can be calculated using information on their legal base, binding character, monitoring bodies, correction mechanisms and resilience to shocks.[2] It is worth noting that although the number of rules increased significantly after 2013, their strength (measured by the Fiscal Rules Index) varies greatly. With the average for the EU countries in 2019 at 1.6, several countries definitely stood out. The highest scores (approximately 3.0) were observed in the Netherlands, Bulgaria, and Lithuania, while in Hungary, Greece, Slovenia and the United Kingdom they did not exceed 1.

Exceeding the threshold set for fiscal rules results in the launch of the excessive deficit procedure (EDP). As an outcome of the GFC, the fiscal positions of most EU countries deteriorated so severely that in 2009 the Council took

18 decisions initiating an EDP, and in 2010 another 4 (European Court of Auditors, 2016, p. 22). Although public finances deteriorated in the EU countries severely also during the pandemic crisis and the debt and deficit limits were exceeded, no new EDP was triggered. In March 2020, the European Commission concluded that the fiscal effort needed to mitigate the crisis and to support the economy, justified the use of the general escape clause. This clause allows for coordinated and orderly temporary deviation from established budgetary requirements due to a severe economic downturn.

As most budgetary decisions have effects far beyond the scope of a single budget, it is important to place it within the framework of longer-term plans, hence the high level of importance attached to the medium-term budgetary framework (MTBF). The MTBF is intended to guarantee the time consistency between policies and targets, and they are needed for converting fiscal targets into detailed revenue and expenditure plans (Fall et al., 2015, p. 47). The obligation of preparing plans over a longer term has been included in the EU legislation. Since 1998, EU countries have been required to provide such plans as part of their stability programs (euro area countries) or convergence programs (non-euro area countries). Provisions related to the MTBF have been strengthened especially with the adoption of Council Directive 2011/85/EU, being a part of the "six-pack." Pursuant to this Directive, EU countries establish a credible, effective medium-term budgetary framework enabling the adoption of at least a three-year term for budget planning. This is to ensure that national budgetary planning is based on a long-term perspective.

Although medium-term budgetary plans are currently provided by all EU countries, they differ significantly in terms of their coverage, level of detail, and procedures for drawing them up. There are also differences relating to the connectedness between the targets/ceilings in national medium-term fiscal plans and the annual budgets.[3] As Fall et al. state (2015), this relationship is crucial for effectiveness of the MTBF. The annual budgets should respect the limits set in the MTBF and should be targeted on longer-term policy priorities. A fundamental feature from the point of view of fiscal surveillance is the possibility of making changes to the MTBF. Various approaches are used here – from allowing very little flexibility depending on strictly defined conditions, to virtually complete freedom, without the need to present any justifications for the changes. It is worth emphasizing that the lessons learned from the GFC have slightly changed the approach to the issues related to the restrictive application of the MTBF arrangements. As Sherwood (2015, p. 6) points out, it may be desirable to allow some flexibility as long as it is economically viable and the transparency criteria are met.

EU regulations concerning fiscal governance frameworks[4] underline that a EU country shall have an independent body to monitor compliance with fiscal rules. This can be performed by fiscal councils, which are independent public institutions aimed at promoting the sustainability of public finances, in particular by assessing the budget and its execution, and by evaluating or providing macroeconomic and budgetary forecasts (IMF, 2013, p. 1).

Fiscal councils differ in terms of their competences, tasks, legal form and scope of independence. Despite all these differences, they share the role of watchdog and a non-partisan role in the budget process and public debate (IMF, 2013). As the IMF reports, in 2020 there were 51 fiscal councils in the world, of which 31 were in Europe.[5] The number of fiscal councils increased significantly after 2005. Among the EU countries, only Poland did not establish such an institution. The research carried out by the IMF (2013, p. 26) suggests that the mere presence of a fiscal council in a given country is not a factor in increasing the effectiveness of fiscal policy. The effectiveness of these institutions depends on some of their features, for instance the degree of their independence and the scope of activities, in particular the monitoring of compliance with fiscal rules. It should be noted that since fiscal councils usually combine several functions, it is difficult to accurately identify "sufficient features" for their effectiveness. The latest IMF report on this matter (Davoodi et al., 2022) underlines the key role of a fiscal council during a pandemic.

3.1.4 Financial assistance facilities

Financial distress of EU countries has been addressed by different financial assistance facilities, some of them are targeted towards the eurozone, towards non-euro area countries.

The European Stability Mechanism (ESM) was established in October 2012, as a successor of temporary stabilization mechanisms from 2010 set up by the eurozone – European Financial Stability Facility (EFSF). Both the EFSF and other EU temporary mechanisms, namely the European Financial Stabilization Mechanism (EFSM), were established to protect the EU's financial stability by providing rapid assistance to countries with severe economic difficulties, to mitigate the effects of financial turmoil. Although the European Stability Mechanism is considered to be a successor to the EFSF (ESM, 2019), its establishment did not mean the immediate liquidation of the former. The EFSF continued previous aid programs, but from July 2013 it could no longer engage in new activities.

The European Stability Mechanism is to be one of the main permanent mechanisms in the strategy of restoring financial stability to the euro area. The assistance offered by the ESM includes loans to countries experiencing or threatened by severe financial problems, purchase of bonds of an ESM member on primary and secondary markets, a prudential credit line (the Precautionary Conditioned Credit Line and the Enhanced Conditions Credit Line), and loans for indirect bank recapitalization and direct recapitalization of financial institutions (see BRRD, Section 2.2).

Financial assistance for eurozone countries was provided by the EU (through temporary facilities and the ESM) but also from other sources, mainly the International Monetary Fund (IMF). For the moment, aid has been granted for countries with severe financial problems within a

Table 3.1 Financial assistance provided by the EFSM, EFSF and ESM

Country	*Facility*	*Loan disbursements*	*Amount (EUR billion)*
Ireland	EFSM	January 2011 to March 2014	22.5
Ireland	EFSF	February 2011 to December 2013	17.7
Portugal	EFSF	June 2011 to April 2014	26.0
Portugal	EFSM	May 2012 to November 2014	24.3
Greece	EFSF	March 2012 to August 2014	141.8
Spain	ESM	December 2012 to February 2013	41.3
Cyprus	ESM	May 2013 to October 2015	6.3
Greece	ESM	August 2015 to August 2018	61.9

Source: Own work based on EC and ESM data.

macroeconomic adjustment program (Cyprus, Greece, Ireland and Portugal) and for indirect bank recapitalization (Spain). The largest beneficiary was Greece (see Table 3.1), which received three aid packages (2010, 2012, 2015, more in Section 3.2.2).

The total financing of the macroeconomic adjustment program for Ireland was set at EUR 85 billion, while for Portugal it was EUR 78 billion. The Portuguese government decided to terminate the aid program without using the full agreed amount of the loan from the EFSM (EUR 23.3 billion instead of the granted EUR 26 billion). The financial assistance granted for the Spanish banking system was up to EUR 100 billion, but the actual amount needed turned out to be much lower (EUR 41.3 billion, disbursed by the ESM). The total volume of assistance for Cyprus was agreed at EUR 10 billion, of which approximately EUR 7.3 billion was used, including EUR 6.3 billion from the ESM and the rest from the International Monetary Fund.

As the ESM provides financial assistance only for the eurozone, there is also a special mechanism for non-euro area countries, with severe difficulties as regards their balance of payments. This is called the Balance of Payments (BoP) assistance facility and it was established in 2002, however became particularly useful during the GFC. The BoP assistance takes the form of medium-term loans granted if a country adopts suitable economic policy measures to ensure balance of payments sustainability. As in the case of assistance to euro area countries, the loans are typically granted by the EU together with other international institutions or countries.

In October 2008, financial assistance was approved for Hungary, EUR 6.5 billion of which was from the BoP (EUR 20 billion in total). Eventually, Hungary received EUR 14.2 billion, EUR 5.5 billion of which was under BoP. Similarly, Latvia did not use the entire amount of aid granted in December 2008 (EUR 7.5 billion). The disbursed amount was EUR 4.5 billion, EUR 2.9 billion of which was under BoP. The third country to receive BoP assistance was Romania. Pursuant to the agreement of May 2009, Romania was to receive EUR 20 billion, EUR 5 billion of which was under the BoP assistance program. The EU support was disbursed in full. Romania subsequently (in 2011 and in 2013) made two more requests for assistance, but they were treated as precautionary and were not followed by any disbursements.

In April 2020, the ESM became a part of the safety net in response to the COVID-19 pandemic crisis. Each of the euro area countries can apply for the support of up to 2% of its GDP (as at the end of 2019). The European Investment Bank is also part of the safety net, which provides support for enterprises while SURE focuses on workers.

SURE (Support to mitigate Unemployment Risks in an Emergency) is a COVID-19 crisis instrument established to help EU countries protect jobs and employees' income threatened by the pandemic. The decision to establish SURE was taken in April 2020, and in May the Council adopted a regulation on this matter. Financial assistance under SURE takes the form of a loan and cannot exceed a total of EUR 100 billion. To finance SURE, the Commission was empowered to issue bonds,[6] and all EU countries agreed to provide bilateral guarantees supporting the loans. The assistance under SURE became available in September 2020, and most of it was distributed from October 2020 to May 2021.

Financial aid was granted to 19 countries for a total amount of EUR 94.3 billion, of which EUR 3.7 billion was allocated under additional funding in 2021 in connection with the next wave of the pandemic. More than half of the funds went to two countries – Italy and Spain, but Poland and Belgium were also significant beneficiaries (see Figure 3.1).

According to European Commission estimates (2021), in 2020 approximately 31 million people (22.5 million employees and 8.5 million self-employed

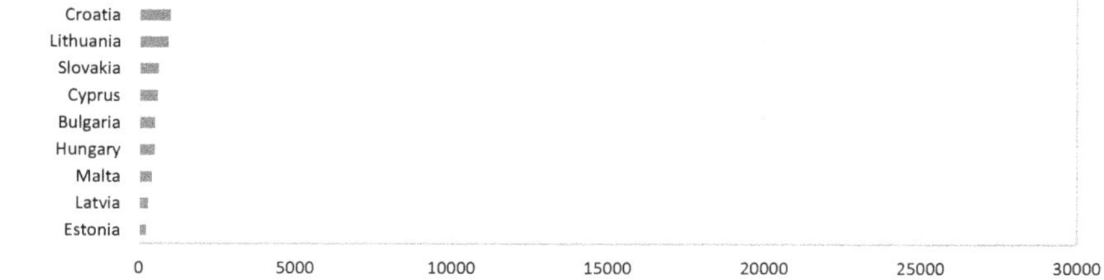

Figure 3.1 Support granted under SURE from October 2020 to May 2021 (EUR million).

Source: Own work based on (European Commission, 2021).

persons) and 2.5 million enterprises were supported under SURE. The funds were primarily intended to support short-time work schemes. Almost 1.5 million people were prevented from becoming unemployed thanks to SURE support. EU countries benefiting from the aid made savings in interest payments of EUR 8.2 billion. These savings are related to the preferential interest rate on SURE loans and their long average maturity.

3.2 Support measures for the financial system – case studies

The global financial crisis triggered state aid to financial institutions on an enormous scale. The vast majority of the aid to financial institutions was approved in 2008 (EUR 3,372 billion) and it was mainly assistance in the form of guarantees (Table 3.2). In the following years, the amount of approved aid gradually decreased, until 2012, when it was increased due to the sovereign debt crisis. The approved aid was used systematically, although not all forms of aid proved to be equally applicable.

Even in 2008, state aid for financial institutions was provided by a total of 11 EU countries for a total amount of EUR 265.7 billion. A year later, the value of the used aid was more than three times higher, and in 2010 it reached a record level – over EUR 1,005 billion. In the following years, financial institutions were still supported from public funds, but the scale of this aid was systematically decreasing. In 2008, the most important form of provided aid was recapitalization and guarantees. The share of guarantees then significantly increased, and in 2009–2011 they constituted on average 88% of all aid granted. Later, an increase in the importance of impaired assets measures could be observed. After 2014, the effects of the financial and sovereign debt crisis were less and less reflected in the volume of aid provided to financial institutions, nevertheless in some countries (in particular in Greece in 2015), these amounts were still significant.

Table 3.2 State aid to financial institutions in 2008–2014 in EU (approved and used, in EUR million)

	2008	*2009*	*2010*	*2011*	*2012*	*2013*	*2014*
Total aid approved	**3 372 005**	**536 168**	**316 800**	**223 470**	**584 075**	**120 265**	**62 532**
Recapitalizations	269 868	110 038	184 010	37 470	150 804	29 556	20 316
Impaired asset measures	4 800	338 503	77 980	6 300	157 480	14 730	3 536
Guarantees	3 097 337	87 627	54 810	179 700	275 791	75 979	38 680
Total aid used	**265 731**	**882 986**	**1 005 202**	**712 011**	**698 142**	**510 494**	**352 739**
Recapitalizations	115 003	110 815	22 751	38 815	91 140	26 566	7 625
Impaired asset measures	0	0	81 708	50 847	162 685	97 305	81 074
Guarantees	150 728	772 171	900 743	622 349	444 317	386 623	264 040

Source: Own work based on the EC State aid Scoreboard.

Table 3.3 State aid to financial institutions in 2008–2014 (by country, used, in EUR million)

	2008	*2009*	*2010*	*2011*	*2012*	*2013*	*2014*	*2008–2014*
European Union	**265 731**	**882 986**	**1 005 202**	**712 011**	**698 142**	**510 494**	**352 739**	**4 427 305**
of which								
Ireland	65 111	228 281	344 665	219 992	42 572	23 729	13 589	937 939
Germany	28 725	155 510	222 282	92 080	135 226	82 816	79 475	796 114
United Kingdom	96 385	197 177	136 513	100 023	22 458	14 611	14 177	581 344
France	21 056	98 983	83 883	62 561	54 675	61 616	53 865	436 639
Spain	0	35 266	66 666	70 482	149 354	71 407	22 130	415 305
Greece	0	5 519	24 307	56 969	90 044	66 820	58 623	302 282
Belgium	24 018	54 367	32 925	28 858	46 155	40 235	39 830	266 388
Italy	0	4 050	0	375	85 441	87 965	39 131	216 962

Source: Own work based on the EC State aid Scoreboard.

Financial institutions did not benefit from state aid in only seven EU countries (Bulgaria, Czechia, Estonia, Malta, Romania, Slovakia, and Finland). In nominal terms, the bulk of aid (approximately 90% on average) went to institutions in eight countries, almost all of which (except the UK) were in the eurozone (Table 3.3). Ireland clearly stands out, as in 2009–2011 the Irish government provided financial institutions with almost EUR 800 billion in total.

The GFC had the greatest impact on banking systems of advanced European countries. However the magnitude of the crisis and necessary government response was also strongly related to the characteristics of the systems. For example, the crisis was not so devastating for banks in Norway, heavily strengthened after the Nordic banking crisis of the nineties. The crisis also affected the two largest Swiss banks, and in the case of one of them, (UBS) intervention turned out to be unavoidable. The aid package provided by the Swiss government, the Swiss Federal Banking Commission and the Swiss National Bank assumed transfer of up to USD 60 billion of illiquid assets to a special purpose vehicle (SPV) and CHF 6 billion in capital injection. Nevertheless, this support did not have a significant impact on Swiss fiscal stability, while in many countries support for financial institutions constituted an extraordinary burden for public finances. During the GFC, this is the best illustrated by the case of Ireland, as such support exceeded twice the amount of GDP in the peak year (2010). During the sovereign debt crisis, Greece's pressing problems with public finance imbalances were further exacerbated by financial instability, and the value of government interventions in 2012 amounted to almost 48% of GDP. Both the Irish and Greek cases are described below. The third chosen case is Cyprus, which is interesting for two reasons. First, the straightforward reason for Cypriot banks' problems was not so much the global financial crisis as the crisis in Greece. Second, the Cyprus bail-in can be considered as a game changer in bank resolution (ESM,

2019, p. 271), as this solution was applied for the first time, even before the BRRD was adopted.

3.2.1 Ireland

Severe problems for the Irish financial system had already emerged in 2007, related to the real-estate bubble and the banks' over-exposure to the property sector, and the financial crisis exacerbated the situation.

In September 2008, the Irish government announced a two-year guarantee on banks' liabilities (Credit Institutions Financial Support Scheme), with the exception of any intra-group borrowing and any debt due to the ECB arising from Eurosystem monetary operations. The support was addressed to six domestic credit institutions, and was worth EUR 375 billion, more than twice Ireland's GDP at that time. While many aspects of this form of support have been criticized, it initially proved to be an effective liquidity measure, however not sufficient to restore market confidence (Baudino et al., 2020, p. 12). The first guarantee scheme was replaced by another (Eligible Liabilities Guarantee Scheme) which was launched at the end of 2009. At the beginning, the new scheme covered around EUR 139 billion in liabilities, while in mid-2010 it was EUR 153 billion (Simon, 2020). The deteriorating Irish fiscal position weakened the credibility, and hence the effectiveness of government guarantees in the banking sector (European Commission, 2011a, p. 5).

In December 2009, the National Asset Management Agency (NAMA) was established with the aim of protecting the value of property development loans and maximizing the state's return. Five financial institutions participated in the program: the Anglo Irish Bank, Allied Irish Bank, Bank of Ireland, Irish National Building Society, and Educational Building Society. A special purpose vehicle (SPV) set up by NAMA was responsible for the purchase, management and sale of loan assets. The purchases were financed by issuing securities (by the SPV), most of which were secured by government guarantees. As the SPV was majority owned (51%) by private investors and met conditions stipulated by Eurostat, it is not considered as a part of general government and consequently its liabilities did not increase public debt.

According to the government's announcement of December 2008, the banks were to be recapitalized with up to EUR 10 billion. The first injections were to go to the Anglo Irish Bank (Anglo, EUR 1.5 billion), Allied Irish Bank (AIB) and Bank of Ireland (BOI) (EUR 2 billion each), by subscribing to preference shares to be issued by those banks (Baudino et al., 2020, p. 16). Estimated capital needs turned out to be insufficient, so instead of the announced amounts, in February 2009, AIB and BOI were injected with EUR 3.5 billion each. Anglo was nationalized in January 2009 and in mid-2009 it was recapitalized with EUR 4 billion. However, its funding position continued to get worse, mainly due to impairment of the loan portfolio (Igan et al., 2019). In 2010, the Irish government issued promissory notes for Anglo three times for the total amount of EUR 25.3 billion. The total amount of the capital injections into five Irish banks (Anglo, AIB, BOI, the Irish Nationwide Building Society and EBS Building Society) in 2009–2010 was EUR 46.3 billion (European Commission, 2011a).

In November 2010, Ireland requested international financial aid, and the approved assistance program (set at EUR 85 billion) provided up to EUR 35 billion for banking system support in 2011–2013. The strategy set for the financial sector envisaged fundamental downsizing and reorganization of the banking sector. The smaller and stronger banks were expected to be viable in the long run without state support. Pursuant to the strategy of March 2011, the domestic banking system was to concentrate on two pillar banks, with BOI as "pillar one" and AIB as "pillar two." It was also decided to merge the EBS Building Society with AIB. Non-viable banks were resolved, and the viable part of the banking system was recapitalized. The recapitalization was completed by July 2011 and out of the total EUR 24 billion, the state contribution was EUR 16.6 billion (European Commission, 2015).

In 2013, the Irish government liquidated the Irish Bank Resolution Corporation (IBRC). This triggered compensation under the ELG Scheme (Simon, 2020). Also in 2013, Ireland completed an assistance program that helped to improve the situation of the financial sector and regain market confidence, however some serious challenges for Irish banks and public finances still remained ahead.

3.2.2 Greece

The first assistance program addressed directly to the Greek financial institutions was approved in November 2008 (European Commission 2008b). The program was aimed at ensuring the stability of the financial system through the Bank Recapitalization Scheme, the Guarantee Scheme and the Bond Loan Scheme. The program was later modified and extended, though it was originally intended to last six months.

Under the Recapitalization Scheme, the government was to acquire the preferred shares of credit institutions to help fulfil the required capital thresholds. The budget for this scheme was set at EUR 5 billion. The wholesale Guarantee Scheme provided state guarantees for newly issued debt instruments with maturities ranging from three months to three years, with the exception of subordinated debt and interbank deposits. With the limit of allocation of EUR 15 billion, it was aimed at re-opening the market for short- and medium-term wholesale financing. Under the third scheme, the Greek government authorized the issuance of Greek special purpose securities, i.e. bonds, with a maturity of up to three years. Banks – a participant in the scheme – were required to use the bonds as collateral in refinancing or marginal lending facilities of the European Central Bank and/or as collateral in interbank transactions for liquidity purposes. The limit of the scheme was set at EUR 8 billion. By May 2009, 40% of the total budget had been allocated (EUR 11.25 billion out of the total EUR 28 billion), most of which was for the recapitalization scheme (around EUR 4 billion) and the bond loan scheme (EUR 4.5 billion). In September 2009, it was decided to change and extend these support measures for banks for the first time. The subsequently introduced changes consisted, in particular, in raising the ceiling for the Guarantee Scheme (Boudghene et al., 2011).

In April 2010, Greece made a formal request for international financial support and then a EUR 110 billion bailout package was accepted (Greek Loan Facility, of which EUR 73 billion was disbursed). There were not many fiscal measures addressed to the financial system in the first Economic Adjustment Programme for Greece (European Commission, 2010a). Importantly it was decided to safeguard financial stability by establishing a special fund to provide capital to Greek banks in case of a significant decline of capital buffers. This fund, which was the Hellenic Financial Stability Fund (HFSF), was created in July 2010 as a legal entity governed under private law. Its capital was set at EUR 10 billion, to be financed under the EU-IMF financing package by the Greek government.

The severe problems of the Greek banks coincided with the sovereign crisis. High losses on government bonds and a deep and protracted recession, which led to a sharp increase in the default rates of Greek households and companies, presented major challenges for financial institutions. The significant deterioration of the banks' financial condition was also caused by the PSI (Private Sector Involvement) program, which assumed a 53.5% debt write-down for private holders of Greek bonds. This debt haircut amounted to approximately EUR 107 billion and, as Xafa (2013) states, it was the biggest sovereign default in history and the first in the eurozone. In March 2012, the second aid package was approved, under which EUR 141.8 billion was disbursed from the EFSF and EUR 12 billion from the IMF. The costs related to bank recapitalization and resolution were estimated at EUR 50 billion. As stipulated in the programme, two banks were resolved, and Proton Bank was the first case in which the provisions of the law concerning the resolution of credit institutions were implemented in Greece.

Proton Bank was a small bank focused on investment banking, characterized by a risky business model, poor quality of the loan portfolio, and – since the outbreak of the GFC – liquidity problems. Under the Greek bank support scheme, Proton Bank received (April–May 2009) Greek government securities of EUR 78 million, a EUR 80 million government capital injection, and a government guarantee for issued bonds with a nominal value of EUR 149 million (European Commission, 2012a). Two options of Proton Bank resolution were under consideration – transfer (sale) of assets to another bank, or establishment of an interim credit institution. As there was no interest in acquiring Proton's assets, only the second option remained (Bank of Greece, 2014). Proton Bank was liquidated (October 2011), and at the same time Nea Proton Bank was established, the sole shareholder of which was the HFSF. Capital claims, subordinated debt, deferred taxes and high-risk loans remained with Proton Bank (put into liquidation), while all deposits and selected assets (loans and securities portfolio) were transferred to Nea Proton Bank. The Greek government also contributed, as government bonds were transferred to the bridge bank at 50% of their nominal value. Nevertheless, despite the further help from HFSF, Nea Proton Bank's financial situation was still deteriorating considerably, and in 2013 it was acquired by Eurobank Ergasias S.A.

The second resolved bank was T-Bank, but that was only the beginning. In 2011–2013, the resolution mechanism was applied to a total of 12 banks, at a cost of EUR 14.8 billion. The highest resolution costs were incurred in the case of ATE-Bank and Hellenic Post Bank (Table 3.4).

In the years 2012–2013, four core banks (National Bank of Greece, Piraeus Bank, Alpha Bank and Eurobank) were also recapitalized for a total amount of EUR 24.4 billion, most of which (36%) was addressed to the National Bank of Greece. However, this was not the end of the problems of the Greek financial system. The economic situation of Greece deteriorated significantly, and the threat of Greek default and its potential withdrawal from the eurozone were visible. At the turn of July and August 2015, banks in Greece remained closed, and cash withdrawals were limited. Finally, an agreement was reached, and a third assistance program was approved by the Greek

Table 3.4 Resolution of Greek credit institutions in 2011–2013 (in EUR million)

Resolved banks	*Date of resolution*	*Resolution tool*	*Acquirer*	*Resolution cost**
Proton Bank	09.10.11	Bridge bank	-	1 122
T-Bank	17.12.11	Sale of business	Hellenic Post Bank	677
Cooper. Lesvou-Limnou	23.03.12	Sale of business	National Bank of Greece	56
Achaiki Cooperative	23.03.12	Sale of business	National Bank of Greece	209
Cooper. of Lamia	23.03.12	Sale of business	National Bank of Greece	55
ATE-Bank	27.07.12	Sale of business	Piraeues Bank	7 471
Hellenic Post Bank	18.01.13	Bridge bank	-	3 733
First Business Bank	10.05.13	Sale of business	National Bank of Greece	457
Probank	26.07.13	Sale of business	National Bank of Greece	563
Cooper. of West Macedonia	08.12.13	Sale of business	Alpha Bank	95
Cooperative of Evia	08.12.13	Sale of business	Alpha Bank	105
Cooper. of Dodecanisou	08.12.13	Sale of business	Alpha Bank	259

Source: Mavridou et al., 2016.

* Funded by the HFSF, only in the case of Proton Bank and T-Bank with participation of Hellenic Deposit and Investment Guarantee Fund (in total for EUR 1312 million).

Parliament in August 2015. It was financed exclusively from the ESM funds (EUR 61.9 billion) and provided a buffer of up to EUR 25 billion for possible recapitalization and resolution of Greek banks. In December 2015, the Greek government received EUR 5.4 billion from ESM for recapitalization of the National Bank of Greece and Piraeus Bank.

In 2018, Greece concluded the third assistance program, with a strengthened financial system, but still with a significant stock of NPL. Fiscal sustainability was restored as regards the budget balance, nevertheless the level of general government debt was the highest among all EU countries (about 186% of GDP).

3.2.3 Cyprus

According to Zenios (2016), there were three distinguishable phases of the Cyprus crisis. The first one, which was due to the onset of the financial crisis in 2008, can be described as a time of excessive debt accumulation, especially by households and corporations, and heavy inflow of foreign deposits. Significant real estate and risky cross-border exposure as well as a substantial share of Greek government bonds and loans to the Greek private sector in major Cypriot banks' assets (Bank of Cyprus, Hellenic Bank and Cyprus Popular Bank, also called Laiki Bank) determined subsequent events (Brown et al., 2017).

In the second phase (2008–2011), the Cyprus government lost access to the capital market and Cypriot banks recorded severe losses due to the Greek PSI. The progressive downgrading of sovereign bonds, resulting from macro and fiscal imbalances, began in the summer of 2010 and by May 2011 the government had completely lost access to international markets. Initially, Cyprus did not seek EU or IMF assistance, as it received a loan from Russia (EUR 2.5 billion), but it turned out to be one-off and insufficient. In Cyprus, the impact of the PSI on the economy became even more severe than in Greece (Clerides, 2014; Zenios, 2016), although the losses of Cypriot banks (namely the Bank of Cyprus, Laiki) amounted to EUR 4.5 billion and the losses of Greek banks were more than nine times higher. Nevertheless, in the case of Cyprus, these losses amounted to almost 25% of GDP, while in Greece this ratio was 18%.

The haircut on Greek government bonds led Laiki Bank to the brink of collapse, and the Bank of Cyprus was also endangered. Laiki Bank did not meet the European Banking Authority minimum regulatory capital requirements, and the only option was its nationalization, which took place in June 2012. The cost of Laiki recapitalization amounted to EUR 1.8 billion and in return the government obtained 84% of shares in the bank (ESM, 2019, p. 266). At the same time, the Cypriot government requested financial support from the Troika (European Commission, European Central Bank and International Monetary Fund), however negotiations proved to be conspicuously long.

The first Eurogroup decision made on 16 March 2013 turned out to be unacceptable for Cyprus, as together with the financial assistance it introduced a one-off stability levy on all deposits, including insured ones. This proposal aroused great controversy, not only among Cypriots (Brown et al., 2017), so consequently, pursuant to the second Eurogroup decision, of March 26, deposit write-off was applied, but only in the case of the uninsured ones. The approved assistance program was aimed at restoring financial stability, reducing the size of the financial sector, fiscal consolidation, and implementing structural reforms to support competitiveness and sustainable and balanced growth. Financing was agreed at EUR 10 billion, of which around EUR 2.5 billion was for recapitalization and banks' restructuring needs (European Commission, 2013).

After the three-year assistance program, Cyprus modernized, restructured, downsized and recapitalized its banking sector. The financial regulation and supervision were also improved and market access restored. In 2015, the general government deficit was reduced (to 0.9% of GDP), however public debt remained at 107.2% of GDP.

3.3 Support measures for the real economy – case studies

In order to stem the decline in demand caused by the financial crisis, and to support growth and employment, EU countries introduced a number of individual stimulus measures, under the European Economic Recovery Plan. The size and composition of discretionary measures varied significantly across EU countries, depending, in particular, on their fiscal needs and fiscal space. The biggest volume of discretionary stimulus was recorded in Spain, Finland, Germany and Austria. In each of these countries, the aggregate value of the fiscal packages for 2009–2010 corresponded to 4%–3.5% of their GDP, while in Bulgaria it was only 0.1% GDP (European Commission, 2009). In the majority of countries, financial support was focused on the labour market, mainly on retraining and activation. A considerable number of measures were directed at increasing households' purchasing power, especially through the reduction of taxes and social security contributions and through direct public expenditures, such as financing of social benefits. Many countries undertook sizeable public investments, primarily in physical infrastructure and energy efficiency. The governments' policy was also aimed at business support, mainly through relaxed access to finance, but also in the form of sectoral support (automotive, tourism, construction).

State aid to the real economy as a response to financial crisis was not of significant volume. Up until the end of 2010, the aid approved under the temporary crisis framework amounted to approximately EUR 82.9 billion, while the aid used was about EUR 32.8 billion (European Commission, 2011b). The limited amounts of aid were the most frequently used temporary support measures. Many countries benefited also from export credit insurance and guarantees. Only a few countries chose the remaining measures and

2011 turned out to be a time when interest in measures under the temporary crisis framework decreased significantly (to EUR 4.8 billion). This could be explained both by the strict rules of granting the aid and by budgetary constraints of most EU countries (European Commission, 2011b).

COVID-19 proved to be an unprecedented shock for the economies of the world. It also quickly turned out that government interventions on an unprecedented scale would be indispensable. Their purpose was primarily to ensure macroeconomic and financial stability.

Direct fiscal measures included mainly subsidies for non-financial enterprises, financing of short-time work schemes, transfers for households (social benefits). All of these measures increased government expenditure. Revenue measures were also introduced, such as reduction of tax and social security contributions, but also accelerated asset depreciation, broadened tax deductibility, tax credits or tax exemptions. In terms of financial measures, there were measures aimed at liquidity and solvency support, such as loans, equity acquisition or state guarantees (Girón, Rodríguez-Vives, 2021; Lacey et al., 2021).

According to preliminary data (Collin et al., 2021), state aid of EUR 2,969 billion (21.3% of GDP) was approved in 2020, of which more than half was authorized for Germany (46.1% of GDP) (Table 3.5). State aid under the temporary legal framework was a frequently used anti-pandemic measure. From March 2020 to the end of 2021, the Commission took 620 approval decisions in this matter, most in April 2020 (70), and in July 2020 and March 2021 (48 each). More than 120 aid decisions were authorized additionally under the TFUE regulation.[7] Most of the aid approved by the European Commission was sector neutral. The only exceptions are those sectors that were particularly affected by the pandemic, such as the airlines and aviation sector.

Table 3.5 State aid in 2020

	State aid approved			*COVID-19 State aid expenditures*		
	EUR billion	*% GDP 2019*	*EU 27 = 100*	*EUR billion*	*% GDP 2019*	*EU 27 = 100*
EU 27*	**2 969.32**	**21.26**	**100.00**	**544.11**	**3.90**	**100.00**
of which:						
Germany	1 588.48	46.05	53.50	104.25	3.02	19.21
Italy	454.57	25.40	15.31	107.94	6.03	19.89
France	430.00	17.73	14.48	155.36	6.40	28.62
Spain	149.05	11.97	5.02	90.85	7.30	16.74
Poland	63.31	11.89	2.13	19.15	3.60	3.53
Belgium	56.08	11.78	1.89	3.64	0.77	0.67
Austria	45.76	11.51	1.54	10.99	2.76	2.02

Source: Collin et al., 2021.

* As at the end of 2020, i.e. not including the UK.

In 2020, the amount actually spent was EUR 544 billion (3.9% of GDP). The bulk of COVID-19-related expenditure was incurred in the first months of the pandemic. By the end of June 2020, EUR 325.2 billion had been spent, mainly by France (EUR 123 billion). Importantly, these amounts reflect only support in the form of expenditure, while a large proportion of the aid was of a non-expenditure nature. According to International Monetary Fund estimates, fiscal liquidity support in all forms in the EU countries in 2020 amounted to 6.8% of GDP. Among all EEA countries, the highest total support was registered in Italy and Germany (42.3% of GDP and 38.9% of GDP respectively), while the lowest was in Croatia and Romania (5.5% of GDP each) and Denmark (6.0% of GDP).

The measures undertaken helped to improve the economic situation, and while all EU countries recorded a decline in GDP, it was lower than initially estimated. According to the EC's forecasts published shortly after the outbreak of the pandemic, the GDP drop in the euro area was expected to reach 7.7%, and 7.4% in the entire EU, while in fact it amounted to 6.4% and 5.9%, respectively. The largest decreases were recorded in Spain (10.8%), Greece (9.0%), Italy (8.9%) and Portugal (8.4%). Among the non-euro area countries, the largest decreases were observed in Croatia (8.1%). All these countries are highly tourism-dependent, and tourism was one of the sectors most affected by the COVID-19 pandemic.

The EU unemployment rate also turned out to be lower than initially forecast. In the EU as a whole, it amounted to 7.1% (forecast 9.0%), and in the euro area to 7.9% (forecast 7.1%). Greece and Spain, with unemployment at 16.3% and 15.5%, deserve more attention, but these figures are comparable to those recorded in previous years. However, in the first pandemic year, Greece recorded a debt of more than twice GDP, and its deficit in relation to GDP was greater than 10%.

As far as the other analyzed non-EU countries (as of the end of 2020) are concerned, their fiscal responses were similar, however, the scale and effects varied. In 2020, actual Swiss expenditures in response to the pandemic amounted to CHF 17.3 billion, of which most was related to short-time working compensation (CHF 10.8 billion). Additional liquidity measures were estimated at about 6% of GDP. Switzerland recorded a budget deficit, but at a level much lower than the EU average (2.8% of GDP versus 6.9% of GDP), mainly due to a surplus from the previous budgetary year. The decline in GDP (by 2.4%) was also lower than in most EU countries. In Norway, discretionary fiscal measures of an expenditure or revenue nature were estimated at just over 4% of GDP. Government spending was directed for instance at households (e.g. higher social benefits, higher wage subsidies for temporary layoffs), entrepreneurs (reimbursement of fixed costs, subsidies) and healthcare. Revenue measures included, for example, lowering the VAT rate, deferring tax payments, and temporary reduction of social security contributions. Liquidity support, worth approximately 4.5% of GDP, consisted mainly of guarantee and loan schemes for business. Compared to the EU countries, the decline in GDP was not so great (by 0.7%, while in Mainland Norway by 2.5%). In the UK, however, the pandemic had a much more severe impact on the economy and much more fiscal stimulus was needed. According to the IMF (2021), additional spending or foregone revenue amounted to 16.3% of GDP, while liquidity measures (mainly guarantees) were estimated at 16.1% of GDP. The deficit soared to almost 13% of GDP, and public debt increased to 144% of GDP (from 117% in 2019). The decline in GDP was also very significant – by 9.4%.

All the fiscal measures in response both to the GFC and the pandemic crisis were in general of similar nature, however they varied in forms of value and structure. The two case studies described below provide examples of the euro area country (Germany) and non-euro area country (Poland) with the biggest state aid approved in 2020.

3.3.1 Germany

In Germany, the financial crisis triggered a severe economic slowdown in 2008/2009, especially in the export-oriented manufacturing sector (Federal Ministry of Finance, 2010, p. 19). The federal government recognized that measures aimed at stabilizing the financial market should be accompanied by a program that strengthened sustainable economic growth by increasing the willingness to invest, encouraging consumption, and securing the employment market, however without violating the structural consolidation of the budget.

In November 2008, the federal government adopted a set of measures targeted at securing growth and employment, with effects to be expected both in the short- and long-term (*Konjunkturpaket I, Beschäftigungssicherung durch Wachstumsstärkung*). The second program (*Konjunkturpaket II, Entschlossen in der Krise, stark für den nächsten Aufschwung*) of January 2009, was intended to alleviate the looming recession in 2009. The budgetary costs of both programs were estimated at EUR 56 billion in 2009 and 2010, of which EUR 26 billion was related to changes in taxation (Blömer et al., 2015, p. 13).

Important measures included supplementing the KfW banking group lending program with the provision of EUR 15 billion for the private banking sector's loans, limited until the end of 2009. It was also decided to hire 1,000 additional workers for job placement, to intensify the Federal Employment Agency's special program for less qualified and older workers, and to extend the maximum drawing period for short-term-work unemployment benefit. Much emphasis was also placed on boosting innovation and investment in transport (Federal Ministry of Finance, 2008, p. 6).

In 2010, the Act to Accelerate Economic Growth (*Wachstumsbeschleunig ungsgesetz*) was implemented with the aim of targeted tax relief and expansion of renewable energies. It introduced for example significant increases in child benefits, changes in inheritance tax favourable for beneficiaries, and a reduction in the VAT rate for the fee for short-term accommodation services aimed at the operators of hotels, inns, guest houses and campsites.

Additional investment incentives in corporate taxation were also implemented. In 2009 alone, the introduced measures reduced the burden on enterprises by just over EUR 2.5 billion (Federal Ministry of Finance, 2010, p. 11).

All of the economic recovery packages significantly decreased the personal income tax burden, especially by raising the basic personal allowance and reducing the lowest tax rate from 15% to 14 % (from 2009). Additionally, some solutions aimed at helping low-income workers and pensioners were introduced. Important measures included also a reduction in the unemployment insurance rate from 3.2 to 2.8% and for health insurance from 15.5 to 14.9%. As Blömer et al. (2015) remark, most of the tax-benefit changes in Germany had been planned long before the economic turmoil, following court judgments.

The coronavirus pandemic significantly impacted the German economy, and thus the government adopted support measures of considerable amounts. The first German response to the pandemic crisis was to help entrepreneurs in the form of a one-off subsidy. Both small enterprises and self-employed persons could apply for the subsidy, regardless of the industry. The subsidy was granted up to EUR 15,000 for three months (Federal Ministry of Finance, 2021, p. 18). In order to protect larger and medium-sized companies, the federal government established the Economic Stabilization Fund (*Wirtschafts stabilizierungsfonds*, WSF), which provided assistance in the form of guarantees and recapitalization measures. The Fund's total capacity was set at up to EUR 600 billion, of which the envelope for the guarantee program was EUR 400 billion. In March 2020, a special KfW (*Kreditanstalt für Wiederaufbau*) program was launched to provide financing (in the form of low-interest liquidity loans) to companies facing temporary liquidity shortages resulting from the pandemic. In April, the program was extended by 100% guarantees (Anderson et al., 2021, p. 69).

The federal government also introduced measures to prevent layoffs, including increases in short-term benefit payments. Short-time work schemes (*Kurzarbeit*) were used on a much broader scale than in the case of the GFC. In mid-May 2020, there were almost 10 million people using this scheme, while during the GFC it was about 1.4 million (Haroutunian et al., 2021). Special provisions on short-time work schemes were extended until the end of 2021. Some facilities were also introduced, so that more employers could take advantage of the scheme.

As the pandemic developed, an economic stimulus package was agreed in June 2020 of EUR 205 billion for the 2020 and 2021 budgetary years (Federal Ministry of Finance, 2021, p. 19). In order to react as quickly as possible, in many cases the federal government used pre-established programs. Aimed at stimulating consumer demand, various instruments were used to boost the disposable income of private households, including, for example, a temporary reduction in VAT rates, a one-off child bonus per child, or increase in tax relief for single parents. Investment incentives for entrepreneurs included an accelerated depreciation option and extended tax incentives for research. Bonuses addressed to SMEs for offering apprenticeships during the crisis were also introduced.

An initial short-term aid scheme *(Überbrückungs-hilfe I)* was implemented for the period from June to August 2020. The scheme was aimed especially at companies with severe losses in revenue due to the lockdown. They could receive subsidies for fixed costs of up to EUR 50,000 per month for up to three months. Subsequently, entrepreneurs' fixed costs were financed from the second short-term aid program *(Überbrückungs-hilfe II)*. In autumn 2020, enterprises affected by another lockdown could apply for aid under the Extraordinary Economic Aid Program (also known as the November and December Assistance Programmes). The aid was disbursed in the form of a subsidy, and the amount depended on the size of the revenue loss. In 2021, another short-term aid scheme *(Überbrückungshilfe III)* was launched to cover the fixed costs due to loss of revenue incurred from November 2020 to June 2021. Under this scheme, self-employed workers and sole proprietorships could also receive a one-off payment of up to EUR 7,500 as "aid for a fresh start" *(Neustarthilfe)*.

There were also measures addressed directly to the health system, in the form of approximately EUR 2 billion for an increased number of intensive care beds in hospitals and the procurement of ventilation equipment, or EUR 2.8 billion as compensation for postponed treatments. Together with the *Länder*, a Public Health Services Pact was adopted, with the financial contribution from the federal government of EUR 4 billion up until 2026 (Federal Ministry of Finance, 2021, p. 21).

The measures introduced in response to the COVID-19 pandemic caused a significant deterioration in the German fiscal position. For the first time since 2011, Germany recorded a deficit (4.3% GDP), while general government debt increased from 59.7% to 69.8% of GDP.

3.3.2 Poland

Initially, the GFC did not cause major disruption to the Polish economy. The effects of the crisis became more noticeable in the second half of 2008. The government's response to the emerging threat was the "Stability and Development Plan – Strengthening the Polish Economy in the Face of the World Financial Crisis," presented in November 2008. The Polish economy was to be strengthened by the proposed pro-demand measures, aimed both at investment and consumption.

The activities stimulating investment demand included increasing the availability of credit for enterprises, increasing the limit of guarantees, strengthening the guarantee system for small and medium-sized enterprises, introducing higher investment relief for newly established enterprises, enabling the recognition of research expenses as tax costs. Importantly, most of these measures were not of expenditure nature; most of them were only additional guarantees or loans that could be granted.

Measures aimed at reducing tax and quasi-tax burdens were intended to be conducive to increasing consumption demand. These were:

- reintroducing (from 2007) indexation of tax thresholds, the exempt amount and tax-deductible costs in personal income tax;
- gradual reduction of the disability pension contribution, from a total of 13% to 6%;
- replacement (from 2009) of three tax rates (19%, 30% and 40%) with two rates (18% and 32%) for personal income tax.

The amount of the overall program was estimated at PLN 91.3 billion, of which PLN 40 billion was government guarantees securing the banking system against loss of liquidity, and PLN 20 billion was guarantees and sureties for SMEs. The cost of measures supporting the growth of consumer demand was estimated at PLN 10 billion. The economic slowdown and the implemented, mainly pro-demand, measures had a negative impact on public finances. In July 2009, Poland was again placed under the excessive deficit procedure. Therefore, the next government program focused to a much greater extent on fiscal consolidation.

In the case of the pandemic crisis, the Polish government reacted on a much larger scale – the total aid amount was set at PLN 242 billion.[8] The measures were introduced from the end of March 2020, along with the subsequent "anti-crisis shields." Mainly expenditure measures were implemented, but there were also revenue measures such as temporary exemptions or reductions in tax rates or temporary exemptions from social and health insurance contributions (to be covered under the expenditure measures).

In 2020, activities aimed at counteracting the negative effects of the COVID-19 pandemic were financed from three sources: the state budget (PLN 23.2 billion), the COVID-19 Counteracting Fund (PLN 92.7 billion) and the Polish Development Fund (Polski Fundusz Rozwoju, or PFR; PLN 63.5 billion) (Rada Ministrów, 2021). As neither the COVID-19 Counteracting Fund nor the Polish Development Fund were part of general government according to the Polish public finance methodology, the transparency of allocation of public funds decreased significantly.

The state budget expenditures included purchase of personal protection equipment, materials and equipment for healthcare institutions, protection of social care homes against the increase in infections caused by the SARS-CoV-2 virus, and the organization and maintenance of collective quarantine facilities. About PLN 10 billion was transferred to the COVID-19 Counteracting Fund, which was established in the Bank Gospodarstwa Krajowego (the only state-owned bank in Poland) at the end of March 2020. The Fund's financial plan was finally agreed at the end of May 2020 and assumed financing of tasks at the level of PLN 100 billion. During the year, the expenditure plan was increased to PLN 112 billion. The main source of financing of the Fund was issuance of bonds.

Almost 2/3 of the funds from the COVID-19 Counteracting Fund were spent through state appropriated funds (the Labour Fund, the Guaranteed Employee Benefits Fund and the Social Insurance Fund). Spending was mainly on subsidies to salaries and social security contributions, one-off loans and one-off subsidies to cover the current costs of running a business, standstill benefit, solidarity allowance, additional care allowance, and sickness benefits.

The Polish anti-crisis shields included also an assistance program addressed to businesses operated by the PFR in the form of the "financial shields," adopted at the end of April 2020.

The PFR financial shield for small and medium-sized enterprises included two activities:

- PFR financial shield for micro-companies (1–9 employees), under which subsidies were granted depending on the number of employees and the decrease in revenues;
- PFR financial shield for SMEs (10–249 employees), where the amount of aid depended on the decrease in revenues.

By the end of 2020, more than 348,000 firms had received the financing, for a total amount of nearly PLN 61.0 billion (of which SMEs received PLN 42.0 billion). The aid was directed primarily to the trade, construction and industrial processing sectors.

As a part of the PFR financial shield for large companies, the following measures were used: liquidity financing of a fully returnable and payable nature, preferential financing with the possibility of compensation of damage related to the outbreak of the pandemic (loans redeemable up to 75% of their value), investment financing using equity instruments on market terms and under state aid. Under the PFR financial shield for large companies, PLN 1.6 billion was paid in 2020. The Polish Development Fund was also engaged in financial support for LOT Polish Airlines. In 2020, the first loan tranche was released in the amount of PLN 894 million.

In response to subsequent waves of the pandemic, additional fiscal measures were introduced in 2021. Some of the former measures were extended or prolonged as well.

As the Polish methodology of public finance reporting lacks transparency and is susceptible to manipulation, the size of the deficit and public debt in 2020 according to the Polish methodology (based on the Public Finance Act) differs significantly from the amounts reported to Eurostat, according to ESA 2010. In the Polish approach, the deficit in 2020 amounted to 1.3% of GDP, and public debt to 47.8% of GDP, while according to the EU methodology it was respectively 7.1% GDP and 57.5% GDP. Regardless of the way the deficit was presented, it was wittingly deteriorated. The sharp increase in spending at the end of 2020 was not the result of attempts to counteract the effects of the pandemic, but the creation of a financial cushion for the next year, via additional spending on behalf of various extra-budgetary institutions.

3.4 Balancing fiscal and financial stability

Financial crises are costly for the budget not only because of the direct expenditures applied to support financial institutions weakened by crisis, but also because of foregone economic output. Thus, from the early stages of a crisis, governments implement a variety of measures to restore confidence in the banking system and minimize the impact on the real sector (Honohan and Klingebiel, 2000).

The effects of the GFC on EU countries were asymmetric. Some countries, despite serious turbulence, quickly regained fiscal and financial stability. Those countries that previously (before the crisis outbreak) showed significant macroeconomic imbalances and did not have credible budget buffers were most affected. The situation deteriorated after the Greek crisis of confidence, and when the effects of the introduced fiscal stimulus could not be sustained due to a sharp increase in debt (Scheinert, 2016).

The enormous scale of government support for financial institutions in response to crisis necessitated a thorough assessment of the consequences of these interventions on the fiscal position, and in particular their impact on the deficit and public debt. As Reinhart and Rogoff (2011) underline – banking crises often precede or accompany sovereign debt crises.

Due to the variety of forms of support measures applied by EU countries and due to their specificity, Eurostat issued a number of decisions organizing and unifying the statistical recording of such interventions.[9] In 2009, key principles were formulated that should be applied when recording public interventions, including the "substance over form" principle, according to which the accounting treatment of operations should reflect economic reality and not the legal or administrative framework in which these operations are carried out. These principles also included the method of valuation of financial transactions, the definition of contingent liabilities, and the rules of classifying institutional units as the part of the general government sector, which was particularly important when countries established various types of institutions to address specific problems related to the effects of financial turmoil. Eurostat explained also how to classify recapitalization operations, lending, guarantees, and exchange of assets, and how to record certain transactions carried out by public corporations. A special, multi-stage classification procedure was provided for purchase of assets and defeasance (buying impaired assets directly from financial institutions or creating a public body to carry out this task). As the recapitalization of banks became a frequently used aid measure, it became necessary later (2012, 2013) to clarify when to treat capital injection as a capital transfer (increasing the government deficit) or as an acquisition of equity (a financial transaction with no impact on the government deficit).

Figure 3.2 shows the net costs of government interventions to support financial institutions in 2008–2020. The vast majority of aid was granted in the euro area countries, which is illustrated by the slight difference between the amount for the eurozone[10] and the amount for the EU as a whole. However, the figure presents the data for the EU countries as at the end of 2020,[11] i.e. not including the United Kingdom, where government interventions were of significant size, especially in 2009 and 2010. The highest net costs of government assistance fall in 2010, 2012 and 2013, and in some countries (Portugal, Austria, Greece) also in 2014–2015. The slightly higher amount recorded in 2020 was not related to the pandemic crisis but resulted from the reclassification of the Spanish SAREB[12] as the general government sector.

Figure 3.2 also shows the relationship between net costs of government interventions to support financial institutions and the amount of the deficit in relation to GDP. While there was a close relationship between these measures in 2010, the sudden deterioration of deficit ratio in 2020 was due to direct government interventions to support the real economy.

When analyzing the impact of support provided to a financial institution on the general government deficit (surplus), we refer to the net amounts, i.e. the difference between the funds allocated and the funds received from the aid granted. The most important expenditure items are related to capital injections (recorded in statistics as capital transfer), interest payable on

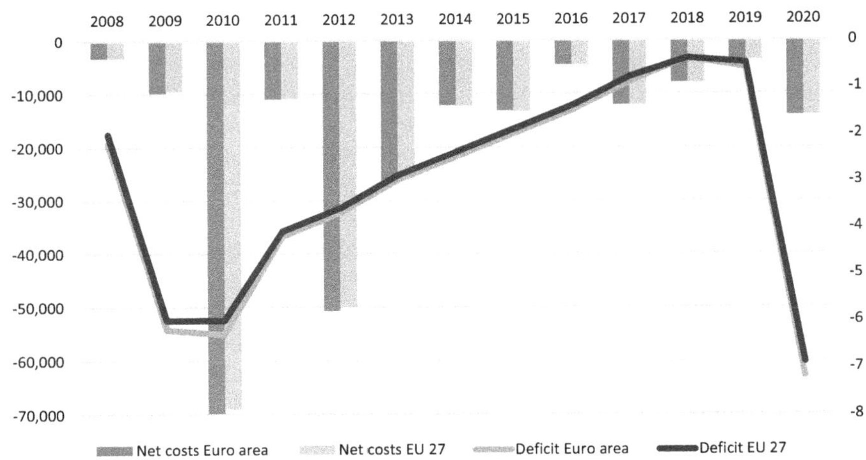

Figure 3.2 Net cost of government interventions to support financial institutions (EUR million, left axis) and general government deficit (% of GDP, right axis) in 2008–2020.

Source: Own work based on Eurostat data.

issued debt instruments, as well as other expenditure, such as asset purchase or commission fees. As concerns guarantees, they do not constitute any government expenditure unless they are called upon. Revenue arising from the government support for financial institutions includes mainly fees received as remuneration for guarantees granted and fees on securities issued under special liquidity schemes, interest on loans granted, and dividends.

The structure of revenues from government intervention has changed over the years. Although in almost every year the most important source of revenue was interest earned on loans granted, the share of fees charged on guarantees clearly decreased while the share of dividends increased (Table 3.6). These changes reflected the reorientation of government interventions – the amount of guarantees granted was limited, and the role of recapitalization was enhanced.

In 2008–2020, the highest net costs of government intervention to support financial institutions were incurred by Spain (in total EUR 58.4 billion), Germany (EUR 49.5 billion) and Ireland (EUR 48.5 billion), while in the case of Germany and Ireland, the peak year was 2010, and in the case of Spain – 2012. High expenditure was related to capital injections (Ireland, Spain) and other capital transfers, e.g. asset purchase (Germany).

There were also countries where support for financial institutions improved the budget result. France's cumulative net revenue for 2008–2020 was almost EUR 2 billion, most of which came from interest and guarantee fees. In a single year (2012), the expenditure related to the granted aid was higher than the realized revenue, due to high capital injection. High cumulative net revenue was also observed in Denmark (EUR 1.5 billion), where pre-BRRD resolution tools were used.

Table 3.6 Impact of government interventions on general government deficit in the EU in 2010–2013 (EUR million)

	2010	*2011*	*2012*	*2013*
Revenue	**21 155**	**26 945**	**29 476**	**21 365**
Guarantees fees	8 879	8 642	7 067	5 552
Interest	10 026	13 979	13 506	10 968
Dividends	1 543	2 731	5 133	3 149
Other	708	1 593	3 769	1 697
Expenditure	**88 226**	**35 768**	**77 100**	**51 019**
Interest	12 552	14 343	14 303	14 044
Capital injection (capital transfer)	38 589	15 155	47 672	26 614
Calls on guarantees	450	1 582	15	0
Other	36 637	4 688	15 110	10 362
Net expenditure	**−67 071**	**−8 823**	**−47 624**	**−29 654**
Net expenditure as % of GDP	**−0.52**	**−0.07**	**−0.35**	**−0.22**

Source: Eurostat, 2014.

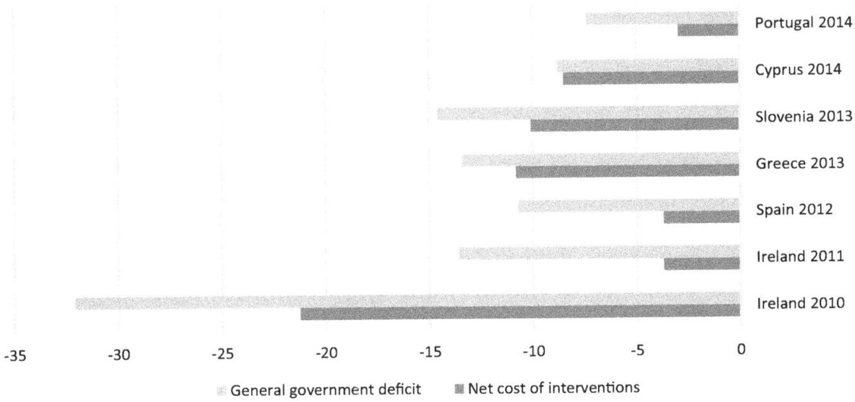

Figure 3.3 The biggest net cost of government intervention to support financial institutions versus general government deficit (% of GDP).

Source: Own work based on Eurostat data.

Many countries have experienced a significant increase in budget deficits due to government interventions to support financial institutions. This impact was particularly large in Ireland in 2010, but also in other countries, such as Slovenia and Greece in 2013, and Cyprus in 2014 (see Figure 3.3). In many countries, the impact was not that huge, but still significant, representing at least 2% of GDP. Such cases included Latvia in 2010 (net costs of 2.2% of GDP) and Portugal in 2014 (3% of GDP), but also countries already mentioned, such as Ireland in 2009 (2.2% of GDP) and Greece in 2012 and 2015 (2.8% of GDP and 2.7% of GDP).

Government interventions affected the amount of public debt, as in most cases, expenditure on supporting financial institutions was financed by incurring liabilities. At the same time, interventions also resulted in an increase in assets related to the granted aid.

The assistance provided to financial institutions is mainly reflected in the balance sheets of the euro area countries. Initially, their assets and liabilities were of comparable size, but since 2010, the growth of their liabilities exceeded the growth of assets. The largest stock of assets related to support provided to financial institutions was recorded in 2010 (EUR 481.7 billion) and since then they have shown an almost continuous downward trend. Liabilities with the highest value observed in 2012 (EUR 597.2 billion), were later decreased slightly (Figure 3.4).

Assets recorded in general government accounts arising from providing support for financial institutions include loans granted by government or purchased from financial institutions, debt securities issued by financial institutions and purchased by governments, and equity and investment fund

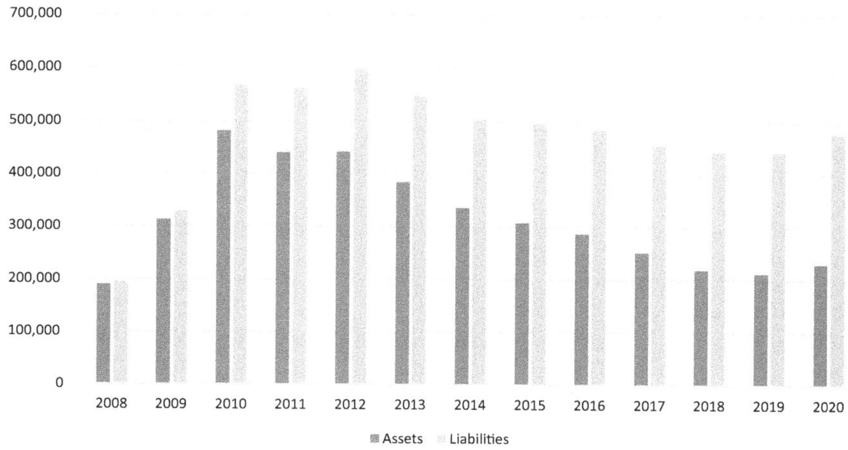

Figure 3.4 General government assets and liabilities arising from support to financial institutions in the euro area in 2008–2020 (EUR million).

Source: Eurostat, 2021.

shares or units, as well as assets of general government entities, such as defeasance structures or special purpose vehicles holding impaired assets.

In 2008–2009, loans and equity and investment fund units had the largest share in the assets of the euro area countries (approximately 70% of the total). Over time, the share of loans decreased significantly, equity remained at a relatively stable level (approximately 30% of the total), and the importance of other assets of general government entities (largely composed of NPLs) increased outstandingly – since 2011 they have accounted for more than half of the assets relating to government interventions to support financial institutions.

Liabilities related to government assistance to financial institutions include primarily loans and debt securities incurred to finance the interventions, as well as other liabilities of general government entities. In 2008–2020, on average, about half of all liabilities were debt securities, while in 2008–2009 their share was even higher, reaching almost 75%. Other liabilities of general government entities were also of great importance, as they accounted for approximately 38% of all liabilities arising from government support for financial institutions in the eurozone (in 2010–2016 even approximately 45%).

In 2020, there was an increase in assets and liabilities related to government interventions compared to the previous year (Table 3.7), which was mainly due to the inclusion of the Spanish SAREB into the general government sector. The increase in liabilities resulting from this change was equivalent to a decrease in contingent liabilities of the same amount.

Table 3.7 General government assets and liabilities arising from support to financial institutions in the euro area and in the EU in 2018–2020 (EUR million)

	euro area			*EU*		
	2018	*2019*	*2020*	*2018*	*2019*	*2020*
Assets	**219 239**	**212 264**	**230 170**	**222 596**	**215 446**	**233 378**
Loans	12 787	11 001	12 129	12 787	11 001	12 129
Debt securities	1 945	1 794	1 143	1 945	1 794	1 143
Equity and investment funds shares/units	64 243	64 368	55 042	64 665	64 632	55 225
Other assets of general government entities	140 264	135 101	161 855	143 199	138 019	164 880
Liabilities	**443 903**	**443 188**	**477 415**	**444 424**	**443 456**	**477 684**
Loans	81 612	81 587	84 093	81 868	81 587	84 093
Debt securities	216 122	219 351	222 765	216 388	219 619	223 034
Other liabilities of general government entities	146 168	142 250	170 557	146 168	142 250	170 557

Source: Eurostat, 2021.

Contingent liabilities are not recorded in government debt statistics as they are of potential nature and may (but do not have to) turn into actual liabilities. The payment obligation arises only when particular future events occur, but these events are uncertain and the amount of government payments to be required is difficult to estimate. Contingent liabilities comprise for instance guarantees granted on financial institutions' assets and (or) liabilities. As the fiscal costs of contingent liabilities are hidden until they fall due, they can be more attractive than direct government support, although they can turn out to be more expensive in the long run (Polackova, 1999). While contingent liabilities do not necessarily require payments, a high level of such obligations can increase the level of fiscal risk. Moreover, payouts related to liabilities usually occur during an economic downturn, which further deteriorates the fiscal position of a country affected by crisis (Bova et al., 2019). Contingent liabilities may also boost moral hazard in the markets, as full government guarantee can entail insufficient analysis and supervision by creditors (Polackova-Brixi and Schick, 2002).

In 2008–2020, the average level of contingent liabilities in the 27 EU countries was EUR 343.2 billion (in the eurozone EUR 332.3 billion). The highest volume of contingent liabilities in the EU countries was recorded in 2009. At that time, they amounted to EUR 723.9 billion, which corresponded to 6.8% of GDP, and in the euro area countries EUR 690.4 billion (7.4% of GDP). Including the UK, which is not currently part of the EU, these amounts increase significantly, as the volume of UK contingent liabilities in the peak year of 2009 exceeded GBP 550 billion, and in the years 2008 and 2010 it was almost GBP 338 billion on average.

Among the 27 EU countries, Ireland clearly stands out, as in 2008–2012 the average value of Irish contingent liabilities amounted to approximately EUR 208 billion, and in 2008 it was EUR 352 billion (Figure 3.5). These liabilities corresponded on average to approximately 120% of Irish GDP, and in 2008 this ratio was as much as 188%. They were mainly related to the Credit Institutions Financial Support Scheme, replaced later by the Eligible Guarantee Scheme.

In 2009–2010, high contingent liabilities were also observed in Germany (EUR 159 billion and EUR 83 billion), but in relation to GDP it was only 6.5% and 3.2%. In 2012–2013, high contingent liabilities in nominal terms were also recorded in Spain and Italy, where they amounted on average to EUR 100 billion and EUR 84 billion (on average respectively: 9.8% of GDP and 5.2% of GDP). High values of contingent liabilities in relation to GDP were noted by Greece in 2010–2015 – on average they amounted to 28% of GDP.

The vast majority of contingent liabilities are related to guarantees granted on the financial institutions' assets and liabilities. In the years 2008–2020, their share in the structure of all liabilities of the euro area countries was on average approximately 81%. The second important item resulted from financial instruments transferred to a special purpose vehicle, especially in 2014–2019, when they amounted to approximately 25% on average. Since 2020, no country has had such commitments anymore, because the last ones were linked to the Spanish SAREB. In some countries, contingent liabilities were observed only until 2013 (the Netherlands), in others until 2014 (Denmark, Slovenia, Sweden). In 2020, the largest contingent liabilities were recorded in France (EUR 30 billion) and Belgium (EUR 29 billion).

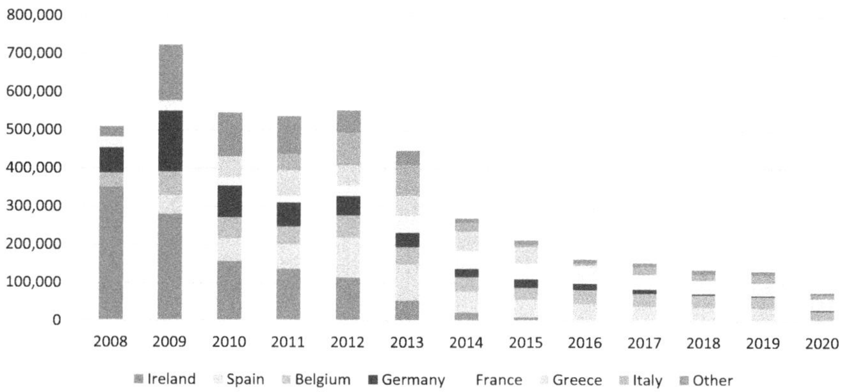

Figure 3.5 Contingent liabilities arising from government intervention to support financial institutions in the 27 EU countries in the years 2008–2020 (EUR million).

Source: Own work based on (Eurostat, 2021).

At the time of the GFC, most fiscal and monetary measures were aimed at supporting the financial sector. Government measures, along with monetary and regulatory policies, restored confidence in the financial sector over time, but the effects of this crisis were also felt in the real economy as well.

The decline in GDP in 2009 amounted to 4.3% in the EU as a whole (4.5% in the euro area), while in Central Europe and the Baltics it decreased by 3.5% (Figure 3.6). Among the euro area countries, the largest decrease was observed in Finland (by 8.1%), but interestingly, during the GFC, it was the Baltic states that experienced the largest decline in GDP of any EU country. After years with a rate of growth of 5–10% annually, 2008 turned out to be a breakthrough. With rapidly growing credit, excessive capital inflows, large net foreign liabilities, a real estate boom, rising inflation and falling GDP, the effects of the financial crisis proved devastating. In all the Baltic states, the balance of public finances also deteriorated significantly, and although in Estonia the threshold of 3% of GDP was not exceeded, in Latvia and Lithuania the general government deficit was even as high as 9.1–9.5% of GDP in 2009. It was also a time of turmoil for Baltic financial institutions, especially for Latvia, where, as a consequence of the problems of the Latvian second largest bank (Parex Bank), the government was forced to request international financial aid. According to Staehr (2013), the recession was so rapid and deep that expansionary policy was unlikely to affect short-term results. The Baltic countries opted for austerity measures to be based on a fixed exchange rate policy and strong fiscal consolidation, with tax increases and expenditure reduction. This approach turned out to be so effective that all the Baltic states managed to maintain the fixed exchange rate system and consolidate public finances, which allowed them to join the euro area (Estonia in 2011, Latvia in 2014, Lithuania in 2015).

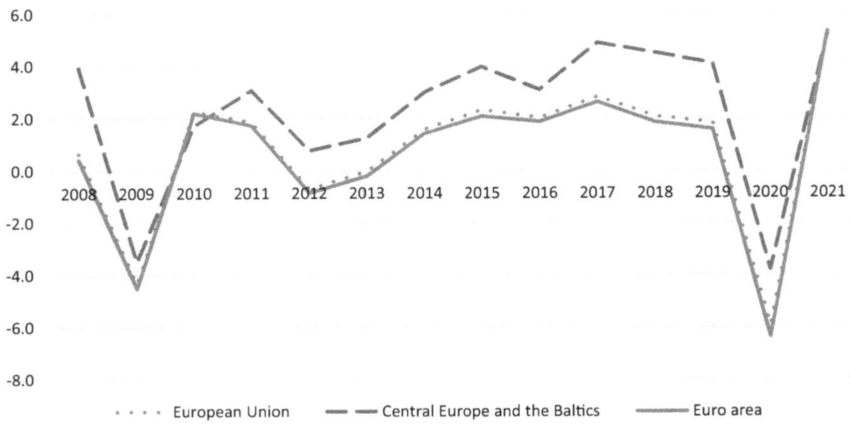

Figure 3.6 GDP growth rate in 2008–2021*.

* 2021 – forecast.

Source: Own work based on World Bank, EBRD.

Financial assistance provided to banks, recession, and an expansionary fiscal policy aimed at supporting the real economy significantly deteriorated EU public finances, and fiscal consolidation has become an increasingly serious challenge, especially for the countries affected by the sovereign debt crisis. In recent years, the economy has operated in a low interest rate environment (LIRE), which contributed to the reduction of the cost of public debt servicing. Nevertheless, a surge in inflation from 2021 means (or could mean in the future) growing interest rates and then an increase in sovereign bond yield. Thus, the risk of instability of public finances may also increase.

Restrictions introduced to contain the spread of the COVID-19 pandemic had a significant negative impact on the economy and international trade. This impact was visible in all EU countries, however the dimension depended not only on the government's response to the pandemic but also on the GDP structure and the significance of sectors most vulnerable to restrictions, such as tourism, transport, hospitality, and culture. The decline in EU GDP of more than 11% in the second quarter of 2020 was the largest drop since the beginning of Eurostat observation in 1995. The falloff was mainly driven by significant declines in private consumption and investment (European Investment Bank, 2021). For comparison, during the GFC, the largest quarterly decline in GDP did not exceed 4%. The third quarter of 2020 was characterized by the highest GDP rebound (by over 12%). The economic recovery was strongly influenced by the lifting of restrictions, nevertheless subsequent waves of the coronavirus forced the imposition of new restrictions, therefore, even from the very beginning, decisive action was needed to limit the negative economic and social effects of the pandemic. All such actions were introduced swiftly, on a large scale and from many directions, which undoubtedly helped reduce the magnitude of GDP decline, compared to the initial forecasts.

Regulations implemented after the outbreak of the GFC strengthened the European financial system, but the magnitude of the pandemic's effects – through increased insolvency of households and enterprises – could also pose a threat to the stability of financial institutions. Monetary, regulatory and fiscal measures were mobilized by the European Central Bank and EU institutions as well as non-euro area central banks and governments of all EU countries. Both standard monetary policy instruments (such as interest rate cuts, liquidity-increasing operations) and asset purchase programs and lending support programs (for more information, see Chapter 2) contributed to maintaining the flow of credit to the economy. By purchasing government securities, central banks were reducing their profitability, thus supporting the financing of fiscal packages. All monetary measures were accompanied by a loosening of the macroprudential policy. The fiscal response was decisive and multidimensional, covering direct financial support for households and enterprises, as well as numerous revenue measures, such as reductions of taxes or social security contributions and measures with indirect impact on public finances (especially liquidity measures like guarantee programs). Most of these measures were planned as emergency and temporary, but successive waves of the pandemic have forced them to be extended.

As noted by Haroutunian et al. (2021), determining the value of the anti-pandemic fiscal packages is a serious challenge, which is related among other things to discrepancies in registering individual forms of support. Undoubtedly, however, the scale of fiscal stimulus was much greater than in the case of the GFC. While the EU discretionary fiscal measures amounted to 1.5% of GDP in 2009 and 1.4% of GDP in 2010 (European Commission, 2010b), according to IMF estimates for 2020 (2021), additional spending or foregone revenues expenditure corresponded to 3.8% of GDP, and liquidity support to 6.8% of GDP.

Complementing the fiscal emergency measures is the NextGenerationEU, which, together with the EU Multiannual Financial Framework, is expected to allow recovery and transform economies to meet the current key structural needs.

Notes

1 This principle means that no measure should lead to significant harm to the environment. For more see Commission Notice Technical guidance on the application of "do no significant harm" under the Recovery and Resilience Facility Regulation, C(2021) 1054 final, Brussels, 12.2.2021.

2 See: https://ec.europa.eu/info/publications/fiscal-rules-database_en.

3 See: Medium-term budgetary frameworks database, https://ec.europa.eu/info/publications/medium-term-budgetary-frameworks-database_en.

4 Such as the Treaty on Stability, Coordination and Governance, Council Directive 2011/85/EU (part of the "six-pack") and Regulation (EU) No 473/2013 of the European Parliament and of the Council of 21 May 2013 on common provisions for monitoring and assessing draft budgetary plans and ensuring the correction of excessive deficit of the member states in the euro area (part of "two-pack").

5 See: https://www.imf.org/en/Data/Fiscal/fiscal-council-dataset. Fiscal councils are often equated with the so-called independent fiscal institutions (IFIs). A database is kept on these institutions by the European Commission (https://ec.europa.eu/info/publications/fiscal-institutions-database_en), however it includes more entities (33 institutions in 2019), because of the broader definition. Independent fiscal institutions are cross-party public bodies, other than the central bank, government or parliament, focusing on promoting sustainable public finances, for example by monitoring compliance with fiscal rules, as well as preparing or endorsement of macroeconomic forecasts for the budget.

6 This was the first EU social bond issuance, and at the same time the world's largest social bond scheme.

7 Article: 107(2)(b), 107 (3)(b) TFEU and 107(3)(c).

8 The total amount of funds for combating the pandemic crisis was set at PLN 312 billion, of which approximately PLN 70 billion was the liquidity package of the National Bank of Poland.

9 The Eurostat decision on this matter can be found at: https://ec.europa.eu/eurostat/web/government-finance-statistics/methodology/decisions-for-gfs.

10 The figure shows the data for the 19 of eurozone, as at the end of 2020, including also (for the full period) Latvia and Lithuania, which joined the euro area in 2014 and 2015 respectively.

11 Including also Croatia (being a EU member country from 2013) for the full period 2008–2020. Whenever aggregated data for 2008–2020 are shown, the data includes EU countries as of the end of 2020.

12 Sareb (Sociedad de Gestión de Activos Procedentes de la Reestructuración Bancaria) was established in 2012 to manage and sell the troubled assets of rescued banks.

References

Amaglobeli, D., End, N., Jarmuzek, M., Palomba, G. 2015. From systemic banking crises to fiscal costs: Risk factors. *IMF Working Paper*, WP/15/166. https://doi.org/10.5089/9781513529356.001.

Anderson, J., Papadia, F., Véron, N. 2021. COVID-19 credit-support programmes in Europe's five largest economies. *Working Paper. 03*. Bruegel.

Bank of Greece. 2014. *The Chronicle of the Great Crisis: The Bank of Greece 2008–2013. Public interventions and institutional actions to safeguard financial stability and overcome the crisis*. Athens.

Baudino, P., Murphy, D., Svoronos, J.-P. 2020. The banking crisis in Ireland, *FSI Crisis Management Series*, No. 2. Bank for International Settlements.

Bellia, M., Calès, L., Frattarolo, L., Maerean, A., Monteiro, D.P., Giudici, M.P., Vogel, L. 2019. The sovereign-bank nexus in the euro area: Financial and real channels. *Discussion Paper*, 122. European Commission. doi:10.2765/67946.

Blömer, M., Dolls, M., Fuest, C., Löffler, M., Peichl, A. 2015. German public finances through the financial crisis. *Fiscal Studies*, Vol. 36, No. 4, 453–474. https://doi.org/10.1111/j.1475-5890.2015.12073.

Bouabdallah, O., Checherita-Westphal, C., Freier, M., Nerlich, C., Sławińska, K. 2020. Automatic fiscal stabilizers in the euro area and the COVID-19 crisis. *ECB Economic Bulletin*, Issue 6.

Boudghene, Y., Buder, M., Dellidou, Z., Galand, C., Iftinchi, V., Lienemeyer, M., Malamataris, Ch., Malvolti, D. 2011. State aid control in a stability programme country: The case of Greece. *Competition Policy Newsletter*, Number 1.

Bova, E., Ruiz-Arranz, M., Toscani, F.G., Ture H. E. 2019. The impact of contingent liability realizations on public finances, *International Tax and Public Finance*, Vol. 26, 381–417. https://doi.org/10.1007/s10797-018-9496-1.

Brown, M., Evangelou, I.S., Stix, H. 2017. Banking Crises, Bail-ins and Money Holdings, *Working Paper*, 2. Central Bank of Cyprus. https://dx.doi.org/10.2139/ssrn.3102815.

Clerides, S. 2014. The Collapse of the Cypriot Banking System: A Bird's Eye View. *Cyprus Economic Policy Review*, Vol. 8, No. 2, 3–35.

Collin, A. M., Boddin, V., van de Casteele, K. 2021. The use of COVID-19 related State aid measures by EU Member States, Competition State aid brief, *Occasional papers by the Competition Directorate–General of the European Commission*, Issue 1.

Davoodi, H. R., Elger, P., Fotiou, A., Garcia-Macia, D., Han, X., Lagerborg, A., Lam, W. R., Medas, P. 2022. Fiscal rules and fiscal councils: Recent trends and performance during the pandemic, *IMF Working Paper*. No. 22/11. International Monetary Fund, Washington, D.C. https://doi.org/10.5089/9798400200472.001.

ESM. 2019. *Safeguarding the Euro in Times of Crisis. The inside story of the ESM*, Luxembourg.
European Bank for Reconstruction and Development. 2021. *Regional Economic Prospects. Bittersweet Recovery*. London. United Kingdom.
European Commission. 2008a. *Communication from the Commission from Financial Crisis to Recovery: A European Framework for Action*. COM(2008)706 final. Brussels.
European Commission. 2008b. *State Aid N 560 /2008 – Greece, Support Measures for the Credit Institutions in Greece*. C(2008) 7382. Brussels.
European Commission. 2009. The EU's response to support the real economy during the economic crisis: An overview of member states' recovery measures, *Occasional Papers*, No 51.
European Commission. 2010a. The economic adjustment programme for Greece, *European Economy Occasional Papers*, No. 61.
European Commission. 2010b. Public finances in EMU – 2010. *European Economy*, No. 4.
European Commission. 2011a. The economic adjustment programme for Ireland. *European Economy Occasional Papers*, No. 76.
European Commission. 2011b. *Report from the Commission State Aid Scoreboard Report on State Aid Granted by the EU Member States. Autumn* 2011. *Update*. COM/2011/0848 final.
European Commission. 2012a. *State aid SA.34488* (2012/C) (ex 2012 */NN) – Greece; Aid to Nea Proton Bank Through Creation and Capitalization of Nea Proton Bank, and Initiation of the Formal Investigation*. C(2012) 5321 final. Brussels.
European Commission. 2012b. *Commission Staff Working Document. Facts and Figures on State Aid in the EU Member States – 2012 Update – Accompanying the Document State Aid Scoreboard 2012 Update. Report on State Aid Granted by the EU Member States*. SWD(2012) 443 final. Brussels.
European Commission. 2013. The economic adjustment programme for Cyprus, *European Economy Occasional Papers*, 149.
European Commission. 2015. Ex post evaluation of the economic adjustment programme Ireland (2010–2013). *European Economy Institutional Paper*, 4. http://dx.doi.org/10.2765/755597.
European Commission. 2021. *Final Report on the European Instrument for Temporary Support to Mitigate Unemployment Risks in an Emergency (SURE) Following the COVID-19 Outbreak Pursuant to Article 14 of Council Regulation (EU) 2020/672 SURE: One Year On*. COM(2021) 596. Brussels.
European Court of Auditors. 2016. *Special Report Further Improvements Needed to Ensure Effective Implementation of the Excessive Deficit Procedure*, No 10, Luxembourg.
European Investment Bank. 2021. *Investment Report 2020/2021: Building a Smart and Green Europe in the COVID-19 Era*.
Eurostat. 2014. *Supplementary Table for The Financial Crisis, Background note*, (October).
Eurostat. 2021. *Eurostat Supplementary Table for Reporting Government Interventions to Support Financial Institutions, Background note*, (October).
Fall, F., Bloch, D., Fournier, J.-M., Hoeller, P. 2015. Prudent debt targets and fiscal frameworks, *OECD Economic Policy Paper*, No. 15. https://doi.org/10.1787/5jrxtjmmt9f7-en.

Federal Ministry of Finance. 2008. *German Stability Programme 2008 Update*. Berlin.

Federal Ministry of Finance. 2010. *German Stability Programme 2010 Update*. Berlin.

Federal Ministry of Finance. 2021. *German Stability Programme 2021 Update*. Berlin.

Girón, C., Rodríguez-Vives, M. 2021. The role of government for the non-financial corporate sector during the COVID-19 crisis. *ECB Economic Bulletin*, Issue 5.

Haroutunian, S., Osterloh, S., Sławińska, K. 2021. The initial fiscal policy responses of euro area countries to the COVID-19 crisis, *ECB Economic Bulletin*, Issue 1.

Honohan, P., Klingebiel, D. 2000. Controlling the fiscal costs of banking crises. World Bank Policy Research Working Paper 2441, Washington. https://doi.org/10.1596/1813-9450-2441.

Igan, D., Moussawi, H., Tieman, A.F., Zdzienicka, A., Dell'Ariccia, G., Mauro, P. 2019. The long shadow of the global financial crisis: Public interventions in the financial sector, *IMF Working Paper*, WP/19/164. https://doi.org/10.5089/9781513508337.001.

IMF. 2009. *Fiscal Rules – Anchoring Expectations for Sustainable Public Finances*, International Monetary Fund, Washington, DC. https://doi.org/10.5089/9781498335164.007.A001.

IMF. 2013. *The Functions and Impact of Fiscal Councils*. International Monetary Fund. Washington, DC. https://doi.org/10.5089/9781498341493.007.A001.

IMF. 2020. *Fiscal Monitor: Policies to Support People during the COVID-19 Pandemic*. International Monetary Fund. Washington, DC.

Lacey, E., Massad, J., Utz, R. 2021. *A Review of Fiscal Policy Responses to COVID-19*. World Bank. Washington, DC. https://doi.org/10.1596/35904.

Laeven, L., Valencia, F. 2010. Resolution of banking crises: The good, the bad, and the ugly. *IMF Working Paper*, Issue 146. https://doi.org/10.5089/9781455201297.001.

Lowe, P. 2009. State Aid Policy in the context of the financial crisis. *Competition Policy Newsletter*, Number 2.

Mavridou, M., Theodossiou, A., Gklezakou, T. 2016. *Greece. Several Greek Banks and Foreign Branches: Resolution Via Public Recapitalization and Bail-In And State Aid Issues (2009–2015)* in: World Bank Group, *Bank Resolution and 'Bail-In' in the EU: Selected Case Studies Pre- and Post-BRRD*. World Bank, Vienna.

Mohl, P., Mourre, G., Stovicek, K. 2019. Automatic fiscal stabilizers in the EU: Size and effectiveness, *Economic Brief*, 045, European Commission.

Polackova, H. 1999. Government contingent liabilities: A hidden risk to fiscal stability. *Policy Research Working Paper*. Washington: World Bank. https://doi.org/10.1596/1813-9450-1989.

Polackova-Brixi, H., Schick, A. 2002. *Introduction. Government at Risk: Contingent Liabilities and Fiscal Risks* in Polackova-Brixi, H., & Schick, A., *Government at Risk: Contingent Liabilities and Fiscal Risks*. Washington: Co-publication of the World Bank and Oxford University Press.

Rada Ministrów. 2021. *Sprawozdanie z wykonania budżetu państwa za okres od 1 stycznia do 31 grudnia 2020 r. Omówienie*. Warszawa.

Reinhart, C. M., Rogoff, K. S. 2011. From financial crash to debt crisis, *American Economic Review*, Vol. 101, No. 5, 1676–1706. https://doi.org/10.1257/aer.101.5.1676.

Scheinert, C. 2016. *Vicious circles. The interplay between Europe's financial and sovereign debt crises*. European Parliament.

Sherwood M. 2015. Medium-term budgetary frameworks in the EU member states, *European Economy Discussion Paper*, 21.

Simon, C. 2020. Ireland's Credit Institutions (Eligible Liabilities Guarantee) Scheme (Ireland GFC). *Journal of Financial Crises*, Vol. 2, No. 3, 773–792.

Staehr, K. 2013. Austerity in the Baltic States during the global financial crisis, *Intereconomics*, Vol. 48, No. 5, 293–302. https://doi.org/10.1007/s10272-013-0472-9.

World Bank. 2021. *Evaluation of the World Bank Group's Early Response in Addressing the Economic Implications of COVID-19*. Approach Paper.

Xafa M. 2013. Life after Debt. The Greek PSI and its aftermath, *World Economics*, Vol. 14, No. 1, 81–102.

Zenios, S.A. 2016. Fairness and Reflexivity in the Cyprus Bail-In, *Empirica*, Vol. 43, No. 3, 579–606. https://doi.org/10.1007/s10663-015-9306-2.

4 Financial market in crisis

4.1 Origin of asset pricing – who drives the market in a crisis?

The financial market is a large shop with plenty of financial instruments traded between numerous participants. The key difference between the goods and services market and the financial market is that the latter relates to intangible instruments. Moreover, market participants can usually both buy and sell them on the transparent and homogenous market. This assumption – in theory – provides more "democratic" access to trading and pricing processes or easy and fast flow of information. In the typical goods and services market, there is a strict division between sellers (producers, shops and service providers) and buyers (i.e. consumers). In the financial market, yesterday's seller can be today's buyer, and you can sell even what you do not possess. The latter phenomenon is known as short selling. Short selling is borrowing in order to sell immediately, which is almost impossible on "ordinary" physical markets.

Although the above-mentioned "democracy" and flexibility foster liquidity, in adverse market conditions they can be a source of disaster. If people "sell short" on a massive scale, it creates bubbles that can burst and accelerate a severe price drop. Short selling increases leverage on the market and the leverage is perceived as a "mother of crises."

Financial markets trade risk. Some agents are eager to buy the risk in order to make a profit, and others want to get rid of the risk in order to be immune to adverse price movements. There are two key factors that determine smooth risk transfer: liquidity and a volatility. Market liquidity is scope for easiness of concluding deals on the financial market. Price volatility is a measure of instability of market prices. If a crisis occurs, liquidity drops and volatility rises. This means two problems: the risk is higher, but it is harder to insure against it. On the contrary, in times of market equilibrium low risk is easy to hedge.

The key evidence of a crisis is increased volatility of prices and decreased liquidity of the market. The crisis means an uncertain and unstable valuation of assets. If the precise value of the owned portfolio cannot be estimated,

DOI: 10.4324/9781003225539-4

risk estimation error is dangerously augmented. As a consequence, market participants bear losses on trading and asset valuation.

The key question is why valuation of financial assets changes? In order to answer this question, one should know and understand determinants of prices of financial instruments that are traded on the market. These determinants can be traditionally split into those that shape demand and those that shape supply of the given asset. However, this attitude is more based on the goods and services market. In the world of finance, a demand-supply relationship is clear on commodities or securities, but rather ambiguous on non-tangible markets such as interest rate instruments or foreign exchange. On off-balance instruments like derivatives especially, instead of the demand-supply ratio a sentiment and in consequence – market flows are analyzed.

Agents active on the financial market do so for various reasons. Some speculate and increase their risky assets in order to make profits. Others hedge to decrease their exposure in order to minimize the sensitivity of their portfolios to price changes. Some look for arbitrage opportunities, but nowadays this is barely possible due to automatization of trading and globalization of information (Pole, 2011; Treleavan et al., 2012; Brogaard et al., 2014).

The key split between market roles is not into buyers and sellers but into market makers and market users. Market makers are liquidity providers and price creators – they quote on a permanent basis. As a result, a market maker is constantly at risk. Market users utilize makers' services and take the prices from them. They trade if they wish to, so they are described as an active side of the market or an aggressor. On the one hand, makers wait passively for users' decisions. On the other hand, they trade among each other so are active in hedging their exposure on a constant basis.

Commonly, market makers are commercial banks for three reasons. First of all, banks are large enough and have sufficient capital to maintain such risky activity like every day market making. Potential losses are relatively low in comparison to the after-tax profit (or loss). Capital is adequate to bear such risk exposure and potential losses. Second, banks have advanced risk management systems that can be used as front office analytical systems for trading. Synergies between a banking book and balance sheet management with proprietary trading and market-making activities are a significant advantage. Last but not least, banks have natural market flows. Customer-based activities mean significant turnover on numerous financial instruments and a permanent need for position management. A market-making overlay is an efficient supplement to such deals. It enriches banks' feeling of the market and improves informational and pricing quality of client services.

Market makers are willing to take a risk because they see numerous advantages. First, they collect margin. They buy low at the bid price and sell high at the ask (offer) price. A bid-ask spread is a measure of indirect transactional costs. These costs favour the market maker.

In the competitive market, the bid-ask spreads are thin – prices are even tighter than short-term volatility of the market. This means losses for the market maker – they trade at the price that is hardly possible to hedge. Even immediate neutralization of the exposure causes a negative result of trading.

In such a situation, market makers search for a second source of revenues – cross-selling. They trade simple and most liquid products at dumping transactional costs, but in parallel they offer more complicated and less liquid products at wider spreads. Simple financial instruments are subsidized by more advanced ones. The first is used for promotion, the latter for making money.

Although a cross-sell may decrease losses on competitive market making, in many cases it is not enough to cover negative results. Then the third advantage is a chance for profits. This advantage is information.

Information is a crucial tool for earning money on the financial market. Trading without information is equal to gambling. Trading with information allows generation of regular profits. Therefore, asymmetry of information is a phenomenon that market makers want to keep. A market maker in the process of quoting at request and trading at their own prices collects information about market flows and market orders. This information allows them to make proper decisions on the basis of forecast changes in market sentiment (Barberis et al., 1998). In the longer term, when an informational advantage is obtained, one can make profits on forecasting shifts in market trends that enable correct market decisions on directional bets.

Trading risk is in fact trading information. This is especially visible on OTC markets. An off-exchange market is less transparent and more dependent on market makers. Tailor-made products offered on that market and the direct relationship between makers and users or bilateral trading among makers create a specific environment for the flow of information.

The flow of information is strengthened by a concept known as a thought contagion (Lynch, 2000; Hirshleifer and Teoh, 2009). Makers try to spread their views on the market. In the daily process of quotes, order execution and deal conclusion, they infect their clients with opinions about future prices. In effect, one observes a phenomenon called behavioural coarsening (Ng, 2010; Shive, 2010). Due to psychological factors, the number of market participants having the same view on future market prices increases. Eventually, this determines a significant sentiment that creates market trends. In fact, the original source of that view are market makers. This is due to the natural process of behavioural imitation (Shiller, 1995; Bikhchandani et al., 1998). Users copy trades concluded by the makers in order to avoid losses. The imitation assures safety of their market exposure. As users know that makers possess informational asymmetry, they want to obtain this unique knowledge indirectly by observing makers' activity. In consequence, the process of copying makers' decisions enhances market trends and is observed as a herding phenomenon or a snowball effect (Brunnermeier, 2001; Chari and Kehoe, 2004). Herding strengthens the initial impulses and accelerates the speed of contagion, and this increases adverse shocks, creating a crisis environment (Lee, 1998; Vives, 2001).

Market prices maintain some cyclicality except where market trends are not augmented by leverage and domination by non-informed participants. If such disequilibrium occurs, markets tend to bubble and bust. It is rather rare for makers to create a bubble, as they tend to be market neutral in the longer term. Dangerous bubbles arise if numerous leveraged users try to earn money on accelerated trends. This ends in a bust which happens at a time of crisis.

Literature gives numerous examples of the role of market sentiment in creating and extinguishing market disequilibria. During the GFC, we witnessed evidence of a correlation between negative sentiment and power on inter-market linkages (Nitoi and Pochea, 2020). The co-existence of sentiment shifts increased integration between dissimilar markets. Sentiment shifts are accelerated by herding behaviour. Bekiros et al. (2017) noticed that the strength of herding is visible at the outbreak of the crisis and its role during the later phases of the turmoil diminishes.

The PIIGS crises was a smooth consequence of the GFC. Moro (2014) analyzes eurozone vulnerability to market sentiment that had a strong impact on the intensification of the PIIGS debt crisis. Research found that sentiment has an influence on market fragmentation across EU national borders that increases liquidity tensions. These changes in local sentiment were created by herd behaviour, as proven by Mobarek et al. (2014). Brooks et al. (2015), in this respect, indicate that herding is present independently at times of crisis and is one of the factors facilitating spreading of negative sentiment in a period of market stress.

The COVID-19 pandemic is different as it was a typical black swan event. Therefore, it was hardly possible to predict its outbreak on the basis of pre-crisis sentiment analysis. Nevertheless, changing sentiment can be a barometer of the market reaction after the outbreak. Kanapickiene et al. (2020), on the basis of interdependence between the economic sentiment and financial markets during the COVID-19 crisis, claim that market users overreact due to false assessment of the received information. The overreaction might be imposed by social media: some research measures the impact of social media news on a decision taken on the equity market and volatility of stocks (Haroon and Rizvi, 2020; Valle-Cruz et al., 2021).

Prices recorded on various segments of the financial markets are of great informational value and can be treated as a thermometer of the market sentiment and the risk aversion. In order to forecast sentiment shifts, one can observe sentiment indicators. They are especially useful and informative on emerging markets that have an embedded asymmetry of risk (more about this asymmetry in Chapter 4.3).

The crucial sentiment indicators are (see Box 4.1):

- asset swap spread,
- OIS spread,
- currency basis spread,
- implied volatility,

Box 4.1 Sentiment indicators

An asset swap spread (ASW) is a price of a strategy built from a debt security (usually it is a treasury bond) and an interest rate swap (IRS). The latter is an instrument swapping fixed interest rate for a floating rate based usually on the IBOR-type index. The difference between a yield of the bond and a yield of the swap is a measure of a relative long-term credit risk of the issuer of the bond versus standard credit risk of short-term interbank borrowing accompanied by the liquidity risk of the security itself. For corporate bonds, an ASW is always positive (a bond's yield over a swap), for safe haven bonds – negative. An ASW is strictly dependent on market sentiment and the current level of the risk aversion – the worse the sentiment, the higher the ASW (more positive or less negative). Therefore, an ASW is a good barometer of the market sentiment – especially on emerging markets (Flavell, 2002).

An OIS spread is the difference between the price of an Overnight Indexed Swap (OIS) and a standard IBOR rate for the same term. An OIS represents a one-day lending risk on the interbank market (it is a forward on the ONIA-type rate). An IBOR reveals an implied cost of the term lending. The term deposits have a higher credit and liquidity risk than the overnight deposits. Hence – the worse the sentiment, the more negative the OIS spread. If market sentiment is poor, the IBOR goes up more quickly than the OIS due to the augmenting risk on the particular money market.

A currency basis spread is the difference between an implied cost of borrowing one currency against the other and a similar cost based on standard IBOR-type rates in those currencies. The currency basis is the price of currency swaps (short-term FX Swaps or long-term CIRS) which are a very popular way of collateralized lending, especially on emerging markets. A currency basis sign is proof of structural imbalances in the cross-border liquidity. At a time of stress, usually a local currency is very cheap for borrowing via a swap as hard currency lending begins to be very expensive for local entities. It is worth adding that a quantitative easing in developed economies has distorted this principle. This has happened because market players have started seeking yields in emerging markets in order to invest locally for the borrowed local currency to avoid foreign exchange risk. An analysis of the currency basis is quite complex, as we have to forecast changes in the relative demand and supply balance in the two currencies simultaneously.

Implied volatility is a key source for pricing options. The higher the risk on a given market, the higher the price to insure its changes via options. The increased instability of market prices usually accompanies a time of stress and augmented risk aversion. Therefore, the implied volatility hikes show the periods of worse sentiment. As option prices relate to the future instability of the underlying asset's prices, volatility is a robust early indicator of a sentiment shift. It is good to add that market analysts use a VIX index as a standard measure of fear on the markets. The VIX is a synthetic volatility index based on prices of options written to the S&P index representing big American stocks (Whaley, 2009). Unfortunately, markets do not offer many more synthetic indices, so an analysis or hedging on the volatility market is only accessible via option contracts.

A risk reversal is also based on option prices, more precisely on the price of the option strategy built on two options. It is of the difference between implied volatilities between low delta calls and low delta puts (so high strikes and low strikes with similar probability of being exercised). A risk reversal represents an expected skew on the market (the asymmetry of sharp price moves). Risk reversals are very popular for foreign exchange options. On emerging currency markets, a sign of risk reversal strategy is always positive. That means that a risk of a strong depreciation of a local currency is always higher than its appreciation. Moreover, it indicates the following rule: the weaker the local currency, the higher its volatilities against major currencies (Rebonato, 2004).

A credit default swap (CDS) represents an insolvency risk of the bond issuer. The majority of CDS relate to sovereign debt. In fact, it is an option where the reference underlying is the event of default. The higher the price, the more probable the default of the issuer. Therefore, high rating issuers have a low price of the CDS and low rating – the opposite. Unfortunately, on emerging markets liquidity of CDS contracts is not sufficient.

- risk reversal,
- credit default swap.

A summary of the sentiment indicators is presented in Table 4.1.

Sentiment indicators will be used in case studies presented in section 4 of this chapter.

Traders and investors use off-balance derivatives to make money on high leverage and to hedge non-linear risks. The overwhelming role of forwards, swaps and options was not limited after the series of crises, although these instruments can be deemed the culprits of market crashes. Trading on derivatives is highly dependent on liquidity. Major (mature) markets offer a wide range of off-balance instruments, both standardized and tailored – the latter used for structured investment products. Emerging (incomplete) markets are scanty in that matter, with a much smaller range of products and fragile liquidity. Pricing emerging derivatives is harder and risk management

Table 4.1 Sentiment indicators – risk and instruments

Sentiment indicator	*Represented risk*	*Embedded instruments*
Asset swap spread (ASW)	Credit & liquidity risk on bonds	Treasury bond and interest rate swap
Overnight Indexed Swap spread (OIS)	Credit & liquidity risk on money market	OIS and IBOR
Currency basis spread (CBS)	Cross-border liquidity risk	FX swap or CIRS
Implied volatility (IV)	Expected instability of prices	ATM option
Risk reversal (RR)	Expected skewness of price changes	OTM options
Credit default swap (CDS)	Credit risk of the issuer	Option on default risk

Source: own work.

is "more art than science.". In such an environment, the role of market makers increases.

Apart from the general rules of pricing, trading, market making and risk management, we can observe idiosyncratic phenomena that distort the process of asset valuation. Since the GFC, central banks (CB) have performed various kinds of expansionary policy that are described as "non-standard" monetary tools. The CB policy focused on pumping up the market liquidity, and this caused a significant increase in the monetary base and radical cut of interest rates. In some currencies, these parked on the negative territory. In general, the policy is known as quantitative easing (QE) and provides extremely low interest rates (zero or negative) and a high demand for privately held securities created by monetary authorities (this is described in Chapter 2). Such expansionary monetary policy is described as unconventional, as the QE is a non-standard tool in central bankers' warehouses. The QE changed the rules of the game, as it heavily affected liquidity and credit risk (Neely, 2015). On the other hand, it created a long-term disequilibrium that could have side effects we cannot foresee at the moment.

Numerous research points out that one observes crowding out effects of QE. Duca et al. (2016) found evidence that central bank purchases crowded out investors and moved portfolio investments to emerging markets. Ferdinandusse et al. (2020) notice crowding out of some traditional buyers decreasing bond liquidity. According to Grimaldi et al. (2021), central bank expansionary non-standard policy has a positive effect on liquidity to some extent, but when the threshold is crossed, this creates a negative effect on the supply side.

In fact, a new style of monetary policy is nowadays treated as the "standard" one, as it is performed by a majority of key central bankers, and this procedure has been conducted over the last decade. This interest rate environment and the incredible activity of central banks both change the rules of the market and behaviour of its participants (Fratzscher et al., 2015). A low-rate environment is a true headache for investors. Due to quantitative easing, the market is flooded by cash, but low-risk instruments offer zero or negative yields. In such circumstances, speculative funds try to use the cheap money to obtain positive returns.

During the pandemic crisis, expansionary tools of monetary policy continued to be used despite growing inflation. In the era of low and negative yields, traders seeking returns are in trouble. Cheap financing can help if a rate differential can be obtained between assets and liabilities. Quantitative easing creates incentives to invest on risky markets, like emerging countries' currencies and low-rated corporate bonds (Lacalle, 2019). The shift to risky assets affects potential disequilibrium and can be a reason for severe turbulences.

The source of the turbulences can be related to inflation in asset prices. The over-liquidity of cash creates an excess demand invested in various securities, pumping its prices over the fundamental levels. This tendency used to create bubbles that can burst, causing price disequilibria (Brown, 2015; Adam and Tzamourani, 2015). Moreover, the QE stimulus increases movement of capital between mature low and negative rate markets and emerging high-yield countries – this was especially visible in the aftermath of the anti-GFC tools (see: Tillmann, 2016; Ramirez and Gonzales, 2017). Sobrun and Turner (2015) indicate that this capital movement is strictly related to near-zero real long-term rates that create incentives to invest in emerging market bonds. These investments bear higher liquidity, currency and credit risk, and this increases the probability of future tensions. Tensions can occur if QE stops ("tapering"). This can have an adverse impact on stability of emerging economies with weaker fundamentals (Rai and Suchanek, 2014; Chari et al., 2017).

One can also observe the QE-origin of the capital flow in emerging Europe in the aftermath of the GFC and PIIGS crises. Horváth and Voslarova (2017) noticed a crowding out effect of ECB monetary policy in local inflation targeting. This had an expansionary effect on the CEE market. As a result, shocks from the eurozone affected small open EU economies with local currencies. Kucharčuková et al. (2016) emphasize the key impact on local foreign exchange rates and fixed income yields. Bluwstein, and Canova (2016) claim that the financial market is a transmitter of these spillovers, due to risk and portfolio rebalancing (more about this subject in the last section of this chapter).

The extraordinary situation during the COVID-19 pandemic changed again the rules of play and created challenges for investors. The monetary stimulus is accompanied by a fiscal one augmenting up-to-date over-liquidity in the system. According to literature, the pandemic brought increased volatility of asset prices (Albulescu, 2021), augmenting the scope of uncertainty and breaking linkages between the stock markets (Zhang et al., 2020). The reaction of the markets moved in line with the following pandemic waves (Ali et al., 2020, and had a reciprocal influence on monetary policy, rendering it less efficient (Wei and Han, 2021).

As a monetary and fiscal stimulus can have side effects, it should be analyzed together with a post-crisis regulatory environment. Both streams, economic and legal, create a contemporary marketplace increasing linkages between mature and emerging markets at a time of stress. Regulations having direct influence on trading are described in the next section.

4.2 Financial markets in crisis – a victim or a culprit?

All kinds of crises distort credibility of market users and endanger stability of trading. The GFC was especially acute for perception of the financial market as a credible and stable marketplace. In consequence, authorities were forced to take steps to improve credibility and assure long-term stability of dealing. This chapter will focus on these issues, looking at two-way interdependence between market liquidity and regulations.

For centuries, trading was bilateral. One person eager to buy had to find another eager to sell. Both sides of the deal bear the risk of the counterparty. This manner of trading is called over-the-counter (OTC) trading. Exchanges, introduced more widely in the late 18th century, allowed more concentrated and safer securities trading, however the phenomenon of trading off-exchange survived. Nowadays, a bulk of instruments are predominantly traded over-the-counter.

The key difference is legal: on an exchange, agents do not trade directly with each other but deal with the exchange. The exchange matches buyers and sellers and steps in between them. On an OTC market, trades are performed directly between both sides of the deal. The trading agreement is purely bilateral (Nysted, 2004; Switzer and Fan, 2007).

The legal difference implies a different source of credit risk. On an exchange, the counterparties bear the risk of the exchange itself, and all have to obey the same rules to make trading safe. In OTC trading, the rules are described in the deal agreement in a discretionary manner, and the agreement shapes the obligations and rights of the counterparties if one defaults.

The crucial kinds of credit risk related to OTC trading are settlement and pre-settlement risk. Market players have developed efficient tools to limit these risks. Firstly – a delivery-versus-payment procedure was introduced to liquidate the risk on a settlement date. Secondly – a collateral agreement is a must to decrease losses on the off-balance valuation in the event of default. Therefore, pre-settlement risk is sufficiently limited (Bliss and Kaufmann, 2006; Morgan, 2008; Singh, 2010; Close, 2011).

As a result, when the crisis occurred, just a handful suffered losses due to the credit risk itself. The main source of problems experienced by the financial market was a negative valuation connected with bad sentiment and a liquidity squeeze (Duffie and Lubke, 2010).

Clearly, financial markets had created disequilibria that had detrimental effects on the real economy, but two issues need to be borne in mind: first – financial instruments are not the only reason for the economic problems, and second – the financial market itself is affected by negative trends in the economy.

A crisis comes when market sentiment is bad and risk aversion is high. A financial market instantly shows the change in both indicators. However, there is a causality conundrum: does sentiment worsen because financial instruments are mispriced and "mis-sold,", or do prices of the instruments drop as a consequence of the deteriorating economy?

The answer to this question depends on the relationship between the size of the financial market and the size of the real economy. In mature economies with well-developed financial markets, leverage causes overgrowth of the financial market itself. Hence a "tail" can wag a "dog." However, in emerging markets, the financial market is immature and smaller than a growing economy. In such markets, disequilibria on local financial instruments cannot severely affect the real economy (for more see Chapter 5), but global financial instruments can. The latter effect is known as "contagion." This is described in Section 4.3 of this chapter.

Regulators who observe an adverse impact of financial markets on the economic stability are forced to act. The most profound wave of new regulations was introduced in the aftermath of the GFC (Biggins and Scott, 2012; Sidanius and Wetherilt, 2012). It was a direct response to the past danger caused by financial engineering. However, all antidotes have side effects.

The new regulations crucial for financial markets cover three areas: financial benchmarks, customer protection, and market infrastructure. They are described below.

4.2.1 Financial benchmark regulation

The GFC changed many rules of the game in the financial markets. One such change relates to the perception of interest rates as a cost of money.

Numerous examples of manipulations were demonstrated on the -IBOR and FX markets (Abrantes-Metz et al., 2012; Hou and Skeie, 2014; Gandhi et al., 2015). Manipulations had two aims: making profits on cash-settled derivatives indexed to reference rates, and hiding the increased financing cost to the public. In both cases, the reference rates were artificially moved in order to set them at the required level divergent from real market rates.

This misconduct forced the regulator to pass new legislation on financial benchmarks (Kirti, 2017). The law is focused on consumer protection and imposes several constraints that indices published on financial markets must meet. However, the -IBOR reform is problematic as the reference money market disappeared after the subprime crisis. As a result, benchmark administrators cannot meet regulatory requirements promoting deal-based indices at the expense of the present expert judgement. Therefore, the benchmark revolution is shaped not only by legal forces but also by economic incentives. This causes a huge compliance risk of legacy contracts that in some cases cannot be amended (Perkins and Mortby, 2015).

Following the famous Wheatley Report (2012), both IOSCO and BIS published in 2013 guidelines for benchmark providers and data suppliers all over the world (HM Treasury, 2012, BIS, 2013, IOSCO, 2013). Moreover, the European Parliament voted to adopt in 2016 the special Benchmark Regulation – BMR (EP 2016) and ESMA imposed several regulatory technical standards that describe the correct behaviour of administrators, banks and other financial institutions engaged in calculation and publication of financial benchmarks.

Due to its origin, special attention is paid to interest rate indices that determine the cash flows in floating rate loans, bonds and derivatives and are used for valuation of such products. Importantly, misconduct of some banks before and during the GFC was a primary reason, but not the crucial factor in the above-mentioned regulatory changes. The key determinant of changes in the benchmark world is a significant structural transformation observed in the interbank money market.

Increased credit risk and an augmented possibility of sudden liquidity squeezes limit the unsecured lending in contemporary markets. Market participants look for alternative ways of cash distribution that can be both cheaper and safer than traditional funding. Secured financing is the answer.

According to Brousseau et al. (2013) and Duffie and Stein (2015), banks transformed their funding structure from wholesale- to more retail-based due to Basel liquidity rules (LCR and NSFR, explained in Chapter 2). Nowadays, liabilities of banks are based on corporate and retail deposits. An interbank market is limited to one-day deposits and secured deposits. The reasons for this change are threefold:

1. The enhanced credit risk decreased credibility of prime banks and the augmented liquidity risk discouraged lending cash for longer terms.
2. The crowding-out effects of the expansionary central bank policy injected huge liquidity into wholesale markets, reducing the need to refinance on the B2B (bank-to-bank) market.
3. Basel liquidity regulations penalized unsecured assets located in other banks.

In effect, a non-short-term unsecured interbank deposit is a peculiar rarity. They were fully replaced by three types of liabilities: O/N interbank, wholesale repo, and mid-term unsecured non-financial deposits.

The key consequence of this structural change was a loss of the market basis for IBOR-type interest rate benchmarks. Previously, inputs for LIBOR had been the expert judgement only, but the level had been based on market prices. The disappearance of the term deposits meant that the -IBOR rates were no longer referred to any concluded deals. The expert judgement was founded on the void. In this environment we witnessed an increased risk of allegations of manipulation. In effect, the number of panellists quoting inputs for the IBORs had decreased significantly.

The BMR accelerated the reform of indices. LIBOR for all currencies except USD was liquidated at the end of 2021 and the dollar benchmark will disappear in mid-2023. The Euribor introduced a new waterfall methodology to prolong its existence.

ISDA, ESMA and central banks cooperated with the market society to develop new benchmarks that can replace IBORs. The majority of alternative rates are based on risk-free rates (RFR) that are calculated on the basis of one-day secured or unsecured wholesale deposits. Usage of RFRs has quite a long tradition on the financial market. In 2010, the compromised LIBOR was replaced by an OIS curve for discounting cash flows in banks' books and for collateral calculations (Bianchetti, 2010; Whitall, 2010).

A drawback of the RFR is a lack of credit component embedded into the rate. Moreover, the RFR itself does not have a yield curve as it relates to one single point on the curve – day 1. The difference between the IBOR rate and the RFR might be significant, and this divergence widened during the crises. In March 2020, i.e. at the beginning of the COVID lockdown, the difference between USD LIBOR and USD RFR (SOFR) was almost 150 bp.

The structural change introduced in the aftermath of the GFC seems to be permanent. Professional participants adapted to the new environment quite smoothly. The problems occurred in relations with consumers.

Use of an RFR is suitable for derivatives. However, for bonds and loans there is a problem with lack of knowledge about the basis for future cash flows. The IBOR is a term rate, which means that the magnitude of future interest payments is known in advance. The RFR – as a one-day rate – must be compounded in order to be treated as the alternative to the term rate. As a result, the accommodation of the RFR requires *in arrears* methodology, when the basis of the interest is known *ex-post* and not *ex-ante*.

A professional market can smoothly accommodate this feature of new benchmarks, but in relations with customers, banks have to take care of reputation and ensure legality.

The problem with amendment of the index used in long-term assets (especially in floating rate mortgages) is a challenge especially on emerging markets. In mature markets, the standard in consumer loans is a fixed-rate contract in which the interest rate benchmark is unnecessary. In some emerging markets, a large share of IBOR-based loans means that annexes are needed to the contracts with customers or regulatory-based conversion of whole stock has to be introduced.[1]

In general, despite some problems with implementation, the BMR brings many advantages for the market:

- it increases market informational transparency;
- it promotes transaction-based indices that decreases the probability of manipulation;

- it encourages building competition in the world of financial benchmarks, favouring a multi-index environment and augmenting the spectrum of choices for the users;
- it protects consumers against any misconduct in the process of the benchmark's usage.

4.2.2 MiFID customer protection

Another regulatory stream relates to the relationship between financial institutions and their clients on the financial market. The aim of this activity is normalization of the B2C (bank-to-client) market to enhance consumer protection and eradicate any mis-selling. A key regulation in that area is the Market in Financial Instruments Directive – MiFID.[2]

MiFID's key objective is to protect investors. It came about due to evidence of mis-selling and financial institutions taking advantage of asymmetry of information about the state of the market and a risk profile of offered instruments. The scope of protection depends on the client profile (retail, professional or eligible), the relation framework (order execution, investment advice, portfolio management) and the type of deal (agency or principal). The regulation is set out not only to strengthen investor protection, but also to reduce the risk of market disorder and a systemic risk, and to make financial markets more efficient.

The early MiFID (2004) introduced a concept of a Systematic Internalizer (SI). This was obligatory from the beginning for equities, and subsequently for all products except foreign exchange. An SI is an investment firm that leads the regular, daily activity on the financial market for sizeable volumes on its own account. This firm executes client orders outside the organized market. Size limits introduced in MIFiD2 (2014) reserve SI status for large investment banks.

In consequence, MiFID regulates agency and principal dealing. Principal dealing means concluding transactions on one's own account. Agency dealing is a process in which a broker quotes a price and executes an order but does not bear the market risk of the deal. The broker passes the exposure on to another counterparty. In order to assure proper protection of clients, the regulation defines a number of distinct types of transactions – see Table 4.2.

Table 4.2 Types of deals under MiFID

Agency dealing	*Principal dealing*
• Execution of orders on an execution venue • Execution of orders by means of agency matching	• Dealing solely on one's own account • Concluding deals through systematic internalization

Source: Busch (2016).

As far as agency dealing is concerned, an investment firm executes a client's orders. One option is an execution venue, i.e. an exchange or a multilateral trading facility (MTF). The latter is a trading venue operated by an investment firm where various investment firms conclude agreements on behalf of their clients. The other option is matching, which is finding another client with an opposite order to match it. An organized trading facility (OTF) can be used to find a matching order. An OTF is defined in MiFID as a multilateral system which is not a regulated market, or an MTF, and in which multiple third-parties buying and selling non-equity interests are able to interact in the system provided by a discretionary operator. An OTF operator can engage in matched principal trading in bonds, structured finance products, emission allowances and derivatives. Moreover, they are obliged to comply with the numerous investor protection obligations such as information management, suitability, best execution, and client order handling. According to regulations, all agency crossing systems require a high duty of care in relation to both clients.

Principal dealing can be performed twofold, through direct bilateral trading with a client against proprietary capital resulting in the conclusion of transactions, or internalization. Dealing on one's own account is perceived as imposing limited duties of care for an investment firm. That is why for many years after introduction of MiFID a significant share of B2C trading on emerging markets was performed in such a way, to avoid any order execution and decrease regulatory burdens. Busch (2016) claims that this wicket weakens market homogeneity and can endanger proper observance of a client's rights.

However, the situation changes if an investment firm collects and executes orders against its own inventory (therefore without engaging any execution venue). This activity is known as internalization. For large banks, acting in their own name while executing the orders is a common daily practice. If this happens, systematic internalization occurs, and the bank is described as an SI. This investment service requires a high level of attention to the client needs and avoidance of conflicts of interest in order to assure best execution and reporting obligations.

An entity classified as an SI is obliged to offer pre-trade transparency, publishing firm quotes for liquid instruments and post-trade reporting sending transactional data to the national competent authority.[3] Being an SI is perceived to be a regulatory burden, but on the other hand it has some significant advantages for a liquidity provider. It facilitates the buyside to avoid the reporting obligation. The obligation is automatically transferred to the SI – therefore trading with an SI is more competitive for clients.

According to MiFID, an SI is a counterparty, not a trading venue. However, despite lack of organized multilateral system, an SI is obliged to report all quotes and trades in order to ensure equal treatment of its clients. A given institution can be an SI in some market segments only – in those asset classes where it crosses volume thresholds. Deals concluded by an SI are treated as executed orders in which client protection is a must (ESMA, 2017).

Importantly, ESMA imposed strict limits on building non-official trading venues consisting of numerous systematic internalizers matching riskless trades as agency dealing. Such networks can circumvent MiFID obligations specified for operators of the trading venues as broker crossing networks (BCN). The intention of ESMA was twofold: it was intended to maintain transparency and information flow of trading venues, and also to protect an added quality of an SI – risk-taking in order to provide liquidity for the market.

Moreover, MiFID regulations are intended to mitigate two drawbacks of the OTC market – market fragmentation and growing dark pool trading. Large deals are dealt in block trading in order to avoid price impact and delay information flow about the deal. In MIFIR (articles 4–5), the regulator introduces a mechanism increasing equity market transparency, which is Double Volume Caps (DVC). A DVC aims to limit trading in non-displayed liquidity (i.e. dark pools) by capping use of transparency waivers (negotiated price and reference price). Bearing in mind that big deals are excluded from the pre-trade transparency mechanism, one can expect growth of Large in Scale trading (LIS). This means aggregation of single equity deals to reach a volume threshold allowing for exclusion.

The general aim of MiFID is convergence of regulated and non-regulated markets in order to increase transparency, decrease informational asymmetry for retail investors, prevent market distortions, and strengthen market supervision (Nögel, 2017). Enhanced governance and control arrangements lead to additional costs. This decreases investment firms' profitability and sets entry barriers for new firms. Regulatory Technical Standards for MiFID II (RTS 25) even impose clock synchronization for high-frequency algorithmic trading, requiring one microsecond granularity and 1/100 microsecond divergence tolerance from UTC for time stamps in reporting data.

Significant changes in EU market infrastructure and liquidity should be expected, with some dark pool liquidity moving to less regulated markets.

4.2.3 EMIR infrastructure

The third pillar of the new regulatory infrastructure is the European Market Infrastructure Regulation (EMIR). Its twin brother in the United States is the Dodd-Frank Act. Both augment market transparency and decrease credit risk on the market.

The main requirements of EMIR are: (i) mandatory central clearing of certain classes of OTC derivatives imposed for certain types of counterparties; (ii) collection of a margin in respect of uncleared OTC derivatives between certain types of counterparties; (iii) reporting of all eligible OTC derivatives to authorized trade repositories; (iv) other risk mitigation requirements for OTC derivatives (Genito, 2019).

EMIR is intended to increase safety and transparency of OTC trading. The former is realized by imposing an obligation of CCP settlement, the latter by introduction of deal repositories. Central clearing reduces contagion risk and improves transparency of pre-settlement risk. Migration of huge off-balance exposures and its risk compression are perceived as key benefits of the EMIR infrastructural reform.

Concentration of credit risk in CCPs creates, however, new systemic risk. Clearing houses became a new "too big to fail" institutions. Moreover, the centrally cleared market exhibits asymmetrical fragmentation, which means that major turnover is concentrated in large CCPs (like SwapClear at LCH) but some portion of volume is cleared by local CCPs that do not have interoperability arrangements (Garvin, 2012; McPartland and Lewis, 2016).

However, not all segments of the market have been moved to CCPs. The CCP settlement obligation applies to large institutions concluding large and eligible deals. For smaller entities (not breaching particular volume thresholds – see table) and for some market instruments (like currency swaps or options), trading is still not cleared and is hence bilateral. Table 4.3 presents the various types of counterparties.

For uncleared OTC transactions, EMIR is gradually imposing new constraints relating to risk management requirements such as timely confirmation, proper valuation, bilateral reconciliation and periodical compression of portfolios. One of the most significant developments is the Initial Margin (IM). OTC markets used to require a variation margin only under the ISDA Credit Support Annex collateral regime. Now, collateral is extended by exchange-style initial margins. An initial margin is the amount of collateral required to open a position in the market. It is always required by exchanges and CCPs, but seldom by brokers or banks. EMIR imposes an obligation of reciprocal exchange of the margin at the inception of the deal. According to BSBC-IOSCO guidelines (2013), an initial margin covers the risk arising between the last variation margin exchange and the liquidation of a position upon default by a counterparty. The margin is calculated on a gross basis, and thus cannot be netted like variation margins if a master agreement is signed between the parties.

Proper calculation of the initial margin is supported by ISDA. This publishes industry standards for concluding, confirming and settling OTC transactions. ISDA publishes the Standard Initial Margin Model (SIMM), which is designed to provide a common methodology for calculating the initial margin for uncleared OTC derivatives. The initial margin calculation is both counterparty- and portfolio-based, with a strict distinction between

Table 4.3 Types of counterparties under EMIR

	Above the threshold	*Below the threshold*
Financial counterparty	FC+	FC−
Non-financial counterparty	NFC+	NFC−

Source: Becker, Maxwell (2014).

the cleared and uncleared part of the exposure. The standardized approach allows easy reconciliation of the required collateral between the parties.

When implementing the standardized model, ISDA (2016) followed the BCBS-IOSCO rules that assume: non-procyclicality, easy replication, transparency, quick calculation, extensibility potential, predictability (calibration stability), reasonable operational costs and burdens, and governance and appropriateness (not overestimating risk). However, Cont (2018) claims that the initial burden for uncleared derivatives is exaggerated. An uncleared market has to calculate risk on the basis of a window that is twice as long as the cleared one. It augments the risk assessment by 40% and does not take into consideration hedging activities of the non-defaulting party before the final close-out of the defaulted transaction.

Importantly, an OTC market has powerful tools in order to reduce its off-balance uncleared exposure. These tools are (Giada and Nordio, 2013; Edsparr and Fischer, 2014; Garcimartín and Saez, 2015):

- multilateral compression auctions for interest rate derivatives;
- break clauses and currency set-off clauses for currency swaps.

IR and FX derivatives are a bulk of the off-balance exposure of financial institutions. Under the EMIR collateral requirements, FIs are highly motivated to reduce the exposure that is not centrally cleared. For IR derivatives, a compression mechanism can be used that unwinds the derivative transaction that can be netted with exposure neutrality and cash settlement of the value. For liquidity derivatives based on foreign exchange, clauses can be used that drop down both a horizon and scale of pre-settlement risk created by long-term FX forwards. This activity has significant added value on emerging markets with higher volatility.

4.2.4 Discussion

The regulations are a response to a risk of instability coming from the financial markets. However, this remedy might have harmful consequences. In some cases, we may observe decreased liquidity of the market and higher access costs for market participants.

If a regulation introduces some penalties for any misconduct on the financial market, this means that it imposes several constraints on trading activities. Market participants who determine trading liquidity are market makers. How do new regulations limit market makers' willingness to provide liquidity for market users?

MiFID imposes client protection and trade transparency, and EMIR defines strict trading rules for some instruments. Both obligations can have adverse effects on market making.

Client protection increases onboarding costs. Each new client must be analyzed and checked. The MiFID analysis is added to previous standard checks related to "know-your-client" (KYC) procedures, including AML (Anti-Money Laundering) and CFT (Countering the Financing of Terrorism). The cost of the analysis might be higher than revenues coming from doing business with the client. Therefore, client protection may limit access to some market segments for smaller clients. In fact, concerns related to mis-selling eradicate some of the more complicated products from the product range – especially for consumers. This reduces turnover and may have adverse effects on market maker revenues and liquidity.

The obligations related to trade transparency decrease informational asymmetry that benefits market makers on the OTC markets. Asymmetry is one of the advantages that creates incentives for the risky process of market making. Market makers trade information, and it is in their interest for this to be private, not public.

The EMIR regime increases costs of professional activity on the financial market. Obligatory settlement novation for interest rate derivatives with wholesale amounts means Central Counterparty infrastructure has to be used. In fact, direct membership of a global CCP (like LCH) is expensive due to operational and infrastructural costs (Wendt, 2006). For smaller financial institutions, the only efficient solution in indirect access to the CCP. The indirect access implies intermediary fees. Moreover, activity in CCP-settled operations demands intra-day collateral management, which increases liquidity requirements. In effect, turnover and outstanding principal in the OTC derivatives initially dropped when the EMIR regime was introduced (Ehlers and Hardy, 2019) – see Figure 4.1. However, 2019 pre-pandemic data were much more optimistic due to the increased market activity focused on hedging global interest rate risk and significant share of administrative deals (portfolio compression and back-to-back operations). Undoubtedly, a lower credit risk implied by the nature of a CCP fosters higher volumes in OTC derivative exposures, especially for large banks. Meanwhile, the pandemic diminished this rising trend (Clarus Financial Technology, 2021).

Eventually, new EMIR requirements introduce an obligatory initial margin in non-cleared OTC transactions (Wallin, 2013). These augment usage of the collateral. According to Credit Support Annexes (CSA) the collateral used to be limited to the variation margin. On the one hand, this requirement strengthens safety of trading and reduces the pre-settlement risk. On the other hand, it increases liquidity demand in the collateral management.

Regulations aimed at financial stability have a strong impact on resilience of financial institutions and safety of financial markets. However, post-crisis financial markets are more expensive when providing liquidity. This is due to regulatory constraints increasing the cost of banking capital, imposing operational burdens on dealing infrastructure, creating new liquidity requirements related to high-quality collateral management, and hampering leverage. In effect, regulations reduce incentives for dealers to make markets as in the past.

According to Duffie (2018b), the aim of the financial market and banking regulations should be focused on the efficient frontier of potential levels of

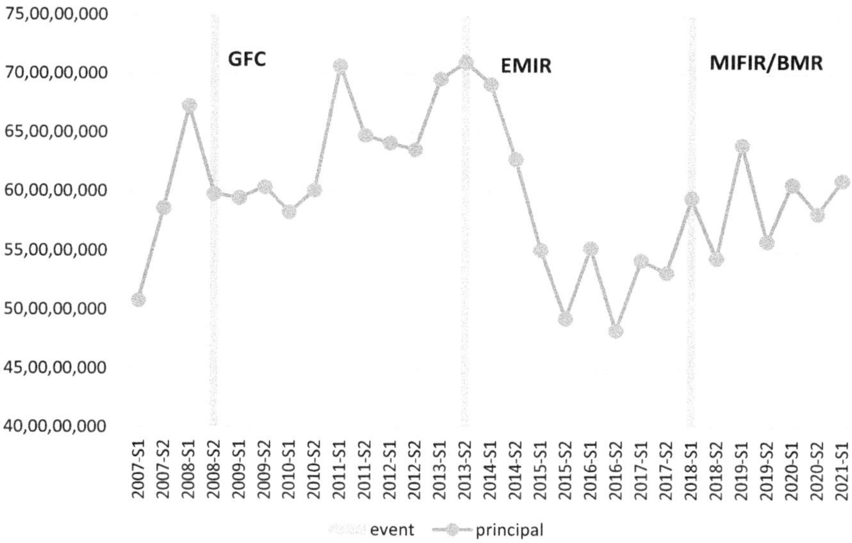

Figure 4.1 OTC principal vs regulations.
Source: Own work on the basis of BIS data (2021).

market efficiency and financial stability. The first is targeted towards market liquidity, the latter comes from leverage constraints and appropriate bank capital. At the optimal level of regulatory constraints, banks are able to offer to buy-side firms' sufficient access to their balance sheet. One of the methods of doing this is encouraging market infrastructure to reduce capital needed to conduct the trade. The encouragement comes from proper formulation of EMIR and MiFID technical rules.

The lost liquidity of OTC bilateral and fragmented markets can be recovered by trading venues and multilateral platforms. This would be in line with the modified behaviour of market makers. The market makers, in the present regulatory environment, prefer to avoid high risk. This means a switch from principal to agency trading, and the latter is feasible with the assistance of trading venues. In parallel, a C2C market starts to be likely as dealers' intermediation must be on "democratic" platforms. In effect, contemporary markets might be more liquid and less costly than opaque bilateral trading.

Duffie (2018a) notes a lack of international regulatory coordination. Despite having much in common, US Dodd-Frank and EU EMIR/MiFID infrastructure create divergences regarding the pace of implementation, scope of regulation and its specific solutions. Currency derivativities cause an additional problem. They are not centrally cleared, and requirements regarding margining are much weaker than for interest rate and credit swaps. This is due to drawbacks coming from transborder coordination and huge liquidity needs connected with deliverable currency exchanges. This causes underregulated systemic risk. According to Duffie (2018a), EU regulations are broader and more precise, but are implemented more slowly than in the US.

Nevertheless, the regulations make the financial market safer and more transparent. Moreover, they protect weaker market participants against negative consequences of any market abuse operations. The side effects for the financial market are of minor importance, as a wholesale market and professional participants have the bulk of tools to decrease the negative impact of the new regulatory environment.

The following section concerns the post-crisis environment in emerging markets.

4.3 Emerging markets asymmetry – how contagion works

A crisis creates market disequilibrium that influences market prices and volatility. Prices are affected by weakening market sentiment and rising risk aversion. Market participants face contagion effects and spillovers that spread turbulences to various market segments, both in terms of asset and location (Iwanicz-Drozdowska et al., 2021). These phenomena are especially acute on emerging markets, due to the asymmetry of risks.

Emerging market prices behave in a different way than for major markets. First, the spectrum of available instruments is limited, so hedging of many kinds of risks is not possible. Second, market liquidity is fragile, and this means that open exposure can be difficult to close in the future. Third, price patterns do not reflect standard assumptions of risk modelling. Therefore, trading on such markets is riskier and requires extensive analysis. A limited number of market makers and a fragmentation of the market increase the asymmetry of information between residents and non-residents. The markets are incomplete, so smooth and efficient position management may be distorted.

The reward for such unpleasant behaviour of the market prices is a higher expected return and lower competitiveness. The latter is of great value for market makers who are daring enough to provide liquidity. The collected information on the emerging markets has "double value" in comparison to the mature markets.

In order to analyze emerging markets, one should be aware of the scope of non-normality of daily returns. The density function has the following features:

- Skewness – the probability of significant jumps is higher than significant drops ("significant" means over two daily standard deviations). It is a measure of the asymmetry of risk. On a typical emerging FX market, probability of sharp local currency depreciation is much higher than for the respective appreciation. A right-hand fat-tail illustrates an increased risk of a currency crisis (Campa et al., 1998; Dumas et al., 1998; Duan, 1999).

- Leptokurtosis – volatility of volatility (instability of a variance). Numerous financial assets are leptokurtic, which means that a density function of its daily returns has fat-tails and a tapered mean. A market has two states: calm and panic, and a measure of a standard deviation is misleading (Cont, 2007).

The misleading standard deviation means that the "standard" is rare. Statistical measures are a mixture of high and low volatilities. The average of the high and low number can in fact never be registered in a given population.

The misleading measure of a variance means that a market cannot rely on historical data for statistical tools in the process of risk assessment. In order to forecast a possible future price range and scope of the instability of prices, the implied – not realized volatilities have to be examined. The implied volatilities embedded in option prices are an objective indicator of what the market thinks about the future uncertainty. It is based on concluded derivative transactions, so it is much more credible than statistical forecasts based on historical data.

In practice, on the emerging markets with non-normal distributions, implied volatility is higher than realized volatility. This does not mean that the market is erroneous (Taleb, 1997). Market players take into consideration higher moments (skewness and kurtosis) and demand a premium for the non-normality. If we hedge the option book, the non-normality is advantageous for option buyers. It creates additional demand on the buy side. This behaviour moves option prices – hence the implied volatility – upwards.

As a consequence of the above-described phenomenon, market makers on options quote not only an expected variance but also expected skewness and kurtosis. An option price always has the embedded future distribution of spot prices. For this reason, options have huge informational content – they can serve as a source of the implied density function of underlying prices.

Skewed and leptokurtic distributions mean that a given market has "a weak side." Its prices behave in an asymmetrical way. The speed of a local asset's depreciation is always higher than in the opposite direction. A local asset means a local currency, local bonds, and other interest rate-related products, and, last but not least – local equities. Moreover, one observes co-movement of a price and its volatility. On the equity market, the lower stock prices, the higher the volatility of the stocks. On the currency market, the weaker the local currency against major currencies (like EUR or USD), the higher the volatility (both realized and implied) of the FX rate (Rafferty, 2012). It can be observed that:

(1) Correl (dS, dIV) >>0
where:
dS – log-return of the spot price of the major currency against the local
dIV – change of the implied volatility of the FX rate

Table 4.4 Correlation between log-returns of FX Spot and daily changes of implied volatility (3M ATM)

6M period	*EUR/PLN*	*EUR/CZK*	*EUR/HUF*	*EUR/USD*
GFC (Sep 2008–Mar 2009)	21%	10%	13%	−3%
COVID (1st wave Mar–Sep 2020)	39%	33%	40%	−5%

Source: Own calculation on the basis of Refinitiv data.

The table demonstrates correlation for CEE emerging currency pairs during the GFC and COVID crisis with the key major currency pair – EUR/USD. The results are given in Table 4.4.

It is clear that CEE currency rates are much more positively correlated with their volatilities than the EUR/USD rate. The latter does not exhibit any directional interdependence between the spot and volatility time series. Moreover, the first wave of COVID crises brought higher spot-volatility interdependence than the GFC, despite much lower absolute levels of volatility itself. This is in line with evidence published by Gunay (2021). This relationship has a strong impact on volatility modelling. This subject will be examined further on.

The asymmetry of risk is a consequence of specific capital flows on emerging markets. Such markets have a wide entrance and a narrow exit, which means that capital inflow is slow, and occurs over a longer period and outflow occurs rapidly in a short time. This asymmetry works as follows: foreign capital is tempted by a positive carry and attractive yields. If sentiment is good, this process is undistorted. A crisis means a sudden change in sentiment. Foreign investors wish to sell local assets and escape from the market as soon as possible. The given market loses its liquidity and experiences increased volatility and discontinuous jumps in prices of instruments representing the local risk.

A crisis can have both endogenous or exogenous origin. An endogenous crisis arises from local economic problems: high inflation, drop in output, a current account deficit, rising public debt, or political instability. The exogenous factors arise abroad due to the contagion effect.

Contagion is a process of spreading of negative sentiment through various markets. Disequilibria in developed countries increases the risk aversion exported to spots with high risk and increased leverage. Negative sentiment born from risk aversion moves to weaker economies (emerging countries) and forces investors to unwind their exposure in such markets. The outflow of capital in such an environment is not connected with local fundamentals. The mechanism is more based on psychological factors related to a thought contagion phenomenon (mentioned in the previous section of this chapter).

The process of shock propagation is difficult to forecast and measure. The key problem is heteroskedasticity of time series of prices – volatility of returns is dependent on price levels, and this means a significant scope of instability of the variance (Rigobon, 2016).

A distinction has to be made between contagion and classic spillover. The first is related to negative sentiment and is born at a time of crisis. Hence its impact is usually much stronger than for normal interdependence between market prices. Spillover can be defined as a linkage between assets that determines their co-movement. It can be observed also in a positive sentiment environment. This means that spillover contains both positive and negative shocks, while contagion contains only the latter. Transmission of shocks after the specified event is known as shift-contagion. This is sudden acceleration of a strength of co-movements after the negative shock (Frank and Hesse, 2009; Ammer et al., 2010).

Emerging markets include small open economies with their own currency, a liberal currency law and a liquid financial market. These economies offer profound and undistorted content on information and a wide scope of investment and hedging tools. Those positive features also mean: (i) higher yields, (ii) increased and instable volatility and (iii) volatile liquidity. Therefore, all three above-mentioned risk components of such markets need to be analyzed.

The "height" of yields cannot be measured in absolute values. Its value is dependent on financial risk and the cost of financing. The former comes from a market, credit and liquidity risk, and the latter relies on transborder liquidity ratios and the investor's own risk. The market risk arises due to volatility of interest rates. The credit risk is a mixture of an issuer's risk and pre-settlement risk on the given market. The liquidity risk can be analyzed twofold: as the easiness of a potential resale of financial assets, and as an ability to refinance the exposure in a local currency. However, even if refinancing is smooth, its cost can convert a high-yield investment into an unattractive one.

Non-residents looking for portfolio investments have a few opportunities to invest on the local market. One is a purchase of securities (stocks or bonds) and the other is a carry trading.

When buying a security denominated in a local currency, the liquidity exposure must be refinanced. There are two basic ways to obtain the local currency required for a security purchase:

1. the local currency bought on a FX spot market (through a currency conversion), which implies currency risk;
2. the local currency borrowed on a FX swap market (via a collateralized loan), which means liquidity and interest rate risk.

In the first option, the result is dependent on the relationship between the FX rate change and a surplus of gains in the security in comparison to the base currency financing costs. In the latter option, the profit is generated by the surplus between a yield on the security and an interest rate related to the cost of funding.

In a carry trading, there is always currency risk. In order to create positive carry exposure, a low-yield currency is borrowed and converted into a high-yield currency. The conversion opens foreign exchange exposure. The net result is dependent on the difference between the interest rate disparity and the FX rate change at the time of the deal.

The key issue is measurement of the cost of funds. This mostly depends on the way the investor borrows funds on the market. On transborder markets, the standard instruments for borrowing a local currency are currency swaps. Therefore, an implied interest rate from currency swaps is a real measure of the cost of funds.

The world of homogenous interest rates has come to an end (Bianchetti, 2010; Mercurio, 2010; Stelmach, 2010). Nowadays, one observes a heterogenic yield spectrum with numerous yield curves in the given currency representing various market segments. Meanwhile, investors should pick up an appropriate yield in order to value their portfolio correctly. The adequate interest rate represents a specific cost of funds, taking into account both liquidity and credit risk. This mainly means two things. From a regulatory point of view a set of different market interest rates can assist banks in decomposition of their interest rate banking book risk (IRBB) in line with Basel guidelines. From an accounting point of view, correct pricing is a must for the proper net present value (NPV) valuation of portfolios. The latter is crucial in the presence of collateral management – interest bearing call accounts determine valuation of yield-sensitive assets.

All modern markets cope with heterogenous yield curves that can be applied for various participants and versatile instruments. A typical small open economy with its own currency has the following yield curves:

1. swap curve,
2. bond curve,
3. OIS curve,
4. repo curve,
5. currency basis curve,
6. deposit curve.

These curves differ in liquidity – some start late but typically they end early. This means that the given curve cannot be used as a discount curve for long-term cash flows. The GFC created curve differentials, and the PIIGS crisis deepened the differences. Therefore, the multi-curve environment is a given state in the COVID crisis.

Table 4.5 summarizes the risk embedded in the mentioned yield curves.

The key issue related to the yield curves is spreads between the curves. A swap curve is used as a benchmark (subtrahend) and other curves are treated as risk factors (minuend). Some of the spreads are the typical sentiment indicators described earlier (i.e. asset swap spread, OIS spread, currency

Table 4.5 Risk embedded in yield curves and their liquidity

Yield curve	*Represented risk*	*Liquidity*
Swap curve	IBOR (short-term), FRA (mid-term), IRS (long-term)	Very good (up to 20–30 years)
Bond curve	Treasury Bonds	Very good (up to 20–30 years)
OIS curve	Swap on ONIA (O/N depo index)	Majors – very good (up to 10–15 years) Emerging – limited (up to 3M)
Repo curve	Secured deposits	Majors – very good (up to 2 years) Emerging – limited (up to 1W)
Currency basis curve	FX Swaps (short-term), CIRS (long-term)	Very good (up to 10–15 years)
Deposit curve	Unsecured term deposits collected by banks from non-financial clients	If rates are negative – current accounts only If rates are positive – up to 1Y

Source: Own work.

basis spread). Others are rarely used, such as repo spread or deposit spread, but also can be treated as an indicator of the state of the market.

Apart from the ambiguity of yield curves, one should observe inconsistency of foreign exchange rates. An estimation of a currency basket is the crucial task to provide a prudent analysis of a value of a local currency. The currency basket is the optimal combination of various currency pairs that minimize risk. Hence – a currency pair (a single a few pairs combined) with minimum volatility is a measure of the strength of the local currency.

Table 4.6 presents the optimal share of EUR and USD for the selected currencies calculated in the long period of 2008–2021. Currencies are selected from the ensuing groups in order to spot the geographical and economic influence on the basket composition:

- key majors (GBP, CHF, JPY),
- CEE Europe (PLN, CZK, HUF),
- frontier Europe (TRY, RUB),
- Latam and Africa (BRL, MXN, ZAR).

We can note particular regularities:

- the EUR share is not correlated with a standard deviation of the basket;
- the EUR share is 100% for CEE currencies due to their tendency for the eurozone convergence;
- the USD share is over 50% for two currencies only;
- the currency spread is negative if the EUR share is over 50% (the higher share the more negative spread);
- the currency spread is almost zero if the EUR share is close to 50%.

Table 4.6 Volatility and basket statistics for the selected currencies

Currency	*GBP*	*CHF*	*JPY*	*PLN*	*CZK*	*HUF*	*TRY*	*MXN*	*ZAR*	*BRL*	*RUB*
EUR share (%)	64	79	22	100	100	100	58	51	80	40	53
Standard deviation (%)	8.1	7.6	9.6	8.7	5.9	9.2	14.3	13.2	15.3	17.1	14.5
Currency spread (pp)	−1.3	−2.8	+2.3	−5.5	−6.0	−5.6	−0.5	−0.1	−1.6	0.5	−0.2

Source: Own calculations.

Notes: The period 31.12.2007–12.10.2021. The EUR share equal to 100% means no USD in the basket. The USD share is equal to 100% minus the EUR share. The standard deviation is an annualized rate calculated on daily log returns for the optimal basket. The currency spread is calculated as the difference between standard deviations for EUR/XXX and USD/XXX, where XXX is a local currency.

Table 4.7 Statistical moments for the elected currency pairs

Currency pair	*Average return (M1) %*	*Standard deviation (M2) %*	*Skewness (M3)*	*Kurtosis (M4)*
EUR/GBP	0.00	8.8	0.3	4.4
EUR/CHF	−0.01	7.9	−7.0	277
USD/JPY	0.00	9.8	−0.1	4.2
EUR/PLN	0.01	8.7	0.2	10.3
EUR/CZK	0.00	5.9	0.6	15.3
EUR/HUF	0.01	9.2	0.4	9.0
EUR/TRY	0.05	14.9	0.6	28.6
EUR/MXN	0.01	14.0	0.7	7.4
EUR/ZAR	0.02	15.4	0.5	3.2
USD/BRL	0.03	17.5	0.2	5.0
EUR/RUB	0.02	15.1	0.7	23.6

Source: own calculations.

For the same period, we have calculated four statistical moments (M1–M4) for the dominating currency pair on the given market (therefore pairs attached to the currency with a bigger share in the optimal currency basket) – see Table 4.7.

The conclusions are as follows:

- emerging market currencies have significant positive skewness and relatively high kurtosis;
- the higher volatility of emerging currencies is accompanied by a positive value of the average return (a long-term depreciation of the local currency) and bigger higher moments;
- the EUR/CHF extreme kurtosis and the deep negative skewness is due to one observation: 15% revaluation of the Swiss franc on January 14, 2015;
- a single currency pair always has higher volatility than the optimal basket volatility;
- the EUR volatility is equal to the optimal basket volatility if the basket is dominated in 100% in euro.

Eventually, we checked the behaviour of the selected currency pairs during two crises: the GFC+PIIGS and COVID. In order to do so, we extracted two crisis periods from the time series:

1. the GFC+PIIGS from 15.09.2008 (the Lehman bankruptcy) to 8.03.2012 (the Greece default);
2. the COVID from 9.03.2020 (a general lockdown implementation) till the end of the series.

The results are presented in Table 4.8.

Table 4.8 Standard deviation of the elected currency pairs

Currency pair	*General SD ()*	*GFC+PIIGS SD ()*	*COVID SD ()*
EUR/GBP	8.8	11.2	8.3
EUR/CHF	7.9	10.8	3.9
USD/JPY	9.8	12.2	6.8
EUR/PLN	8.7	14.2	6.6
EUR/CZK	5.9	8.3	6.8
EUR/HUF	9.2	14.2	7.3
EUR/TRY	14.9	14.0	15.7
EUR/MXN	14.0	17.2	16.3
EUR/ZAR	15.4	16.5	14.6
USD/BRL	17.5	21.4	19.8
EUR/RUB	15.1	10.7	15.9

Source: Own calculations.

What we see in the data:

- for a majority of European currency pairs and for Japan, volatility during the GFC+PIIGS crisis was higher, and during the COVID crisis it was lower than volatility for the whole time series;
- for Turkey and Russia in Europe and for non-Europe emerging markets, we observed constant increased volatility, which in some cases is even higher during the COVID crisis than the GFC (TRY, RUB).

As a consequence of a non-normal distribution of returns, one observes a volatile and skewed implied volatility of assets. Firstly – the volatility is not stable (however mean reverted), secondly – the speed of the volatility changes is different upwards and downwards. Eventually – the volatility is dependent on the underlying price level.

The periods of calm spot prices are accompanied by low volatilities. On the contrary, in periods of panic, the volatility increases sharply. Moreover, the upward move is faster and stronger than the downward one. Therefore, the implied volatility expresses similar skewness to the underlying price. It is caused by the phenomenon of co-integration between spot prices and its volatilities.

On an emerging FX market, the higher the spot, the higher the volatility. For comparison, on the equity market the lower the stock indices, the higher the prices of options. A weak local currency or a low value of stocks means bad sentiment and a higher susceptibility to a market crisis. In such an environment, risk aversion is high, and this increases the scope of expected instability of market prices and increases the cost of insurance against it (i.e. prices of options that are fully determined by the implied volatility).

Such interdependence can be described by the following simple function:

(2) dVol = f(dSpot)

In more detail, if we use an error correction model (ECM), we see:

(3) $dy_t = \alpha_1 * dx_t + \alpha_2 * dx_t\text{-}1 + \lambda*(y_{t-1} - \beta_0 - \beta_1 * x_{t-1}) + \varepsilon_t$

where:

$\lambda<0$ (error correction component)
dy_t – a change of the implied volatility for the ATM FX option (for zero-delta straddle, ZDS)
dx_t – a change of the FX rate of a local currency against a major currency

The relationship between spot and volatility is crucial for understanding the mechanics of the option market. The consequence of this phenomenon is a constant presence of a volatility smirk (Zhang and Xiang, 2008). The smirk is a variant of the volatility smile. This means that high strikes are much dearer than low strikes. This can be explained threefold:

1. positive skewness of the density function of daily returns implies that a pricing model which assumes a normal distribution underprices high strikes – a volatility hike is a remedy for such limitation;
2. if we know that an upward spot move hikes volatility, the higher volatility for high strikes is a forecast of the ATM level if the spot reaches this level of prices – the same, low strikes have lower volatility as people forecast a volatility drop if a local currency appreciates;
3. if we know that an upward spot risk is higher than a downward risk (if we take into consideration a conditional volatility, i.e. significant price moves only), there is a surplus of the demand on hedging against a currency crisis, and this means a sharp depreciation of a local currency – this demand augments prices of high-strike options, hence the higher volatility of such contracts; in parallel, there is a surplus of the supply related to low-strike options as they are written in order to finance high-strike contracts through zero-cost strategies – investors are not afraid of short low delta puts as they are naturally hedged by their basic long local currency exposure.

Apart from the spot-vol model, it is possible to build the subsequent volatility models:

(4) dRR = f(dSpot)
(5) dFLY = f(dSpot)

(6) $dCS = -f(dVol)$
(7) $dVol = f(d\Delta R)$

In model 4, we assume a relationship between a risk reversal and a spot. A risk reversal (RR) is an option strategy built of two OTM options with a similar probability – one bought and the other sold. The purchased contract is financed by the written one and the total premium is often close to zero – hence this such combination of options is described as a zero-cost strategy. As ZDS is a bet on the variance, RR is a bet on the skewness. The price of RR is a difference between volatilities of the low delta call and the low delta put. Although they have similar probability (identical absolute value of delta coefficient), their risk is different due to the skewness of returns. Hence, we observe a higher volatility on the higher strike.

A spot increase means worse sentiment and higher risk aversion, therefore, both the ATM volatility and risk reversal prices go up when a local currency depreciates.

In model 5, one assumes dependence between a butterfly and a spot. A butterfly (FLY) is an option strategy built of four options: two OTM and two ATM (in practice it is a combination of straddle and strangle). In a vega-neutral butterfly, we bet on the future scope of the kurtosis. If we buy a strangle against selling a straddle, we bet on the kurtosis increase against the expected levels. Butterfly prices are positive as a volatility of the strangle is always higher than a volatility of the straddle. It is because the average of the OTM volatilities is higher than the ATM volatility (with a volatility smile it is obvious but with a volatility smirk it is due to its asymmetrical shape (surplus for a higher strike is bigger than dearth for a lower strike).

A spot rise means higher volatility and also increased instability of volatility. Therefore, higher leptokurtosis and butterfly prices are expected to go up.

In model 6, we analyze the shape of the volatility curve, i.e. dependence of the volatility on maturity of the contract. If the volatility is low, the shape of the volatility curve is normal (contango). This means that the market accepts low present volatility but in the longer term expects some rise in volatility. In a high-volatility environment, the volatility curve is negative (backwardation). This is because market players observe high short-term volatility but expect volatility decreases in the future.

To summarize – high volatility implies a negative curve and low volatility – a positive one. Such behaviour of the volatility curve results from the phenomenon of mean reversion. The low volatility (like an interest rate) has a tendency to rise to the long-term mean, and the high volatility does the opposite.

The detailed model 6 is as follows:

(8) $dCS_t = \alpha + \beta * dMID_t + \varepsilon_t$

where:

$\beta < 0$ (negative correlation between the level and the shape)
CS_t = ZDS(1Y) – ZDS(1M) (a calendar spread built on a one-year ZDS and a one-month ZDS)
MID_t = ZDS(3M) (a three-month ZDS as an approximate geometrical middle of the curve)

Model 7 expresses a co-dependence between the FX volatility and the interest rate differential. The assumption is that the higher the difference between interest rates in two currencies, the higher instability of a currency rate built on these currencies. The rationale of such phenomenon is that a high difference in interest rates means a significant carry that provokes investors to buy a local currency and make money on a carry trading. An initial capital inflow and an eventual sharp capital outflow during a crisis determines the augmented volatility of the FX rate (Brunnermeier et al., 2008).

The augmented volatility is accompanied with a drop of market liquidity. Unlike on developed markets, illiquidity on emerging markets is temporary and sentiment-dependent. It is good enough if the risk aversion is low (from a statistical point of view in the majority of observations in the long-term time series) but it disappears if the sentiment deteriorates. Low market liquidity means lack of reliable information on prices and a scarcity of hedging tools as standard financial instruments like derivatives can evaporate (Köksal and Orhan, 2013; Rösch and Kaserer, 2014).

4.4 Case studies for foreign exchange, interest rate, liquidity and equities

Crisis and related illiquidity create disequilibria in demand and supply, hampering smooth forecast of future prices and – hence – proper valuation of assets. This means an increase of uncertainty causing higher volatility of prices. We prepared five case studies presenting extraordinary behaviour of different market segments in the crisis environment. They are as follows:

1) CEE currency rates in autumn 2008
2) Euro fixed income and money markets in late 2011
3) Currency basis for PLN in early 2015
4) Global equity market in spring 2020
5) CEE markets in 2020–21

The first case refers to the GFC on emerging markets, the second and third cases represent turmoil in transborder EU liquidity as a consequence of the PIIGS crisis. The two latter cases happened during the early stage of the COVID crisis.

4.4.1 CEE currency rates in autumn 2008

The contagion exploded after Lehman Brothers went bankrupt on September 15, 2008. This event breached fragile sentiment and accelerated a rise in risk aversion. It caused a sharp and simultaneous increase of market, credit and liquidity risk. Volatility went up and turnover on financial markets plummeted due to an immediate freeze in credit lines. Moreover, strong changes of prices intensified collateral calls, and this made it harder to manage liquidity exposure.

Some assets stopped trading, and this hampered ability to reduce risk. The losses of market players were incurred on the devaluation of assets held in portfolios that were almost impossible to sell. In investments, the rule of maximizing “return on capital” was replaced by the rule of obtaining “return of capital.”

In this environment, banks and financial institutions tried to reduce their negative valuations by concluding deals that created antifragility. In order to be anti-fragile, one has to open an exposure that earns money on a further worsening of the market sentiment (Taleb, 2012). This was only possible on large market segments with enough liquidity.

Having that in mind, some markets observed an increased supply in comparison to others. On illiquid markets, trading was very limited due to volume constraints. In consequence, the supply from small markets moved to bigger markets where trading was still possible.

CEE FX markets are a good example of such phenomenon. If we compare the performance of various currency rates against the euro (September 1, 2008 basis set as 100 – see Figure 4.2) we see huge differences in price change direction and price ranges of various currencies. We selected 7 rates against the euro: 2 major, treated as safe-haven (USD and CHF) and 5 from emerging Europe (PLN, HUF, CZK, RON and TRY). Both major currencies appreciated after LB’s collapse and all emerging – depreciated. The highest loss of value was recorded in February 2009 for PLN (45% against EUR), the lowest for CZK (18% against EUR). The remaining currencies depreciated approximately 20–30%. The question is why PLN witnessed the biggest drop in value in the region.

The answer is market liquidity. PLN was liquid enough to be efficiently sold. This happened despite strong macroeconomic fundamentals, far better than for the other CEE markets. Market participants suffering losses on Hungarian, Czech, Romanian and Turkish markets could not successfully manage their exposure in order to square the currency position. Moreover, as stated by Kočenda and Moravcová (2019), the GFC crises strengthen emerging markets’ volatility spillovers and heavily increase the hedging costs. In such an environment, a tool to decrease the losses was found on the neighbouring Polish market, where non-residents were able to both sell and borrow the local currency in significant amounts. The ability to borrow

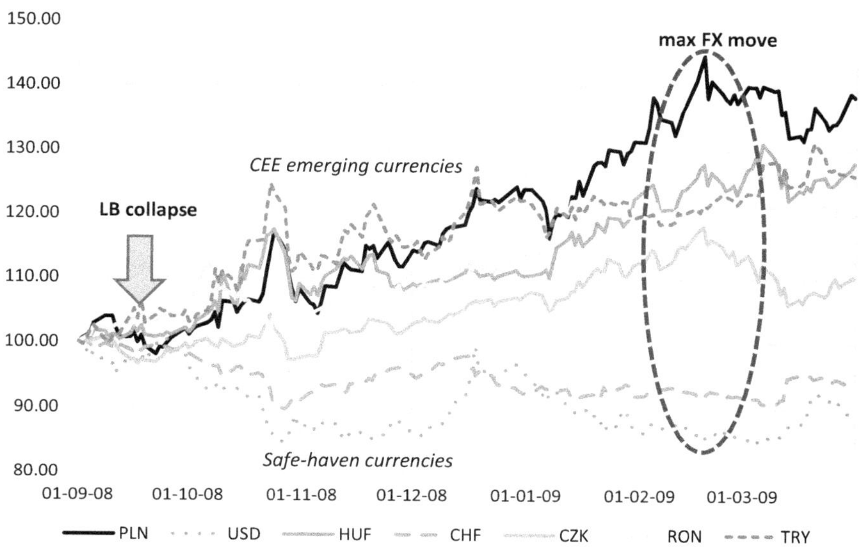

Figure 4.2 Currency rates after Lehman collapse.

Source: Own work on the basis of Refinitiv data.

(through currency swaps) meant that short selling could be organized at the turn of the year. The proof of this activity is seen in Figure 4.3.

The chart presents the FX spot rate on the background of the currency basis implied from 3M EUR/PLN FX Swaps (calculated as the difference between the swap PLN borrowing rate and the local money market rate – 3M WIBOR). The basis was close to zero before the subprime crisis and went down slightly during the early stage of the GFC. It started to be very volatile after the LB collapse. In the acute phase of the GFC, it reached 123 bp in October and −225 bp in February following the bad sentiment and the rising risk aversion. This environment hampered local banks in borrowing hard currencies through swaps, but in parallel it meant very cheap PLN borrowing costs (WIBOR minus over 1pp). Speculators took advantage of this situation to borrow PLN in order to sell it short. In effect, the currency basis jumped unexpectedly, and the PLN depreciation path received additional fuel for the speculative attack.

Therefore, we observed the classical stages of currency turmoil. In the first stage, non-residents sell local bonds and get rid of the obtained local currency on the foreign exchange market. In this stage, the amount of sold currency is equal to the amount of currency that had been purchased during the period of good sentiment. The only difference is speed: the capital inflow lasted for years and the capital outflow takes a few weeks. In the second stage,

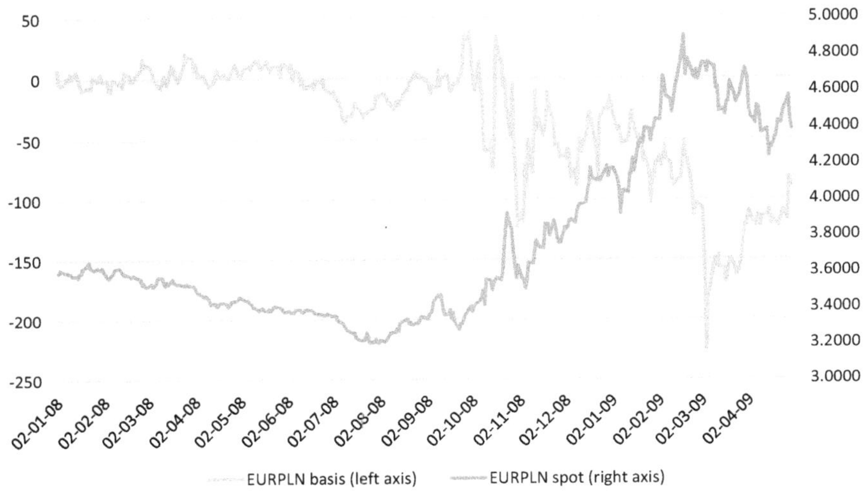

Figure 4.3 Currency 3M basis spread and FX spot in EUR/PLN during GFC.
Source: Refinitiv.

speculators try to borrow a local currency in order to sell it short. This is the additional fuel that enhances the weakening wave of the local currency (see Krugman et al., 1999).

Currency turmoil can become a currency crisis if the market is drained of liquidity and the foreign exchange rate starts to move in discontinuous jumps (Eichengreen et al., 1996). This was observed for example on the Russian rouble in August 1998. However, in the analyzed case, the turmoil did not become a crisis: the central bank's intervention and the verbal intervention from the fiscal authorities was enough to stop the sharp upward move in the EUR/PLN rate. Moreover, strong monetary and fiscal intervention on the US market improved the global sentiment in spring 2009 after the half-year period of severe tensions.

4.4.2 Euro fixed income and money markets in late 2011

Eurozone PIIGS crises started as an aftermath of the GFC turmoil. Budgetary problems and external imbalances of peripheral eurozone economies were transferred to prices observed on the financial market. We analyze two sentiment indicators: asset swap for local treasury bonds and OIS and epo spreads against Euribor. Both analyzes are performed during the exacerbation of the crisis. This peaked at the turn of 2011/2012.

Figure 4.4 presents relative yields for bonds in three PIIGS countries (Spain, Italy and Portugal) and one safe-haven country (Germany). It is clear

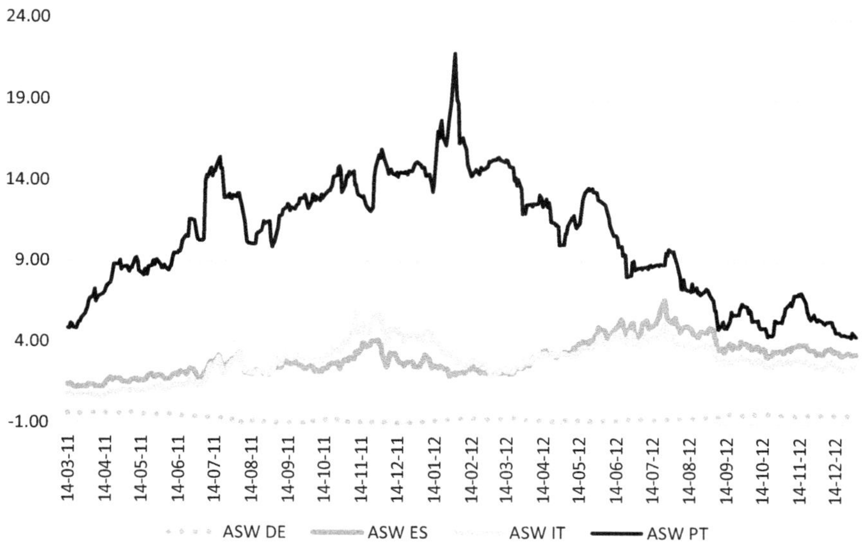

Figure 4.4 5Y Asset Swap spreads for some EMU markets.
Source: Refinitiv.

that safe-haven bonds are insensitive to the loss of credibility of the eurozone, unlike the peripheral bonds. The highest asset swap spread was recorded for Portugal in early 2012 – over 20 p.p. over EUR swap. At the same time, the asset for German bunds was negative. There was significant correlation between daily yield changes for Spain and Italy (77% in the analyzed period) and negative correlation between all PIIGS yields and the German one.

Figure 4.5 below shows parallel behaviour of OIS and repo markets. In these markets, the more negative the spread against Euribor, the worse the sentiment on the market (due to the increased credit and liquidity risk). The greatest negative spread was recorded at the same time as the maximum for the asset swaps – at the turn of 2011 and 2012. Note that the OIS spread was greater than the repo one, which means that a one-year unsecured deposit was perceived as riskier against one-day unsecured risk than against one-year secured risk.

In general, we observed co-movement of the capital and money market sentiment indicators (if risk aversion rises, asset swap becomes more positive and OIS/repo spreads more negative). These phenomena are in line with conclusions drawn by Kazemi and Sohrabji (2012), who claimed that in the analyzed period we witnessed a shift-contagion that increased cross-market linkages. The safe-haven treatment of German bonds is close to Büchel (2013), who stated that German and ECB representatives had a strong impact on market sentiment, unlike representatives of peripheral EMU countries.

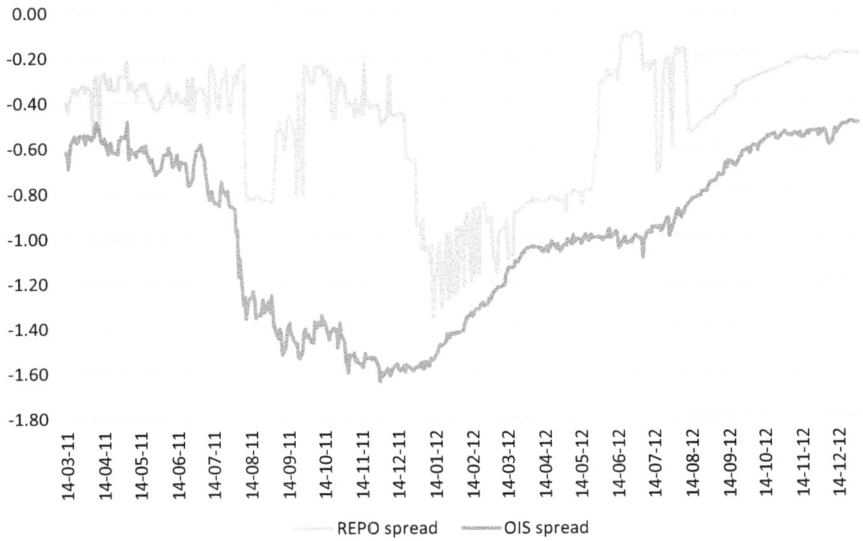

Figure 4.5 1Y Euribor spreads for OIS and Repo markets.
Source: Refinitiv.

4.4.3 The currency basis for PLN in early 2015

In general, the currency basis in emerging markets used to be local IBOR negative (i.e. hard currency IBOR positive). This means that it is cheaper to borrow a local currency than a foreign one in comparison to the IBOR interest rate parity (Baba and Packer, 2009; Borio et al., 2016). The stylized fact has the following rationale:

1. Due to a lack of capital and high local yields, local entities prefer a foreign currency borrowing. Local banks must finance foreign currency assets on the currency swaps market. If the market faces increased risk aversion, the pressure on borrowing the hard currency is stronger.
2. Non-residents can diversify their emerging market risk while investing in local securities with a borrowed but not bought local currency. This method means that currency risk can be avoided. If sentiment is bad, non-residents stop their emerging market investments and thus do not need the currency swaps anymore.

Local entities use currency swaps to refinance foreign currency assets and they *must* do this during a liquidity squeeze. Non-residents use currency swaps to refinance their emerging market investments and they *can* do this if they need to. The "must" side creates stronger demand than the "can" side. This moves the currency basis sign to the negative territory.

With this in mind, the currency basis is a sentiment indicator. If risk aversion rises, the currency basis should widen, making hard currency refinancing more expensive for local banks. This was observed after the Lehman collapse. Before the GFC, the currency basis was close to zero because the relative cost of financing was very similar to the IBOR parities. The GFC changed the rules of the game: the IBOR lost credibility as a robust indicator of cost of funds and real refinancing cost diverged from the IBOR curves. In parallel, the liquidity situation on emerging markets was much worse than in mature economies. Local debtors started to have acute problems with borrowing hard currencies. In effect, the currency basis widened to 200 bp, which meant that local banks had to pay 2 pp over the LIBOR or (which is the equivalent) had to place PLN collateral 2 pp below the WIBOR.

The phenomenon of very expensive hard currency liquidity was observed over a few months after the LB collapse and again during the PIIGS crisis. This situation changed rapidly in early 2015 – the currency basis switched its sign (see Figure 4.6).

The reasons for such unusual behaviour of the currency basis were as follows:

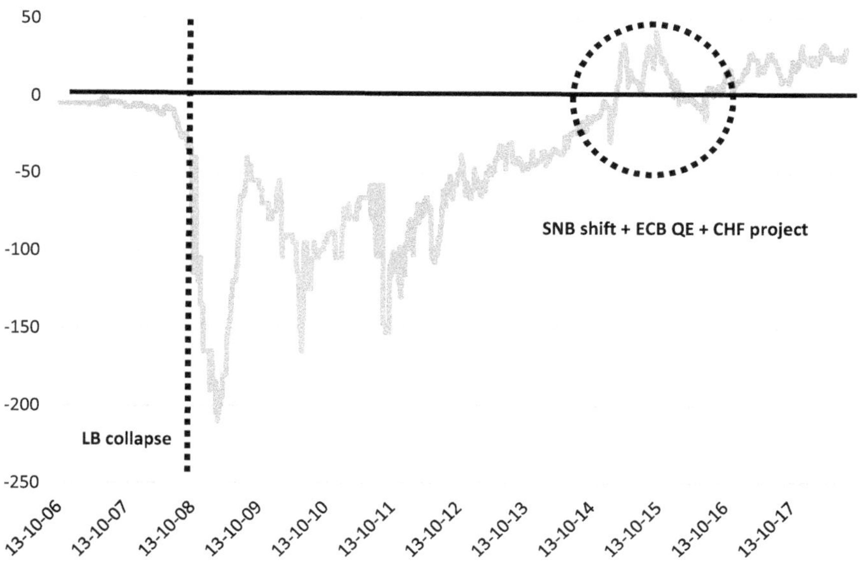

Figure 4.6 Currency basis spread in 5Y EUR/PLN 2006–18.

Source: Own work on the basis of Refinitiv data.

1. In late 2014, Hungary forced through a law converting old CHF mortgage loans into HUF. Polish politicians announced similar move, and investors started pricing probability of a strong reduction of banks' Swiss franc assets. Such forecasts implied limited demand for hard currency in currency swaps, and the currency basis moved towards zero.
2. On January 15, 2015, the SNB decided to stop defending the EUR/CHF parity at 1.2 and reduced the key interest rate to −0.75. In consequence, Swiss franc immediately appreciated approximately 20%. This move had two repercussions: (i) it increased the necessity to convert the CHF debt into local currencies in the CEE region; (ii) it augmented outflow from negative yield safe-haven assets to emerging markets.
3. On January 22, 2015, the ECB announced a plan of the heavy quantitative easing policy, which permanently moved EUR rates to negative territory and increased demand for emerging market positive-yielding assets (Falagiarda et al., 2015; Ciarone and Colabella, 2016).

Since then, there has been constant demand for PLN assets (bonds and equities) purchased without FX risk. In order to avoid this risk, funds borrowed PLN through currency swaps moving the currency basis to the positive side. In parallel, demand created by local banks diminished as Polish authorities planned to introduce a formal conversion of Swiss franc mortgages to PLN (as in Hungary). The fact that the plan has still not been implemented is a different matter.

4.4.4 The global equity market in spring 2020

In early March 2020, all the major economies witnessed the outbreak of the COVID-19 pandemic that started in January 2020 in China. Authorities introduced spectacular lockdowns that limited the virus transmission but had deep negative effects on the real economy. Thus, GDP and employment indicators plummeted. The US economy registered the biggest ever drop in the non-farm payrolls (NFP): in April the labour market lost over 20 million jobs, surpassing the previous 75-year-old record more than 10 times and the GFC worst NFP result over 20 times. Unemployment went from 4.4% to 14.7% (see Figure 4.7).

However, the terrible news announced in early May was interpreted as "good news" compared to the March data, which revealed only 700k jobs losses. The reason was the relationship between the figures and the consensus. In March, the consensus was −100k and the realized figure was 7 times worse. The April expectation was set at 1.5M worse than the final publication.

The market reaction is not based on economic absolute data but on the gap between the consensus and the publicized figures. If data are bad but eventually better than expected, it is interpreted as good news. Otherwise – if figures are objectively positive but worse than expected – it is treated as bad news.

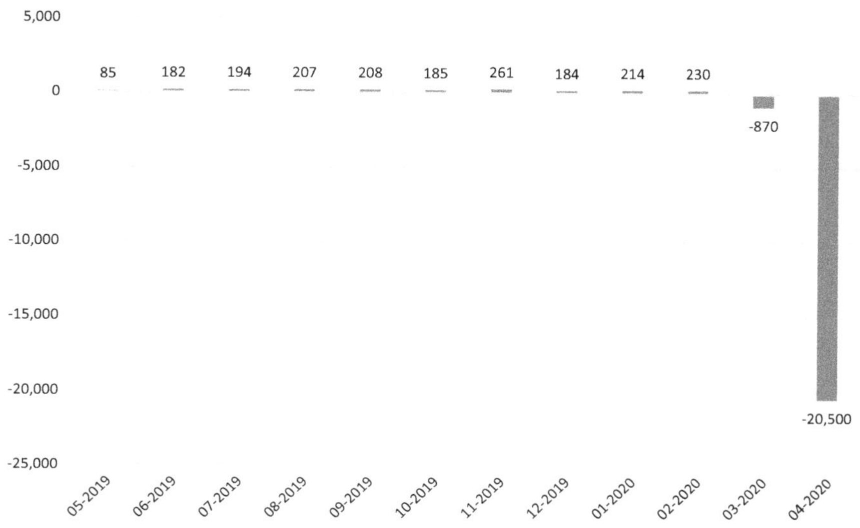

Figure 4.7 US payrolls in early COVID pandemic.
Source: US Bureau of Labor Statistics.

Therefore, the equity market reacted positively, and stock prices rose. This happened in a manner contrary to macroeconomics. Although the positive surprise on NFP was one of the reasons, the rationale for the upward trend had more profound grounds.

According to Krugman (2020), the market resumed buying stocks just a few weeks after the COVID negative shock hit the economy. The reason is connected with the expansionary monetary and fiscal policy in the US. The immediate reaction of the Fed was to inject a huge amount of money into the economy, and interest rates dropped almost to zero. Moreover, a fiscal program of the anti-pandemic shield meant a significant inflow of cash to the corporate sector. The financial market was flooded with cheap money that was invested in the equity market – having in mind that yield on the alternative bonds market fell rapidly.

The divergence between anti-COVID restrictions and equity indices is clearly seen in Figure 4.8.

The Covid Stringency Index in the US jumped in March from 10 to 70 and Standard & Poor's Index dropped 35%. CSI has been stable since then, and the S&P500 entered a constant upward trend reaching February levels in August and rising within 12 months by 85%. The disconnection between the real economy and the stock market was clearly visible.

Similar behaviour was observed on the EU market due to strong interdependence of global capital markets (Bessler and Yang, 2003; Samarakoon,

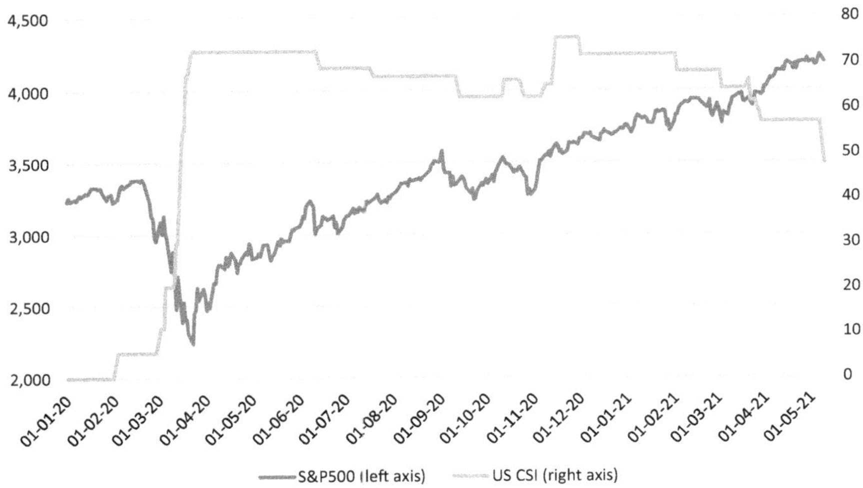

Figure 4.8 S&P 500 index vs Covid Stringency Index in the US.
Source: Refinitv, Blavatnik.

2011). For example, S&P 500 and DAX correlation of log-returns in the period of 2008–2021 was recorded at 63%, increasing during the COVID-19 crisis to 70%. US stimulus explains parallel movement of EU indices both in "old" and "new" Europe.

The case study shows that the COVID crisis is perceived as temporary and not originated by economics. Investors look at interest rates, liquidity and cash flows – in that environment, macroeconomic figures like unemployment and GDP have no impact on financial market decisions (more about these phenomena: Ashraf, 2020, Baker et al., 2020, Cepoi, 2020).

4.4.5 CEE markets in 2020–21

The outbreak of the COVID-19 crisis increased global risk aversion. As described in the previous case study this effect was very short-term. However, on emerging markets, the adverse contagion effects on the process were stronger and of long duration. The evidence of that phenomenon is seen on the sentiment indicators.

Figure 4.9 presents asset swap spreads for non-euro area CEE countries: Poland, the Czech Republic and Hungary. It is clear that in comparison to German bunds, the reaction of CEE markets is much stronger. Nevertheless, it was observed in the first wave of the pandemic only. The following waves did not have a significant impact on the process of the local treasury bonds. The reason for this are government shields that injected money for corporates and the expansionary monetary policy of local central banks cutting yields

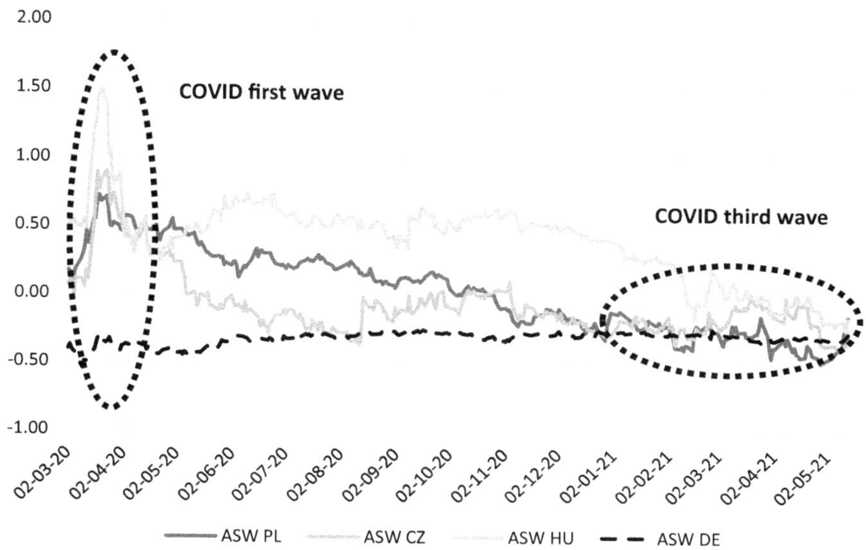

Figure 4.9 Asset Swaps in EU during COVID-19.

Source: Own calculation on the basis of Refinitiv data.

to zero-levels. For example, in Poland over-liquidity of the banking system tripled in the first year of the pandemic. In consequence, bond yields dropped, and asset swap spread went back to negative territory.

The situation on the foreign exchange market was slightly different. Figure 4.10 shows spot, volatility and risk reversal for the EUR/PLN cross during the first 15 months of the pandemic.

As described in a previous section of this chapter, ATM volatility and risk reversal are robust sentiment indicators, especially in small open economies with their own currency. The first wave of the pandemic caused the sharpest upward move of both indicators in line with local currency depreciation. The impact of the following waves was weaker, but still the FX market was negatively affected by global disequilibria creating shift-contagion effects. This evidence is close to Aslam et al., (2020), which proved decreased efficiency of currency markets jolted by the COVID black-swan event. This efficiency drop is especially visible on emerging currencies. Gunay (2021) noticed this, as he compared the FX impact of the COVID crisis with the GFC, showing much stronger spillover effects in the contemporary crisis. However, in the case of CEE currencies, one should take into account the negative impact of the expansionary monetary policy on carry trading efficiency. This can have adverse effects on nominal FX rates but in the longer term can reduce FX volatility.

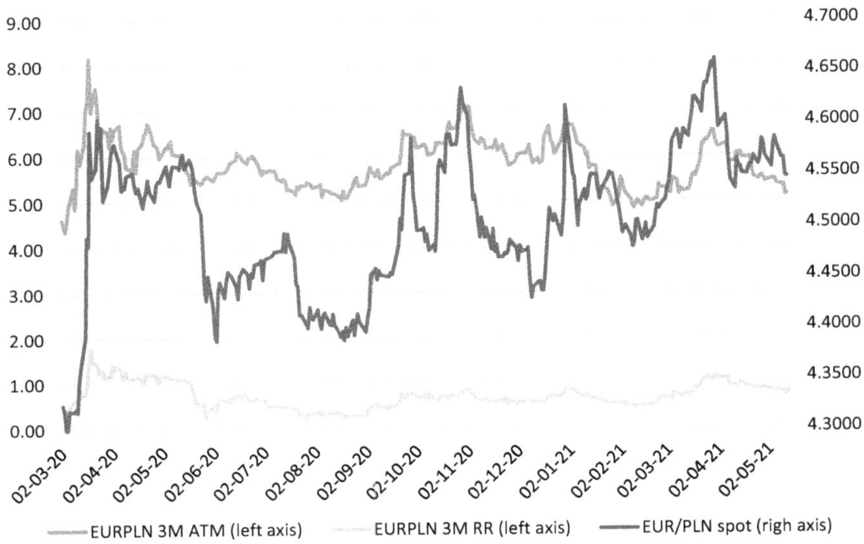

Figure 4.10 EUR/PLN FX market during COVID-19.
Source: Refinitiv.

Economic turbulences occur with increased volatility and decreased liquidity in the financial market. The emerging currencies' reaction is more dramatic due to the asymmetry of risk recorded in these markets. One observes that the skewness of returns as depreciation of local assets is much faster that their appreciation. Emerging markets are more fragile than developed markets and therefore are vulnerable to contagion. This chapter describes how to read sentiment indicators in order to assess the state of the market and its scope of risk aversion. However, expansionary central banks' activities and regulatory constraints affect all markets in a similar way and counteract the detrimental effect of negative shocks that create spillovers in a time of crisis.

Notes

1 In October 2021 the European Commission pointed out SARON as a legal replacement of the CHF LIBOR.
2 A directive MiFID (2004/39/EC) was originally published a few years before the GFC with the deadline of implementation set on January 31, 2007, but the process of implementation was delayed, especially in less mature markets. The directive was replaced by MiFID II (2014/65/EC) and accompanied by a regulation MiFIR (600/2014). We refer to legal environment introduced in the aftermath of the GFC.
3 Post-trade reporting is realized by APA (Approved Publication Arrangement). This obligation is implemented for bonds since 2018. It does not refer to illiquid or sizeable one-off transactions.

References

Abrantes-Metz, R., Kraten, M., Metz, A. & Seow, G. 2012. Libor manipulation? *Journal of Banking & Finance*, 36(1), 136–150.

Adam, K., Tzamourani, P. 2015. Distributional consequences of asset price inflation in the Eurozone, CEPR Discussion Paper, DP10897.

Albulescu, C. 2021. COVID-19 and the United States financial markets' volatility, *Finance Research Letters*, 38, 101699.

Ali, M., Alam, N. & Rizvi, S. 2020. Coronavirus: an epidemic or pandemic for financial markets, *Journal of Behavioral and Experimental Finance*, 100341.

Ammer, J., Cai, F. & Scotti, C. 2010. Has International Financial Co-Movement Changed? Emerging Markets in the 2007–2009, Board of Governors of the Federal Reserve System, International Finance Discussion Papers, No. 1006.

Ashraf, B. 2020. Economic impact of government interventions during the COVID-19 pandemic: International evidence from financial markets, *Journal of Behavioral and Experimental Finance*, 27, 100371.

Aslam, F., Aziz, S., Nguyen, D., Mughal, K. & Khan, M. 2020. On the efficiency of foreign exchange markets in times of the COVID-19 pandemic, *Technological Forecasting and Social Change*, 161, 120261.

Baba, N. & Packer, F. 2009. Interpreting deviations from covered interest parity during the financial market turmoil of 2007–08, *Journal of Banking & Finance*, 33(11), 1953–1962.

Baker, S., Bloom, N., Davis, S., Kost, K., Sammon, M. & Viratyosin, T. 2020. *The Unprecedented Stock Market Impact of COVID-19*, No. w26945, National Bureau of Economic Research.

Barberis, N., Shleifer, A. & Vishny, R. 1998. A model of investor sentiment, *Journal of Financial Economics*, 49, 307–343.

Becker, L & Maxwell, F. 2014. Category two confusion, *Risk Magazine*, 32.

Bekiros, S., Jlassi, M., Lucey, B., Naoui, K. & Uddin, G. S. 2017. Herding behavior, market sentiment and volatility: will the bubble resume? *The North American Journal of Economics and Finance*, 42, 107–131.

Bessler, D. & Yang, J. 2003. The structure of interdependence in international stock markets. *Journal of International Money and Finance*, 22(2), 261–287.

Bianchetti, M. 2010. Two curves, one price: Pricing & hedging interest rate derivatives decoupling forwarding and discounting yield curves, *Risk Magazine*, 8.

Biggins, J. & Scott, C. 2012. Public-private relations in a transnational private regulatory regime: ISDA, the state and OTC derivatives market reform, *European Business Organization Law Review*, 13(3), 309–346.

Bikhchandani, S., Hirshleifer, D. & Welch, I. 1998. Learning from the behavior of others: Conformity, fads, and informational cascades, *The Journal of Economic Perspectives*, 12(3) 151–170.

BIS. 2013. *Towards Better Reference Rates Practices: A Central Bank Perspective*, BIS, March.

BIS. 2021. WEBSTATS_OTC_DATAFLOW_csv_col

Bliss, R. & Kaufman, G. 2006. Derivatives and systemic risk: Netting, collateral, and closeout, *Journal of Financial Stability*, 2(1), 55–70.

Bluwstein, K. & Canova, F. 2016. Beggar-thy-neighbor? The international effects of ECB unconventional monetary policy measures, *International Journal of Central Banking*, 45, September 2016.

Borio, C., McCauley, R., McGuire, P. & Sushko, V. 2016. Covered interest rate parity lost: Understanding the cross-currency basis, *BIS Quarterly Review*, September.

Brogaard, J., Hendershott, T. & Riordan, R. 2014. High-frequency trading and price discovery, *The Review of Financial Studies*, 27(8), 2267–2306.

Brooks, S. M., Cunha, R. & Mosley,, L. 2015). Categories, creditworthiness, and contagion: how investors' shortcuts affect sovereign debt markets, *International Studies Quarterly*, 59(3), 587–601.

Brousseau, V., Chailloux, A. & Durre, A. 2013. Fixing the Fixings: What Road to a More Representative Money Market Benchmark? *IMF Working Paper* No. 13/131, 29.05.2013.

Brown, B. 2015. *How Fed Quantitative Easing Spread Asset Price Inflation Globally, in: A Global Monetary Plague*, Palgrave Macmillan, London, 39–72.

Brunnermeier, M. 2001. *Asset Pricing Under Asymmetric Information: Bubbles, Crashes, Technical Analysis, and Herding*, Oxford University Press, New York.

Brunnermeier, M., Nagel, S. & Pedersen, L. 2008. Carry trades and currency crashes. *NBER Working Paper* No. 14.473, National Bureau of Economic Research.

Büchel, K. 2013. Do words matter? The impact of communication on the PIIGS'CDS and bond yield spreads during Europe's sovereign debt crisis, *European Journal of Political Economy*, 32, 412–431.

Busch, D. 2016. Agency and principal dealing under the markets in financial instruments directive, in: *Agency Law in Commercial Practice*, ed. Busch et al., Oxford Scholarship, pp. 141–175.

Campa, J., Chang, K. & Reider, R. 1998. Implied exchange rate distributions: evidence from OTC option markets, *Journal of International Money and Finance*, 17(1), 117–160.

Cepoi, C. 2020. Asymmetric dependence between stock market returns and news during COVID19 financial turmoil, *Finance Research Letters*, 36, 101658.

Chari, A., Stedman, K. D. & Lundblad, C. 2017. Taper tantrums: QE, its aftermath and emerging market capital flows, *National Bureau of Economic Research*, No. 23474.

Chari, V. & Kehoe, P. 2004. Financial crises as herds: overturning the critiques, *Journal of Economic Theory*, 119(1), 128–150.

Ciarlone, A. & Colabella, A. 2016. Spillovers of the ECB's non-standard monetary policy into CESEE economies, *Ensayos sobre política económica*, 34(81), 175–190.

Clarus Financial Technology. 2021. How Much of the Derivatives Market is Now Cleared? www.clarusft.com/how-much-of-the-derivatives-market-is-now-cleared-2021-edition/.

Close, R. 2011. Global Risk Management in Action, in: Hoflich Peter, ed., *Banks at Risk: Global Best Practices in an Age of Turbulence*, Wiley, pp. 159–181.

Cont, R. 2007. Volatility Clustering in Financial Markets: Empirical Facts and Agent–Based Models, in: *Long Memory in Economics*, ed., Teyssière G. & Kirman A., Springer, Berlin Heidelberg, pp. 289–309.

Cont, R. 2018. *Margin Requirements for Non-cleared Derivatives*, ISDA.

Duan Jin, C. 1999. Conditionally fat-tailed distributions and the volatility smile in options, Rotman School of Management, University of Toronto, Working Paper.

Duca, M., Nicoletti, G. & Martinez, A. 2016. Global corporate bond issuance: what role for US quantitative easing? *Journal of International Money and Finance*, 60, 114–150.

Duffie, D. & Stein, J. 2015. Reforming LIBOR and other financial market benchmarks, *Journal of Economic Perspectives*, 29(2), Spring, 191–212.
Duffie, D. 2018a. Financial regulatory reform after the crisis: An assessment, *Management Science* 64(10), 4835–4857.
Duffie, D. 2018b. Post-crisis bank regulations and financial market liquidity, Baffi Lecture.
Duffie, D., Li, A. & Lubke, T. 2010. Policy perspectives on OTC derivatives market infrastructure, March (424), FRB of New York Staff Report.
Dumas, B., Fleming, J. & Whaley, R. 1998. Implied volatility functions: Empirical tests, *The Journal of Finance*, 53(6), 2059–2106.
Edsparr, P. & Fischer, P. 2014. Tail risk and contract design from a financial stability perspective, in: *Developments in Macro-Finance Yield Curve Modelling* (ed. Jaglit et al), Cambridge University Press, 121–140.
Ehlers, T., & Hardy, B. 2019. The evolution of OTC interest rate derivatives markets. *BIS Quarterly Review, December*.
Eichengreen, B., Rose, A. & Wyplosz, C. 1996. Contagious currency crises: First tests, *NBER Working Paper* No. 5681.
EP. 2016. *Regulation of the European Parliament and of the Council* (EU) 2016/1011 of 8 June 2016 on indices used as benchmarks in financial instruments and financial contracts or to measure the performance of investment funds (BMR).
ESMA. 2017. The systematic internaliser regime, in: Questions and Answers on MiFID II and MiFIR transparency topics, ESMA70-872942901-35.
Falagiarda, M., McQuade, P. & Tirpák, M. 2015. Spillovers from the ECB's non-standard monetary policies on non-euro area EU countries: evidence from an event-study analysis, No. 1869, *ECB Working Paper*.
Ferdinandusse, M., Freier, M. & Ristiniemi, A. 2020. Quantitative easing and the price-liquidity trade-off, *Sveriges Riksbank Working Paper Series*, No. 335.
Flavell, R. 2002. *Swaps and Other Derivatives*, Wiley & Sons.
Frank, N. & Hesse, H. 2009. Financial spillovers to emerging markets during the global financial crisis, *IMF Working Papers* WP/09/104, 1–20.
Fratzscher, M., Duca, M. & Straub, R. 2016. ECB unconventional monetary policy: Market impact and international spillovers, *IMF Economic Review*, 64(1), 36–74.
Gandhi, P., Golez, B., Jackwerth, J.C. & Plazzi, A. 2015. Libor manipulation: Cui Bono? finance research seminar, April 2015.
Garcimartín, F. & Saez, M. I. 2015. Set-off, netting and close-out netting, in: *Research Handbook on Crisis Management in the Banking Sector*, ed. Haentjens Matthias, Wessels Bob, Edward Elgar, pp. 331–344.
Garvin N. 2012. Central counterparty interoperability. RBA Bulletin, June, 59–68.
Genito, L. 2019. Mandatory clearing: the infrastructural authority of central counterparty clearing houses in the OTC derivatives market, *Review of International Political Economy*, 26(5), 938–962.
Giada, L. & Nordio, C. 2013. Bilateral credit valuation adjustment of an optional early, termination clause, *arXiv*, 1205.
Grimaldi, M., Crosta, A. & Zhang, D. 2021. The liquidity of the government bond market – what impact does quantitative easing have? Evidence from Sweden, *Sveriges Riksbank Working Paper Series,* No. 402.
Gunay, S. 2021. Comparing COVID-19 with the GFC: A shockwave analysis of currency markets, *Research in International Business and Finance*, 56, 101377.

Haroon, O. & Rizvi, S. A. R. 2020. COVID-19: Media coverage and financial markets behavior – a sectoral inquiry, *Journal of Behavioral and Experimental Finance*, 27, 100343.

Hirshleifer, D. & Teoh Siew, H. 2009. Thought and behavior contagion in capital markets, in: *Handbook of Financial Markets: Dynamics and Evolution*, ed., Thorsten Hens, Schenk-Hoppé Klaus, Elsevier, pp. 1–56.

HM Treasury. 2012. *The Wheatley Review of LIBOR: final report,* HM Treasury, September.

Horváth, R. & Voslarova, K. 2017. International spillovers of ECB's unconventional monetary policy: the effect on Central Europe, *Applied Economics*, 49(24), 2352–2364.

Hou, D. & Skeie, D. 2014. *LIBOR: Origins, Economics, Crisis, Scandal and Reform, Federal Reserve Bank of New York Staff Report* No. 667, March 2014.

IOSCO. 2013. Principles for Financial Benchmarks Final Report, OICU-IOSCO, FR 07/13, July.

Iwanicz-Drozdowska, M., Rogowicz, K., Kurowski, Ł. & Smaga, P. 2021. Two decades of contagion effect on stock markets: Which events are more contagious? *Journal of Financial Stability* 55, 100907.

Kanapickienė, R., Teresienė, D., Budrienė, D., Keliuotytė-Staniulėnienė, G., & Kartašova, J. 2020. The impact of COVID-19 on European financial markets and economic sentiment, *Economy & Business*, 14, 144–163.

Kazemi, H. & Sohrabji, N. 2012. Contagion in Europe: Examining the PIIGS crisis, *International Advances in Economic Research*, 18(4), 455–456.

Kirti, D. 2017. What are reference rates for? *IMFWorking Paper*, WP/17/13, January 2017.

Kočenda, E. & Moravcová, M. 2019. Exchange rate comovements, hedging and volatility spillovers on new EU forex market, *Journal of International Financial Markets, Institutions and Money*, 58, 42–64.

Köksal, B. & Orhan, M. 2013. Market risk of developed and emerging countries during the global financial crisis, *Emerging Markets Finance and Trade*, 49(3), 20–34.

Krugman, P. 2020. Crashing Economy, Rising Stocks: What's Going On? *New York Times,* April 30.

Krugman, P., Rogoff, K., Fischer, S. & McDonough, W. 1999. Currency crises, in: *International Capital Flows*, ed., M. Feldstein, University of Chicago Press, pp. 421–466.

Kucharčuková, O. B., Claeys, P. & Vašíček, B. 2016. Spillover of the ECB's monetary policy outside the euro area: how different is conventional from unconventional policy? *Journal of Policy Modeling*, 38(2), 199–225.

Lacalle, D. 2019. Are the effects of unconventional monetary policy on financial markets causing bubbles? *JBAFP*, 1(1), 95–117.

Lee, I. H. 1998. Market crashes and informational avalanches. *The Review of Economic Studies*, 65(4), 741–759.

Lynch, A. 2000. Thought contagions in the stock market, *The Journal of Psychology and Financial Markets*, 1(1), 10–23.

McPartland, J. & Lewis, R. 2016. The challenges of derivatives central counterparty interoperability arrangements. *The Journal of Financial Market Infrastructures*, 4, 41–51.

Mercurio, F. 2010. Modern LIBOR market models: using different curves for projecting rates and for discounting. *International Journal of Theoretical and Applied Finance*, 13(01), 113–137.

Mobarek, A., Mollah, S. & Keasey, K. 2014. A cross-country analysis of herd behavior in Europe. *Journal of International Financial Markets, Institutions and Money*, 32, 107–127.

Morgan, G. 2008. Market formation and governance in international financial markets: The case of OTC derivatives, *Human Relations*, 61(5), 637–660.

Moro, B. 2014. Lessons from the European economic and financial great crisis: a survey, *European Journal of Political Economy*, 34, 9–S24.

Neely, C. 2015. Unconventional monetary policy had large international effects, *Journal of Banking & Finance*, 52, 101–111.

Ng, L. & Wu, F. 2010. Peer effects in the trading decisions of individual investors, *Financial Management*, 39(2), June, 807–831.

Niţoi, M. & Pochea, M. M. 2020. Time-varying dependence in European equity markets: A contagion and investor sentiment driven analysis, *Economic Modelling*, 86, 133–147.

Nögel, U. 2017. MiFIDII /MiFIR – Boost for Big Data Analytics in Trading?, www.linkedin.com/pulse/mifidii-mifir-boost-big-data-analytics-trading-part-13-nögel/.

Nystedt, J. 2004. Derivative market competition: OTC markets versus organized derivative exchanges, *SSRN working paper*.

Perkins, J. & Mortby, P. 2015. Evolving financial benchmarks: The impact on legacy contracts, *Journal of Securities Operations & Custody*, 7(4), Autumn/Fall, 296–304.

Pole, A. 2011. *Statistical Arbitrage: Algorithmic Trading Insights and Techniques*, Wiley & Sons.

Rafferty, B. 2012. Currency returns, skewness and crash risk, *SSRN Paper* No. 202.292.015.

Rai, V. & Suchanek, L. 2014. The effect of the federal reserve's tapering announcements on emerging markets, *Bank of Canada Working Paper*, No. 2014–50.

Ramírez, C. & González, M. 2017. Have QE programs affected capital flows to emerging markets? A Regional Analysis. *Joint Research*, 155–188.

Rebonato, R. 2004. *Volatility and Correlation: The Perfect Hedger and the Fox*, Wiley & Sons.

Rigobon, R. 2016. Contagion, spillover and interdependence, *ECB WPS*, No 1975, November.

Rösch, C. & Kaserer, C. 2014. Market liquidity in the financial crisis: The role of liquidity commonality and flight-to-quality, *Journal of Banking & Finance*, 45, 152–170.

Samarakoon, L. 2011. Stock market interdependence, contagion, and the US financial crisis: The case of emerging and frontier markets, *Journal of International Financial Markets, Institutions and Money*, 21(5), 724–742.

Shiller, R. 1995. Conversation, information, and herd behavior, *American Economic Review*, 85(2), 181–185.

Shive, S. (2010). An epidemic model of investor behavior. *Journal of Financial and Quantitative Analysis*, 45(1), 169–198.

Sidanius, C. & Wetherilt, A. 2012. Thoughts on determining central clearing eligibility of OTC derivatives, Bank of England, Financial Stability Paper 14.

Singh, M. 2010. Collateral, netting and systemic risk in the OTC derivatives market. *IMF Working Papers*, 1–15.

Sobrun, J. & Turner, P. 2015. Bond markets and monetary policy dilemmas for the emerging markets, *BIS Working Paper*, No 508.

Stelmach, J. 2010. Testing the homogeneous interest rates assumption by principal component analysis: The Euro area case. *Ekonomika*, 89(3), 30–39.

Switzer, L. & Fan, H. 2007. *Interactions between Exchange Traded Currency Futures and OTC Derivatives*, Finance Department, Concordia University.

Taleb, N. 1997. *Dynamic Hedging*, Wiley & Sons.

Taleb, N. 2012. *Antifragility: Things that Gain from Disorder*, Penguin.

Tillmann, P. 2016. Unconventional monetary policy and the spillovers to emerging markets, *Journal of International Money and Finance*, 66, 136–156.

Treleaven, P., Galas, M. & Lalchand, V. 2013. Algorithmic Trading Review, *Communications of the ACM*, 56(11), 76–85.

Valle-Cruz, D., Fernandez-Cortez, V., López-Chau, A. & Sandoval-Almazán, R. 2022. Does Twitter affect stock market decisions? Financial sentiment analysis during pandemics: a comparative study of the H1N1 and the Covid-19 periods. Cognitive computation, *Cognitive Computation*, 14, 372–387.

Vives, X. 2001. The Speed of Information Revelation. *New Research in Financial Markets*, 149.

Wallin, J. 2013. Impact of Reform on Collateral and Margin Requirement Practices, *Journal of Securities Operations & Custody*, 5(4), 299–311.

Wei, X. & Han, L. 2021. The impact of COVID-19 pandemic on transmission of monetary policy to financial markets, *International Review of Financial Analysis*, 74, 101705.

Wendt, F. 2006. *Intraday Margining of Central Counterparties: EU Practice and a Theoretical Evaluation of Benefits and Costs*, De Nederlandsche Bank.

Whaley, R. 2009. Understanding the VIX, *The Journal of Portfolio Management*, 35(3), 98–105.

Whitall, C. 2010. The price is wrong, *Risk Magazine*, 3.

Zhang, D, Hu, M. & Ji, Q. 2020. Financial markets under the global pandemic of COVID-19, *Finance Research Letters*, 36, 101528.

Zhang, J. & Xiang, Y. 2008. The implied volatility smirk, *Quantitative Finance*, 8(3), 263–284.

5 The interplay between the financial sphere and the real sphere

In this chapter, the fourth research hypothesis (H4) is addressed: the relationship between finance and the real economy was different including the direction of causality, during each of the recent turbulences. First, the relevant literature on the interplay between the real economy and the financial sphere for pre-2000 and 2000+ periods is reviewed, with special attention paid to the differences between developed and developing countries. Second, this relationship is analyzed for periods around various crises to show whether the crisis origin impacts this interplay.

5.1 Finance and growth nexus – state of play

There is a plethora of theoretical and empirical research on the relationship between financial development and economic growth (finance & growth nexus, henceforth: F&G), using different methodologies, data sets, and a variety of proxies. The general consensus is that from the theoretical point of view, the financial system plays a crucial role in mobilizing and intermediating savings in the economy. Through economies of scale and scope, financial markets and financial intermediaries (like banks) are able to ameliorate the problems of asymmetric information and high transaction costs between economic agents. Levine (1997) classifies the classic functions of financial systems into the following categories: facilitating trading, hedging, diversifying, and pooling of risk; allocating resources; monitoring managers and exerting corporate control; mobilizing savings, and facilitating the exchange of goods and services in the economy.

Initially, as indicated by a seminal study by Schumpeter (1911), well-functioning financial intermediation spurs growth by fostering and enabling financing of technological innovation and production processes. Further studies argued that a liberalized financial system mobilizes an increased volume of savings and allocates capital in the economy to more effective uses, both of which boost the volume and overall productivity of capital, which ultimately contributes to economic growth. King and Levine (1993) mention that a high level of financial development fosters economic growth, accelerates capital accumulation, and improves the efficiency of capital employed in the

DOI: 10.4324/9781003225539-5

economy. Levine and Zervos (1998) confirm the significant positive role of stock markets and banking development for economic growth, capital stock accumulation, and productivity. Levine (2005) summarizes the theory and empirical evidence on the relationship between F&G, emphasizing the existence of a positive link, but highlighting the implications of various measures of financial development used in many studies.

Thus, in line with Demetriades and Andrianova (2004), conceptually, financial development is, at best, a facilitator of economic growth, rather than its ultimate true cause. The true cause of economic growth is in the real sector: the discovery of natural resources or of alternative ways of using existing resources, creation of new ideas, technological progress, product innovation, etc. Instead, finance is essential in ensuring that new ideas are translated into products, services, and technologies. A well-functioning financial system enables the real economy to fully exploit such new opportunities and facilitate them, but is not the single cause of growth, *per se*. Normally, we expect bidirectional causality between F&G, since when the real economy grows, there should be more savings coming into the financial system, which – given the process of modern monetary creation – will allow banks to increase the extension of new loans.

However, the link from finance to growth might become broken, as with the excessive growth of the financial system, funds are being increasingly diverted to non-productive activities (due to growing inefficiencies in the banking system) e.g. to financing low-quality projects, projects with only shorter-term payoffs or speculative ventures (like financing credit bubbles). This tendency brings diminishing added value to the economy, instead of channeling financial savings into new investments. Kindleberger (1978) claimed that the cyclical instability of expectations and asset speculation regarding over-leveraged investments can have severe negative consequences for an economy. This is in line with the "financial instability hypothesis" by Minsky (1992), arguing that the financial system in a modern capitalist economy becomes inherently unstable, as speculative and Ponzi finance begins to dominate hedge transactions, ultimately leading to endogenously driven cyclical shocks and crises.

What we conclude from the seminal F&G literature in the XX century is that there is a traditional view of a positive linear long-run link between F&G, but there is less certainty about the causality of this relationship (Ang, 2008). Those studies also do not provide a clear explanation of the endogeneity of the variables used, and the results may vary considerably due to different institutional and structural characteristics of each economy and the financial system. Still, the main drawback is often a short estimation period used in many time-series studies, especially given the medium- to long-term nature of financial cycles. This problem is particularly severe for most developing countries where data are scarce. As the F&G time series grows longer, future studies will be able to provide more robust and conclusive results. Determining and untangling the F&G relationship remains important also from a policy perspective, as it helps governments properly formulate growth-enhancing policies.

5.2 Tail wagging the dog?

One of the main topics of F&G research is the question of the strength and direction of causality between the real economy ("dog") and financial intermediation ("tail"). The F&G relationship is highly non-linear and depends on the differences in cyclicality and relation between business and credit cycles, which are rarely synchronous. The studies (as reviewed below) assessing the direction of the F&G causality most often use Granger (or Dumitrescu and Hurlin's modification in the case of panel data) causality tests for that purpose. While the majority of studies use single-country samples, we focus solely on these based on an international sample, which offer more robust results. Empirical F&G studies typically explore the validity of two opposite points of view: the *supply-leading* and *demand-following* hypothesis (Patrick, 1966). The first hypothesis argues that financial development is a necessary pre-condition and "leads" economic growth. On the contrary, the second hypothesis states that finance plays a minor role in economic growth and is merely considered a by-product or an outcome of growth. Research on those hypotheses can be divided into two evolving areas, finding diverse strengths of the F&G link.

The first stream of studies, using mainly pre-2000 data on a large sample of countries, usually confirms the existence of a positive uni- or bi-directional causality between F&G (Calderon and Liu, 2003; Beck and Levine, 2004; Christopoulos and Tsionas, 2004; Apergis et al., 2007; Beck et al., 2014), mainly through financial deepening. These studies indicate a positive and statistically significant relationship between F&G, tested with different financial indicators and proxies. The results show that this positive nexus is stronger in developing countries in the long run, underlining the benefits of reforming the financial system for growth e.g. through liberalization (Bangake and Eggoh, 2011). The positive impact of finance on growth is mainly driven by the bank credit channel, predominantly by enterprise credit rather than consumer credit (Beck et al., 2012). The beneficial (linear) bidirectional F&G link is found mainly in studies on emerging markets, even with post-2000 data, as those have a lower level of financial development, compared to advanced countries (Handa and Khan, 2008; Nguyen et al., 2021). This, however, means that developing economies are simply not at the point at which finance can become a drag on growth. Bidirectional causality link is also driven by the trade channel and trade openness (i.e. via exports and foreign direct investments) leading to a higher supply of external finance (Wajda-Lichy et al., 2019; Kawa et al., 2020). This pro-trade positive impact of higher financial development is more likely to occur in relatively small open economies. While confirming the bidirectional F&G link, Akinci et al. (2014) concur that in countries with less sophisticated financial systems economic growth induces financial development. Positive unidirectional causality is additionally found in countries where the stock market is liquid and highly active (when finance is approximated with stock market variables) both in advanced and developing countries (Levine and Zervos, 1998; Rajan and Zingales, 1998; Lyócsa, 2014). In fact, Botev et al. (2019) show that banking and market financing are complementary and the positive effect of bank credit on growth is larger when stock markets are deeper. In line with the Schumpeterian theorem, Pradhan et al. (2016) and Mtar and Belazreg (2021) argue that it is the innovation and financial development which drive economic growth in the long run (e.g. by leading to more efficient resource allocation and improved performance of knowledge-based economies). Surprisingly, Mhadhbi et al. (2020) show that the direction of causality between banking sector development and economic growth is sensitive to the choice of banking proxies and confirm both the demand-following, supply-leading and complementarity between those hypotheses at the same time.

The second area of studies, usually based on post-2000 cross-country data, indicate that the "waggling of the tail by the dog" (i.e. the positive impact of financial development on growth) is non-linear and loses its strength. Gantman and Dabós (2012) prove that financial development, operationalized as a credit to the private sector, simply does not have a positive effect upon economic growth. At the same time, Demetriades and Rousseau (2016) provide evidence that financial depth over time becomes the less significant determinant of long-term economic growth, as more finance seems not to have resulted in more growth (instead, it is the quality of financial system regulation that matters). Literature mentions several reasons for this phenomenon. The breakdown of the positive F&G link might be driven by a structural break initiated by the occurrence of the GFC, especially in high-income countries, like these in the EU (Luintel et al., 2016). Rousseau and Wachtel (2011) confirm with strong evidence on a wide panel sample, that the increased incidence of financial crises in recent decades is indeed related to the dampening of the effect of financial deepening on growth. Excessive financial deepening or too rapid a growth of credit usually leads to both inflation and weakened banking systems, which in turn gives rise to growth-impeding financial crises. Thus, during and because of the crisis episodes, the benefits of financial deepening on growth disappear. Another reason for the weaker F&G link is suggested by Owen and Temesvary (2014), who show that it exists when the domestic banking sector is not well developed and depends on the type of bank lending. Cheng et al. (2021) further argue that financial development is unfavourable for economic growth, especially in high-income countries, due to the diffusion of information and communication technologies connected with growing financial development. Those doubts about the fading strength of F&G are confirmed by Swamy and Dharani (2019, 2021), who identified that in advanced countries there is presence of nonlinearity and an inverted U-shaped bidirectional relationship between F&G in the long run, thus subscribing to the mentioned threshold effect hypothesis. The fragility of F&G link was additionally found in CESEEs, i.e. due to relatively less developed financial systems, the legacy of socialism, failure to establish robust and prudent legal and regulatory frameworks, low fiscal and monetary disciplines, their experience of banking crises, as well as the role of foreign banks' lending (Berglof and Bolton, 2002; Koivu, 2002; Petkovski and Kjosevski, 2014; Caporale et al., 2015; Iwanicz-Drozdowska et al., 2018). Also, Hsueh et al. (2013) provide no evidence to indicate that financial development is the most important determinant of economic growth in Asian countries. This implies that the causal direction between F&G is sensitive to the country-level financial development specificities (Owen and Temesvary, 2014).

In conclusion, the current verdict of empirical studies on the F&G relationship and their causality still remains inconclusive. As summarized by Bongini et al. (2017), the F&G debate focused at first on the overall impact of the financial system and its depth on economic growth, causality and channels of influence, as well as the conditions necessary to achieve its positive relationship with GDP. The agenda then shifted to comparisons between bank- and market-based financial systems. The debate following the onset of the GFC has tended to employ a systemic perspective to analyze the fragility and limits of "oversized" financial systems in contributing to economic growth. Beck (2009) and Valickova et al. (2015) argue that the unresolved F&G debate is due to different econometric approaches, research designs and cross-country samples applied. Nevertheless, studies using pre-2000 data more often found positive bidirectional link from finance to growth, while those estimated on post-2000 data show this bidirectional link weakened over time or even became negative, especially after financial system development reached its maturity, in developed countries. A vast minority of studies on F&G focus on transmission channels via banking and the stock market, with only a few confirming the existence of bidirectional causality also for insurance (Chang et al., 2014). In the post-GFC period, there is a new consensus that credit expansion has a positive impact on growth, but only up to a critical threshold of financial system development, beyond which the benefits diminish and negative externalities begin to materialize (Cecchetti and Kharroubi, 2012; Beck et al., 2014; Arcand et al., 2015). This has a direct impact on the positive or negative role of finance, contingent on the level of maturity of the country's financial system.

5.3 Financial and real spheres in Western and Eastern Europe

In this part, we present the results of the empirical analysis of crisis events and try to find out empirically if the "tail" is wagging the "dog.". First, we present differences between "new" and "old" European countries using data descriptive analysis. European countries have been divided into two groups: "old," i.e. pre-2004 EU members and mature economies (Switzerland, Norway; we also include the UK in this group) and the "new" EU members. Second, we use Granger's and Dumitrescu-Hurlin's approaches to analyze the interplay between the financial sphere and the real economy.

As our research focuses on crises periods, we use windows one year before and one year after a given crisis event. The data were then gathered in four separate subsets, covering four crisis-around periods:

1) September 2007 – September 2009 – the collapse of Lehman Brothers (15 September 2008);
2) March 2011 – March 2013 – the eurozone sovereign debt crisis (PIIGS, with its culminating point in March 2012);
3) July 2014 – June 2016 – the technical default of Greece (30 June 2015);
4) March 2019 – March 2021 – the outbreak of the COVID-19 pandemic (11 March 2020).

5.3.1 Financial and real spheres in Europe

After WWII, for many years Europe operated under two much different economic and political systems. Therefore, there are still – even after 30 years of economic and political transformation – significant differences between the "old" and "new" European economies. The most important differences, in the context of our analysis, relate to the levels of economic development and financial deepening (see for example Iwanicz-Drozdowska et al., 2018). Both the levels of GDP per capita (GDP p.c.) and typical financial deepening measures (such as bank credit-to-GDP and stock market capitalization-to-GDP ratios) are lower in "new" Europe. According to World Bank data as of year-end 2020 (World Bank, 2022), the average GDP p.c. in the "old" European countries amounted to USD 48,300 (in current prices), while in "new" European countries it was USD 19,400 (in current prices). In the case of financial deepening, the situation in these two groups of countries is also very different. Bank credit to the private sector was on average above 100% of GDP in the "old" and about 50% in the "new" European countries (World Bank, 2022). As not all countries reported to the World Bank their market capitalization of listed domestic companies to GDP, we compare differences based on the limited scope of data. In Central Europe and the Baltics, market capitalization was about 21% of GDP, while for example in Germany and Spain it was about 60% and in Switzerland more than 260%. In recent decades such significant differences also existed (e.g. Bongini et al., 2017), however during the GFC these differences were reduced to some extent, as "new" countries converged (e.g. Iwanicz-Drozdowska et al., 2016).

During the crises that are subject to our in-depth scrutiny, "old" and "new" economies also have shown some differences. In Figures 5.1 and 5.2 we present macroeconomic variables such as inflation, unemployment, production in industry and retail trade around crisis periods.

Except for the periods around the technical default of Greece, inflation in "new" countries was higher than in the "old" ones (including deflation episodes), while the unemployment rate started to be more favourable in "new" countries around the time of the default of Greece. The overall tendencies of these two variables show similarities.

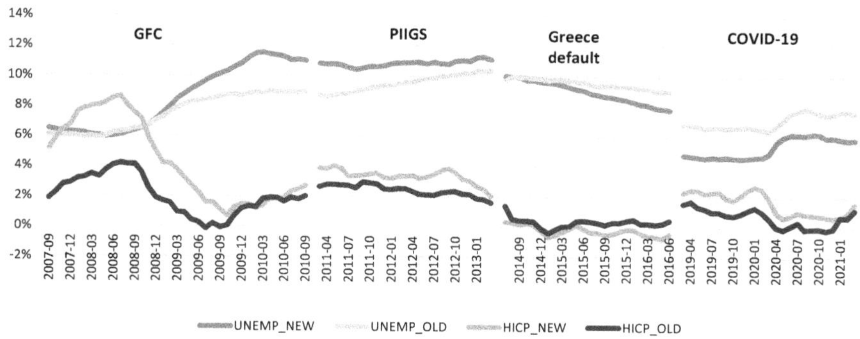

Figure 5.1 Inflation and unemployment.

Source: Own work based on monthly Eurostat data.

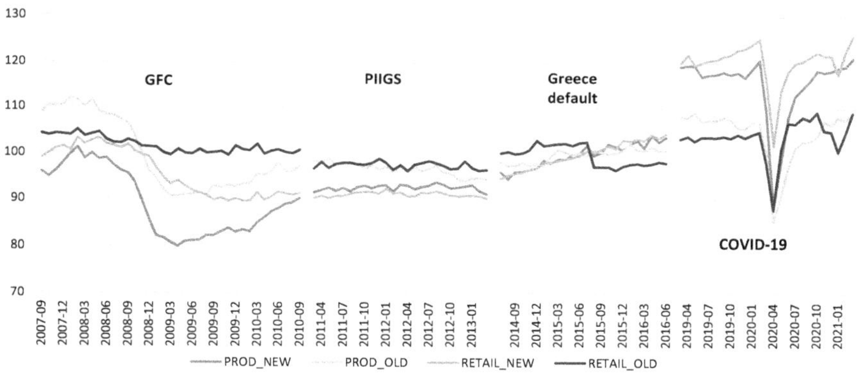

Figure 5.2 Production in industry and retail trade.

Source: Own work based on monthly Eurostat data; index, 2015=100, seasonally adjusted data.

The retail trade index dropped in "new" countries to a larger extent than in "old" Europe during the GFC, and the tendency of the measure of production in industry was similar. During the period around the PIIGS culminating point, both measures showed only minor ups and downs, while around the time of the Greek technical default, only retail trade in "old" countries declined. The external shock caused by the outbreak of the COVID-19 pandemic resulted in a significant drop in these two variables in both groups of countries, with production in industry in "new" countries facing the most severe decline, which may be associated with supply chain disruptions.

In the case of measures of the financial sphere (see Table 5.1), different reactions are observed around crises dates. In the case of sovereign debt crisis events, stock markets in "old" countries reacted with panic. The stock indices

Table 5.1 Changes of market parameters in crisis-around periods

Group of countries and instrument	*GFC*	*PIIGS*	*GR default*	*COVID-19*
OLD – 5Y T-Bond yields (b.p.)	−0.12	−0.12	−0.11	0.08
OLD – TR market index (%)	−3.99	−4.68	0.76	−24.01
NEW- 5Y T-Bond yields (b.p.)	0.11	−0.21	−0.03	0.06
NEW- TR market index (%)	−6.61	−0.35	−0.74	−20.81

Note: own work based on Refinitiv data; change of month_{t-1} and month_{t+1} around the crisis date; monthly averages of daily prices; 5Y T-Bonds yields – yields on 5-year T-Bonds; TR market index – total return stock market index.

plummeted during the COVID-19 outbreak and also T-Bond yields increased at that time. All these are a sign of increased risk in the economy, for both private and public sectors, as perceived by investors. Around the outbreak of the COVID-19 pandemic, no differences between "old" and "new" countries are observed. This situation differs from the GFC and PIIGS events. Upon the outbreak of the GFC, stock market indices suffered, and investors shifted to safe-haven assets, i.e. T-Bonds of "old" European countries. In the case of "new" European countries, their T-Bonds yields reflected a higher risk in the eyes of the investors. As the PIIGS crisis broke out, investors shifted their sentiment to T-Bonds of the "new" countries, regarding them to be less risky, probably because the largest "new" economies were outside the eurozone.

As presented in the above section, crisis events trigger changes in the real and financial spheres, but the question remains whether the "tail" (finance) is wagging the "dog" (real economy). We try to address this problem empirically in the following section.

5.3.2 Data and methodology

One important objective is to identify whether the relationship between the considered indicators representing different spheres exists and how it has changed between the different considered crisis periods. We use the following indicators divided into subsets that represent the different spheres:

(1) Economic indicators (source: Eurostat):
- UNEMP – unemployment rate (seasonally adjusted data),
- PROD – production in industry (manufacturing) index (2015=100, seasonally and calendar adjusted data), i.e. monthly changes in the volume of output;
- RETAIL – retail trade (except for motor vehicles and motorcycles) volume and turnover index (2015=100, seasonally and calendar adjusted data), i.e. monthly changes of the deflated turnover;

(2) Financial indicators (source: Refinitiv):
- TB_5Y – 5-year treasury bond yields, monthly average based on daily data;

- TR – total return index (gross dividends), monthly average based on daily values of stock exchange indices;

(3) Pandemic indicators (source: University of Oxford, Oxford COVID-19 Government Response Tracker, ourworldindata.org):

- COV_STRING – COVID-19 Stringency Index, monthly average based on daily data;
- COV_RESP – COVID-19 Government Response Index, monthly average based on daily data.

Validating research hypothesis 4 (H4) requires identification of the relationships between the aforementioned indicators that belong to different groups and checking whether these relations have remained stable over time and – most of all – during the particular crisis periods.

An important question is the type of the considered relationship. Numerous research in such a case, consists in firstly assuming the direction of the causal relation, then estimating a series of regressions and finally – drawing conclusions from the estimated coefficients and their statistical significance. However, such an approach cannot be applied in our research: it can only be correct if the researcher *ex ante* knows that the potential relationship is causal and can identify its direction. Failing to make proper assumptions might result in wrong conclusions and mistaking coexistence for causality. We thus propose to use Granger-type tests of causality, which allows identification of causality without assuming its direction, as well as bidirectional causality or just coexistence.

Technical details of the procedure are as follows.

5.3.2.1 Step 1 Data curation

The data on the aforementioned indicators were collected. They were published with a frequency ranging from single working days to full months. Thus, we opted for the monthly frequency of the observations – in the case of the daily observations, the monthly average was used in each case.

Obviously, the "pandemic indicators" were only available in the last of the crises, while the other variables were available in each of the periods for all or most of the countries of interest. Table 5.2 provides details regarding the data availability. The entire research is carried out separately for each of the aforementioned crisis periods and each group of countries – the "old" and "new" European countries and the complete set of countries included in the analysis together.

5.3.2.2 Step 2 Stationarity analysis

One potential threat is the issue of the non-stationarity of the considered time series. Not only does it often result in identifying spurious regressions, but it is also an obstacle in the causality study. We thus perform a series of stationarity tests to identify the order of integration of the series of interests

Table 5.2 Data availability

Variable/period	*Lehman Brothers collapse (T=25)*	*Eurozone sovereign debt crisis (T=25)*	*Default of Greece (T=24)*	*COVID-19 pandemic (T=25/15[1])*
UNEMP	Full[2] except CH	Full[2] except CH	Full[2]	Full[2] except CH
PROD	Full[2] except CH	Full[2] except CH	Full[2]	Full[2]
RETAIL	Full[2]	Full[2]	Full[2]	Full[2]
TB_5Y	CH, CZ, DE, DK, ES, FI, HU, IT, LT, LV, NO, PL, PT, RO, SE, SI, SK, UK	CH, CZ, DE, DK, ES, FI, HU, IT, LT, NO, PL, PT, RO, SE, UK	CH, CZ, DE, DK, ES, FI, HU, IT, LT, LV, NO, PL, PT, RO, SE, SI, SK, UK	CH, CZ, DE, DK, ES, FI, HU, IT, LT, LV, NO, PL, PT, RO, SE, SI, SK, UK
TR	Full[2] except UK	Full[2] except UK	Full[2] except UK	Full[2]
COV_STRING	-	-	-	Full[2] except IS, LU
COV_RESP	-	-	-	Full[2] except IS, LU

1 In the case of the variables UNEMP, PROD, RETAIL, TB_5Y and TR the T=15 (starting February 2020), in the case of COV_STRING and COV_RESP the T=15; 2 The complete data set includes the "old" countries: Austria, Belgium, Denmark, Finland, France, Germany, Greece, Iceland, Ireland, Italy, Luxembourg, the Netherlands, Norway, Portugal, Spain, Sweden, Switzerland, the UK and the "new" countries: Bulgaria, Croatia, Cyprus, the Czech Republic, Estonia, Hungary, Latvia, Lithuania, Malta, Poland, Romania, Slovakia, Slovenia. Any missing data are reported in the table.

and, in consequence, the order of their differences that potentially would need to be used to assure stationarity. The data constitute a number of panels of a length of between 15 and 25 periods each (24–25 in most cases). The number of countries varies across the considered variables and groups between 8 and 30. These relatively high frequencies are sufficient to achieve trustworthy test results.

Numerous stationarity tests for panel data exist. We opt for the cross-sectional augmented Im-Pesaran-Shin (CIPS) test proposed by Pesaran (2007). Its key property is that it builds on the earlier Im, Pesaran and Shin (2003) proposal and allows cross-dependence of the series: a feature that seems essential given the character of the data. Pesaran (2007) proposes to use the standard ADF test regressions and augment them with the cross-sectional averages of the lagged levels and first differences of the considered series. Also, it allows for the panel-specific parameter in the ADF test equation. The properties of this test are widely acknowledged, making it a very popular tool. Under the null hypothesis, the series in the considered panel has a unit root. We thus hope to reject the null hypothesis, however, failing to reject it results in the sequential analysis of further differences of the considered series until a stationary series is found. As a result, the order of integration of the considered series is identified. One minor drawback of the CIPS test is that the test statistic does not follow any widely applied distribution and thus the critical values for the test need to be identified via simulation. In consequence, we assume the 5% level of significance and use the critical values for that level provided by Pasaran in the source article from 2007. Also, to ensure the required properties of the error term in the test equations on the one hand and a sufficient number of observations in the series on the other hand, we use the ADF regressions with a single lag. It must be emphasized though that the results are robust to the inclusion of a higher number of lags (up to 3 have been tested).

As expected, not all the considered series are stationary, however, no series is integrated in the order exceeding 1. Characteristically, with no exceptions, the order of integration indicated by the CIPS test is the same for each of the considered series in each of the 4 crisis periods. The details are provided in Tables 5.3–5.6.

Table 5.3 The results of CIPS stationarity test – the fall of Lehman Brothers period

Statistics/Series	*UNEMP*	*PROD*	*RETAIL*	*TB_5Y*	*TR*
CIPS – level	−1,869	−3,228	−3,020	−1,356	−2,080
critical value	−2,110	−2,110	−2,110	−2,250	−2,150
CIPS – difference	−4,229	-	-	−3,687	−4,045
critical value	−2,110	-	-	−2,250	−2,150

Source: own calculations.

Table 5.4 The results of CIPS stationarity test – the eurozone debt crisis period

Statistics/Series	*UNEMP*	*PROD*	*RETAIL*	*TB_5Y*	*TR*
CIPS – level	−1,808	−3,095	−3,039	−2,109	−1,598
critical value	−2,110	−2,110	−2,110	−2,250	−2,150
CIPS – difference	−4,307	-	-	−3,715	−3,954
critical value	−2,110	-	-	−2,250	−2,150

Source: own calculations.

Table 5.5 The results of CIPS stationarity test – the default of Greece period

Statistics/Series	*UNEMP*	*PROD*	*RETAIL*	*TB_5Y*	*TR*
CIPS – level	−2,146	−3,520	−2,189	−1,986	−1,227
critical value	−2,110	−2,110	−2,110	−2,250	−2,15
CIPS – difference	−4,228	-	-	−5,816	−3,640
critical value	−2,110	-	-	−2,250	−2,150

Source: Own calculations.

Table 5.6 The results of CIPS stationarity test – the outbreak of the COVID pandemic period

Statistics/Series	*UNEMP*	*PROD*	*RETAIL*	*TB_5Y*	*TR*	*COV_ STRING*	*COV_ RESP*
CIPS – level	−1,984	−3,250	−2,514	−1,401	−1,433	−2,304	−2,434
critical value	−2,110	−2,110	−2,110	−2,250	−2,150	−2,170	−2,170
CIPS – difference	−3,945	-	-	−3,439	−4,302	-	-
critical value	−2,110	-	-	−2,250	−2,150	-	-

Source: Own calculations.

Following the results, we find that PROD, RETAIL, COV_STRING and COV_RESP ~ I(0) while UNEMP, TB_5Y, TR ~ I(1). In consequence, in the further analysis, we use the levels of the PROD, RETAIL, COV_STRING and COV_RESP variables and the first differences of UNEMP, TB_5Y and TR.

5.3.2.3 Step 3 Identification of causality

Numerous researchers use the word "impact" without actually checking for the causality effects in the considered data. This yields the risk of mistaking causality for coexistence. To address this question, we formally consider and test for the causality in the Granger sense. This approach has the advantage of allowing and testing for causality in any of the two possible directions or even both at the same time.

In the classical paper by Granger, the equation of interest takes the form of

$$y_t = \sum_{k=1}^{K} \gamma_k y_{t-k} + \sum_{k=1}^{K} \beta_k x_{t-k} + \varepsilon_t, \quad t = 1,\ldots,T. \tag{5.1}$$

Let $\{y_t\}$ and $\{x_t\}$ be two stationary series. It is said that x causes (or actually: Granger-causes) y if the past values of x are significant predictors of y, taking account of the past values of y. To put it another way, if the

$$H_0: \beta_1 = \cdots = \beta_k = 0$$

is true then the causality would not be confirmed. Rejecting the null indicated causality in this particular direction. At the same time, we may substitute x with y and test for causality in the opposite direction: it actually is quite typical to identify the bidirectional relation in this framework.

While (5.1) can be estimated both in the time series and in the panel data case, Dumitrescu and Hurlin (2012; DH hereafter) make a note that in the panel data framework (5.1) imposes strong assumption of constancy of the γ_k and β_k across panels. This is equivalent to assuming that the relationship between x and y (as well as the past and the current y) is constant across units, which seems strong in non-homogeneous panels. Alternatively, DH proposed estimating

$$y_t = \sum_{k=1}^{K} \gamma_{ik} y_{i,t-k} + \sum_{k=1}^{K} \beta_{ik} x_{i,t-k} + \varepsilon_{i,t}, \quad t = 1,\ldots,T; i = 1,\ldots,N \tag{5.2}$$

and testing for

$$H_0 : \beta_{i1} = \cdots = \beta_{iK} = 0 \text{ for all } i = 1,\ldots,N$$

While rejecting the null hypothesis in the Granger's framework indicates that x Granger-causes y for all the units (because the relationship is essentially the same in all cases), rejecting the null hypothesis in the DH framework might mean that the relationship exists for any positive number of units, not necessarily all of them. Still, the DH approach has the flexibility advantage, which makes it more trustworthy.

One important issue is the value of K in regressions (5.1) and (5.2). There is no clear clue as to what lag should be used except for the technical limitations in the DH approach. One popular approach is to allow for a certain maximum lag length and allow an algorithmic selection of the optimum length based on the value of information criteria. This is also the approach adopted in this research: we allow for the maximum lag length of 3 and use the BIC criterion to find the optimal lag length, potentially different in each estimated regression.

5.3.3 Results and discussion: Tail (finance) wagging the dog?

Due to differences between "old" and "new" countries, it cannot be assumed that all of them are homogenous. Therefore, we treat the results of Dumitrescu-Hurlin's test as the main procedure, while Granger's test is treated as a robustness check. It must however be emphasized that under the parameter heterogeneity, the results of Granger's test might be misleading and thus the DH results are more credible. In the discussion, whenever the concept of the significance of a variable is used, a 5% level is assumed for brevity. As the analysis was conducted in the four separate subsets, covering four crisis-around periods, we present the results chronologically. Results of the tests are presented in the appendix to this chapter for "old," "new," and "all" European countries. Also, rejecting the null hypotheses does not mean that the effect of causality can be confirmed for each country that constitutes a part of the considered sample. However, failing to reject the null means that in none of the countries has the effect been observed.

In the case of the GFC, there are only a few cases in which the null hypothesis is rejected, i.e. at least for some of the countries causality exists. On the one hand, the "tail" wagged the real economy at least for some "old" European countries, which is confirmed for the pairs: (1) production in industry (or production in further paragraphs) as a dependent variable and 5-year T-Bonds (also confirmed for all countries); (2) retail trade and total return stock exchange index. On the other hand, the "dog" wagged the financial sphere, as the retail trade and production impacted in at least some "new" European countries the stock market return (retail trade confirmed its significance also for all countries). Therefore, one may say that this interplay differed during the GFC between "old" and "new" countries. Granger's test confirmed these findings.

In the case of the PIIGS crisis, null hypothesis is rejected only in a single case, that is the retail trade is dependent on 5-year T-Bonds in "all" countries. Although all PIIGS countries are "old," there is no difference between "old" and "new" countries. However, one should keep in mind that "all" countries are not homogenous as they consist of the peripheral euro area, core euro area and non-euro area countries. Due to the solidarity mechanism, euro area (including some "new") countries provided support to PIIGS. The technical default of Greece, which was analyzed as a separate case, revealed no interplay between the real economy and finance. It also shows that the market discounted before Greek problems and this technical default was irrelevant. Granger's test confirmed these findings.

Against this background, the COVID-19 crisis differs significantly, i.e. the null hypothesis is rejected in numerous cases. The rate of unemployment, production and retail trade as dependent variables were impacted in the various settings of countries by the financial sphere and by COVID-19 measures (with some exceptions). On the other hand, the production impacted T-Bonds yields (except for "new" countries). The situation in which this is a "tail" wagging the "dog" is more visible than the "dog" wagging the "tail." The COVID-19 indices played a significant role for the financial sphere, as they show not only stringency measures (including lockdowns), but also government response in the form of financial support (fiscal stimulus, explained in detail in Chapter 3) or some relief measures for borrowers (explained in detail in Chapter 2). The pandemic situation was a "game-changer" as it has impacted both the real economy and finance. Granger's test confirmed these findings.

In summary, the PIIGS crisis and the technical default of Greece did not show a causality link between the real and financial spheres. In the case of the GFC, the causality has been identified for certain cases as well as the differences between "new" and "old" European countries. In "old" countries it was the financial sphere that impacted the real economy, while in the "new" countries – just the opposite. Such a difference may be plausibly explained by the significantly lower level of financial deepening in "new" countries and the fact that financial intermediaries in "new" countries were not exposed to "toxic" financial instruments circulating in the US and the "old" European countries. The recent COVID-19 crisis reveals other patterns of this interplay, namely the "tail" has been more frequently wagging the "dog" regardless of the group of countries. This may be explained by the fact that the pandemic shock "surprised" all countries in the same way and counter-measures in most of the cases were similar (except for Sweden as far as lockdown, social distancing and isolation are concerned). Moreover, the response to the COVID-19 pandemic impacted both the real economy and finance due to the stimuli, while the stringency of pandemic measures played a far more minor role.

References

Akinci, G. Y., Akinci, M., & Yilmaz, Ö. 2014. Financial development-economic growth nexus: A panel data analysis upon OECD countries. *Hitotsubashi Journal of Economics*, Hitotsubashi University, 55(1), 33–50, DOI: 10.15057/26816.

Ang, J. B. 2008. A survey of recent developments in the literature of finance and growth. *Journal of Economic Surveys*, 22, 536–576. https://doi.org/10.1111/j.1467-6419.2007.00542.x.

Apergis, N., Filippidis, I., & Economidou, C., 2007. Financial deepening and economic growth linkages: a panel data analysis. *Review of World Economics*, 143(1), 179–198, https://doi.org/10.1007/s10290-007-0102-3.

Arcand, J.-L., Berkes, E., & Panizza, U. 2015. Too much finance? *Journal of Economic Growth*, 20(2), 105–148, https://doi.org/10.1007/s10887-015-9115-2.

Bangake, C., & Eggoh, J. C. 2011. Further evidence on finance-growth causality: A panel data analysis. *Economic Systems*, 35(2), 176–188, https://doi.org/10.1016/j.ecosys.2010.07.001.

Beck, R., Georgiadis, G., Straub, R. 2014. The finance and growth nexus revisited. *Economics Letters*, 124(3), 382–385, https://doi.org/10.1016/j.econlet.2014.06.024.

Beck, T., & Levine, R. 2004. Stock markets, banks, and growth: panel evidence. *Journal of Banking and Finance*, 28(3), 423–442, https://doi.org/10.1016/S0378-4266(02)00408–9.

Beck, T. 2009. The econometrics of finance and growth, in: Mills T.C., Patterson K. (eds) *Palgrave Handbook of Econometrics*. Palgrave Macmillan, London. https://doi.org/10.1057/9780230244405.

Beck, T., Büyükkarabacak, B., Rioja, F. K., & Valev, N. T. 2012. Who gets the credit? And does it matter? Household vs. firm lending across countries. *The B.E. Journal of Macroeconomics*, 12(1), 1–46. https://doi.org/10.1515/1935-1690.2262.

Beck, T., Degryse, H., & Kneer, C. 2014. Is more finance better? Disentangling intermediation and size effects of financial systems. *Journal of Financial Stability*, 10, 50–64, https://doi.org/10.1016/j.jfs.2013.03.005.

Berglof, E. & Bolton, P. 2002. The great divide and beyond: Financial architecture in transition. *Journal of Economic Perspectives*, 16(1), 77–100, DOI: 10.1257/0895330027120.

Bongini, P., Iwanicz-Drozdowska, M., Smaga, P., Witkowski, B. 2017. Financial Development and Economic Growth: The Role of Foreign-Owned Banks in CESEE Countries, *Sustainability*, 9(335), 1–25, doi:10.3390/su9030335.

Botev, J., Égert, B., & Jawadi, F. 2019. The nonlinear relationship between economic growth and financial development: Evidence from developing, emerging and advanced economies. *International Economics*, 160, 3–13, https://doi.org/10.1016/j.inteco.2019.06.004.

Calderón, C., & Liu, L. 2003. The direction of causality between financial development and economic growth. *Journal of Development Economics*, 72(1), 321–334, https://doi.org/10.1016/S0304-3878(03)00079–8.

Caporale, G. M., Rault, C., Sova, A. D., Sova, R. 2015. Financial development and economic growth: Evidence from 10 new European union members. *International Journal of Finance and Economics*, 20, 48–60, https://doi.org/10.1002/ijfe.1498.

Cecchetti, G., & Kharroubi, E. 2012. *Reassessing the impact of finance on growth*. Bank for International Settlements. *BIS Working Papers* No. 381.

Chang, T., Lee, C.-C., & Chang, C.-H. 2014. Does insurance activity promote economic growth? Further evidence based on bootstrap panel Granger causality test. *The European Journal of Finance*, 20(12), 1187–1210, DOI: 10.1080/1351847X.2012.757555.

Cheng, C.-Y., Chien, M.-S., & Lee, C.-C. 2021. ICT diffusion, financial development, and economic growth: An international cross-country analysis. *Economic Modelling*, 94, 662–671, https://doi.org/10.1016/j.econmod.2020.02.008.

Christopoulos, D., & Tsionas, E. 2004. Financial development and economic growth: evidence from panel unit root and cointegration tests. *Journal of Development Economics*, 73(1), 55–74. https://doi.org/10.1016/j.jdeveco.2003.03.002.

Demetriades, P. O., & Rousseau, P. L. 2016. The changing face of financial development. *Economics Letters*, 141, 87–90, https://doi.org/10.1016/j.econlet.2016.02.009.

Demetriades, P., & Andrianova, S. 2004. Finance and growth: What we know and what we need to know, in: Goodhart C.A.E. (eds) *Financial Development and Economic Growth*. British Association for the Advancement of Science. Palgrave Macmillan, London. https://doi.org/10.1057/9780230374270_2.

Dumitrescu, E.-I., and C. Hurlin. 2012. Testing for Granger non-causality in heterogeneous panels. *Economic Modelling*, 29, 1450–1460.

Gantman, E. R., & Dabós, M. P. 2012. A fragile link? A new empirical analysis of the relationship between financial development and economic growth. *Oxford Development Studies*, 40(4), 517–532, DOI: 10.1080/13600818.2012.728582.

Granger, C. W. J. 1969. Investigating causal relations by econometric models and cross-spectral methods. *Econometrica*, 37, 424–438.

Handa, J., & Khan, S. R. 2008. Financial development and economic growth: a symbiotic relationship. *Applied Financial Economics*, 18(13), 1033–1049, DOI: 10.1080/09603100701477275.

Hsueh, S.-J., Hu, Y.-H., Tu, C.-H. 2013. Economic growth and financial development in Asian countries: A bootstrap panel Granger causality analysis. *Economic Modelling*, 32, 294–301, https://doi.org/10.1016/j.econmod.2013.02.027.

Im, K. S., M. H. Pesaran, and Y. Shin. 2003. Testing for unit roots in heterogeneous panels. *Journal of Econometrics*, 115, 53–74.

Iwanicz-Drozdowska, M., Bongini, P., Smaga, P., & Witkowski, B. 2018. *The Role of Foreign-Owned Banks in Post-Communist European Countries*, Palgrave Macmillan Studies in Economic Transition, Palgrave Macmillan, DOI: 10.1007/978-3-030-01111-6.

Iwanicz-Drozdowska, M., Smaga, P., & Witkowski, B. 2016. Financial development. Have post-communist countries converged? *Transformations in Business and Economics*, 15(2A) (38A), s. 389–414, 2016.

Kawa, P., Wajda-Lichy, M., Fijorek, K., & Denkowska, S. 2020. Do finance and trade foster economic growth in the new EU member States: Granger panel bootstrap causality approach. *Eastern European Economics*, 58(6), 458–477, DOI: 10.1080/00128775.2020.1762497.

Kindleberger, C.P. 1978. *Manias, Panics and Crashes*. Basic Books, New York.

King, R. G., & Levine, R. 1993. Finance and growth: Schumpeter might be right. *The Quarterly Journal of Economics*, 108(3), 717–737, https://doi.org/10.2307/2118406.

Koivu, T. 2002. *Do Efficient Banking Sectors Accelerate Economic Growth in Transition Countries*, BOFIT Discussion Paper, No. 14, Bank of Finland.

Levine, R., & Zervos, S. 1998. Stock markets, banks, and economic growth. *American Economic Review*, 88(3), 537–558.

Levine, R. 1997. Financial development and economic growth: Views and agenda. *Journal of Economic Literature*, 35(2), 688–726.

Levine, R. 2005. Finance and growth: Theory and evidence, in: P. Aghion, & S. N. Durlauf (Eds.), *Handbook of Economic Growth: Vol. 1A*, pp. 865–934, Elsevier.

Luintel, K. B., Khan, M., Leon-Gonzalez, R., & Li, G. 2016. Financial development, structure and growth: New data, method and results. *Journal of International Financial Markets, Institutions and Money*, 43, 95–112, https://doi.org/10.1016/j.intfin.2016.04.002.

Lyócsa, S. 2014. Growth-returns nexus: Evidence from three Central and Eastern European countries, *Economic Modelling*, 42, 343–355, https://doi.org/10.1016/j.econmod.2014.07.023.

Mhadhbi, K., Terzi, C. & Bouchrika, A. 2020. Banking sector development and economic growth in developing countries: a bootstrap panel Granger causality analysis. *Empirical Economics*, 58, 2817–2836, https://doi.org/10.1007/s00181-019-01670-z.

Minsky, H. P. 1992. *The Financial Instability Hypothesis*. The Jerome Levy Economics Institute Working Paper No. 74, Levy Economics Institute.

Mtar, K., & Belazreg, W. 2021. Causal nexus between innovation, financial development, and economic growth: The case of OECD countries. *Journal of the Knowledge Economy*, 12, 310–341, https://doi.org/10.1007/s13132-020-00628-2.

Nguyen, H. M., Le, Q. T.-T., Ho, C. M., Nguyen, T. C., & Vo, D. H. 2021. Does financial development matter for economic growth in the emerging markets? *Borsa Istanbul Review*, https://doi.org/10.1016/j.bir.2021.10.004.

Owen, A. L., & Temesvary, J. 2014. Heterogeneity in the growth and finance relationship: How does the impact of bank finance vary by country and type of lending? *International Review of Economics & Finance*, 31, 275–288, https://doi.org/10.1016/j.iref.2014.02.007.

Patrick, H. T. 1966. Financial development and economic growth in underdeveloped countries. *Economic Development and Cultural Change*, 14, 174–189, http://dx.doi.org/10.1086/450153.

Pesaran, M. H. 2007. A simple panel unit root test in the presence of cross-section dependence. *Journal of Applied Econometrics*, 22, 265–312.

Petkovski, M., & Kjosevski, J. 2014. Does banking sector development promote economic growth? An empirical analysis for selected countries in Central and South Eastern Europe. *Economic Research-Ekonomska Istraživanja*, 27(1), 55–66, DOI: 10.1080/1331677X.2014.947107.

Pradhan, R. P., Arvin, M. B., Hall, J. H., & Mahendhiran, N. 2016. Trade openness, foreign direct investment, and finance-growth nexus in the Eurozone countries. *Journal of International Trade & Economic Development*, 26(3), 336–360, DOI: 10.1080/09638199.2016.1249392.

Rajan, R. G., & Zingales, L. 1998. Financial dependence and growth. *The American Economic Review*, 88(3), 559–586.

Rousseau, P. L., & Wachtel, P. 2011. What is happening to the impact of financial deepening on economic growth? *Economic Inquiry*, 49, 276–288. https://doi.org/10.1111/j.1465-7295.2009.00197.x.

Schumpeter, J. A. 1911. *The Theory of Economic Development*, Cambridge, Harvard University Press.

Swamy, V., & Dharani, M. 2021. Thresholds in finance–growth nexus: Evidence from G-7 economies. *Australian Economic Papers*, 60(1), 1–40, DOI: 10.1111/1467–8454.12192.

Swamy, V., Dharani, M. 2019. The dynamics of finance-growth nexus in advanced economies. *International Review of Economics & Finance*, 64, 122–146, https://doi.org/10.1016/j.iref.2019.06.001.

Valickova, P., Havranek, T., & Horvath, R. 2015. Financial development and economic growth: a meta-analysis. *Journal of Economic Surveys*, 29, 506–526. https://doi.org/10.1111/joes.12068.

Wajda-Lichy, M., Kawa, P., Fijorek, K., & Denkowska, S. 2019. Trade openness and financial development in the new EU member states: Evidence from a granger panel bootstrap causality test. *Eastern European Economics*, 58(3), 242–263, DOI: 10.1080/00128775.2019.1701498.

World Bank, data.worldbank.org, access in February 2022.

APPENDIX 5.1

Dependent variable	*Independent variable*	*Crisis*	*Group of countries*	*Granger statistic*	*Granger p-value*	*DH statistic*	*DH p-value*
PROD	TB_5Y	GFC	All	29,628	0,000	3,054	0,034
PROD	TR	GFC	All	43,010	0,000	2,132	0,130
PROD	TB_5Y	GFC	New	2,698	0,441	0,726	0,484
PROD	TR	GFC	New	25,097	0,000	1,134	0,327
PROD	TB_5Y	GFC	Old	87,189	0,000	3,350	0,026
PROD	TR	GFC	Old	51,495	0,000	1,849	0,145
RETAIL	TB_5Y	GFC	All	28,221	0,000	−0,536	0,664
RETAIL	TR	GFC	All	0,993	0,803	2,144	0,128
RETAIL	TB_5Y	GFC	New	3,531	0,317	0,236	0,838
RETAIL	TR	GFC	New	3,255	0,354	0,449	0,687
RETAIL	TB_5Y	GFC	old	40,443	0,000	−0,861	0,418
RETAIL	TR	GFC	old	5,905	0,116	2,455	0,068
TB_5Y	UNEMP	GFC	all	1,077	0,584	−0,725	0,488
TB_5Y	PROD	GFC	all	4,671	0,097	−1,325	0,382
TB_5Y	RETAIL	GFC	all	1,004	0,605	0,487	0,679
TB_5Y	UNEMP	GFC	new	6,185	0,103	−0,732	0,455
TB_5Y	PROD	GFC	new	5,946	0,051	0,698	0,479
TB_5Y	RETAIL	GFC	new	6,320	0,097	−0,162	0,900
TB_5Y	UNEMP	GFC	old	3,521	0,061	0,136	0,903
TB_5Y	PROD	GFC	old	8,814	0,003	−1,395	0,340
TB_5Y	RETAIL	GFC	old	4,385	0,036	0,835	0,496
TR	UNEMP	GFC	all	25,512	0,000	0,698	0,616
TR	PROD	GFC	all	21,656	0,000	4,920	0,119
TR	RETAIL	GFC	all	10,635	0,014	4,431	0,036
TR	UNEMP	GFC	new	9,019	0,029	0,256	0,853
TR	PROD	GFC	new	7,509	0,057	3,577	0,070
TR	RETAIL	GFC	new	6,319	0,097	5,206	0,017
TR	UNEMP	GFC	old	15,383	0,002	0,709	0,566

(continued)

Dependent variable	*Independent variable*	*Crisis*	*Group of countries*	*Granger statistic*	*Granger p-value*	*DH statistic*	*DH p-value*
TR	PROD	GFC	old	21,117	0,000	3,400	0,138
TR	RETAIL	GFC	old	16,335	0,001	1,334	0,307
UNEMP	TB_5Y	GFC	all	5,478	0,019	−0,183	0,868
UNEMP	TR	GFC	all	0,000	0,993	−0,666	0,599
UNEMP	TB_5Y	GFC	new	1,016	0,313	0,311	0,743
UNEMP	TR	GFC	new	0,046	0,830	−0,024	0,983
UNEMP	TB_5Y	GFC	old	4,086	0,043	−0,489	0,646
UNEMP	TR	GFC	old	0,066	0,797	−0,875	0,450
UNEMP	TB_5Y	PIIGS	all	0,311	0,577	−0,729	0,459
UNEMP	TB_5Y	PIIGS	old	0,491	0,484	−0,497	0,621
UNEMP	TB_5Y	PIIGS	new	6,946	0,008	0,176	0,864
UNEMP	TR	PIIGS	all	0,484	0,487	−1,230	0,305
UNEMP	TR	PIIGS	old	0,299	0,584	0,072	0,954
UNEMP	TR	PIIGS	new	1,576	0,209	−1,916	0,070
PROD	TB_5Y	PIIGS	all	8,551	0,036	0,638	0,553
PROD	TB_5Y	PIIGS	old	6,156	0,104	1,568	0,100
PROD	TB_5Y	PIIGS	new	10,282	0,016	−1,036	0,227
PROD	TR	PIIGS	all	4,068	0,254	−0,187	0,883
PROD	TR	PIIGS	old	6,142	0,105	−0,331	0,795
PROD	TR	PIIGS	new	2,218	0,528	0,088	0,932
RETAIL	TB_5Y	PIIGS	all	18,619	0,000	−0,987	0,398
RETAIL	TB_5Y	PIIGS	old	23,934	0,000	−0,071	0,946
RETAIL	TB_5Y	PIIGS	new	3,536	0,171	−0,753	0,444
RETAIL	TR	PIIGS	all	2,243	0,524	0,010	0,991
RETAIL	TR	PIIGS	old	3,226	0,358	0,362	0,762
RETAIL	TR	PIIGS	new	10,686	0,014	0,121	0,915
TB_5Y	UNEMP	PIIGS	all	0,154	0,695	0,643	0,503
TB_5Y	UNEMP	PIIGS	old	1,012	0,314	−0,627	0,498
TB_5Y	UNEMP	PIIGS	new	0,654	0,419	1,918	0,054
TB_5Y	PROD	PIIGS	all	7,877	0,049	1,449	0,191

TB_5Y	PROD	PIIGS	old	13,539	0,004	1,704	0,102
TB_5Y	PROD	PIIGS	new	1,247	0,264	0,138	0,885
TB_5Y	RETAIL	PIIGS	all	12,721	0,000	2,086	0,096
TB_5Y	RETAIL	PIIGS	old	7,993	0,005	1,007	0,361
TB_5Y	RETAIL	PIIGS	new	0,065	0,798	2,189	0,054
TR	UNEMP	PIIGS	all	2,819	0,420	−0,492	0,642
TR	UNEMP	PIIGS	old	4,039	0,257	−0,788	0,438
TR	UNEMP	PIIGS	new	0,671	0,880	0,139	0,889
TR	PROD	PIIGS	all	13,326	0,004	1,348	0,320
TR	PROD	PIIGS	old	9,412	0,024	1,303	0,262
TR	PROD	PIIGS	new	19,364	0,000	0,567	0,624
TR	RETAIL	PIIGS	all	12,948	0,005	1,523	0,325
TR	RETAIL	PIIGS	old	12,907	0,005	0,708	0,643
TR	RETAIL	PIIGS	new	12,131	0,007	1,504	0,203
PROD	TB_5Y	Greece	all	13,685	0,003	0,887	0,393
PROD	TR	Greece	all	1,886	0,596	−0,565	0,615
PROD	TB_5Y	Greece	new	17,570	0,001	0,938	0,340
PROD	TR	Greece	new	7,788	0,051	−0,062	0,961
PROD	TB_5Y	Greece	old	1,903	0,593	0,351	0,736
PROD	TR	Greece	old	0,502	0,918	−0,697	0,586
RETAIL	TB_5Y	Greece	all	0,843	0,839	−0,856	0,434
RETAIL	TR	Greece	all	0,240	0,971	−0,592	0,619
RETAIL	TB_5Y	Greece	new	0,629	0,890	−0,425	0,654
RETAIL	TR	Greece	new	3,043	0,385	1,554	0,112
RETAIL	TB_5Y	Greece	old	0,960	0,811	−0,201	0,839
RETAIL	TR	Greece	old	0,083	0,994	−1,187	0,297
TB_5Y	UNEMP	Greece	all	0,037	0,848	−1,181	0,218
TB_5Y	PROD	Greece	all	1,256	0,262	−0,570	0,640
TB_5Y	RETAIL	Greece	all	30,270	0,000	−0,026	0,990
TB_5Y	UNEMP	Greece	new	1,428	0,232	−1,011	0,264
TB_5Y	PROD	Greece	new	1,642	0,200	−0,217	0,845
TB_5Y	RETAIL	Greece	new	47,749	0,000	0,042	0,984

(continued)

Dependent variable	*Independent variable*	*Crisis*	*Group of countries*	*Granger statistic*	*Granger p-value*	*DH statistic*	*DH p-value*
TB_5Y	UNEMP	Greece	old	0,807	0,369	−0,680	0,469
TB_5Y	PROD	Greece	old	0,076	0,782	−0,570	0,603
TB_5Y	RETAIL	Greece	old	0,006	0,936	−0,073	0,957
TR	UNEMP	Greece	all	6,785	0,079	−0,385	0,698
TR	PROD	Greece	all	7,686	0,053	−1,175	0,396
TR	RETAIL	Greece	all	532,355	0,000	−0,928	0,545
TR	UNEMP	Greece	new	11,675	0,009	−0,575	0,585
TR	PROD	Greece	new	47,374	0,000	−1,067	0,321
TR	RETAIL	Greece	new	67,546	0,000	−0,277	0,806
TR	UNEMP	Greece	old	2,606	0,456	−0,009	0,992
TR	PROD	Greece	old	1,247	0,742	−0,627	0,636
TR	RETAIL	Greece	old	72,052	0,000	−0,990	0,488
UNEMP	TB_5Y	Greece	all	1,785	0,182	−0,001	0,999
UNEMP	TR	Greece	all	0,466	0,495	−0,740	0,484
UNEMP	TB_5Y	Greece	new	0,390	0,532	0,843	0,399
UNEMP	TR	Greece	new	0,081	0,775	−0,137	0,897
UNEMP	TB_5Y	Greece	old	1,825	0,177	−0,756	0,446
UNEMP	TR	Greece	old	0,505	0,477	−0,862	0,434
COVID_RESP	UNEMP	COVID	all	97,000	0,000	2,217	0,051
COVID_RESP	PROD	COVID	all	544,146	0,000	5,049	0,026
COVID_RESP	RETAIL	COVID	all	159,927	0,000	3,863	0,056
COVID_RESP	TB_5Y	COVID	all	57,014	0,000	8,182	0,000
COVID_RESP	TR	COVID	all	94,225	0,000	6,879	0,015
COVID_RESP	UNEMP	COVID	new	3,262	0,353	1,962	0,057
COVID_RESP	PROD	COVID	new	372,701	0,000	7,312	0,012
COVID_RESP	RETAIL	COVID	new	122,746	0,000	2,008	0,096
COVID_RESP	TB_5Y	COVID	new	17,038	0,001	10,511	0,000
COVID_RESP	TR	COVID	new	170,008	0,000	6,009	0,015
COVID_RESP	UNEMP	COVID	old	157,667	0,000	1,203	0,135

COVID_RESP	PROD	COVID	old	252,745	0,000	5,445	0,010
COVID_RESP	RETAIL	COVID	old	63,405	0,000	0,799	0,492
COVID_RESP	TB_5Y	COVID	old	197,918	0,000	1,576	0,131
COVID_RESP	TR	COVID	old	81,114	0,000	9,373	0,030
COVID_STRING	UNEMP	COVID	all	62,626	0,000	2,732	0,040
COVID_STRING	PROD	COVID	all	383,369	0,000	4,134	0,057
COVID_STRING	RETAIL	COVID	all	84,775	0,000	0,664	0,641
COVID_STRING	TB_5Y	COVID	all	14,660	0,002	1,814	0,101
COVID_STRING	TR	COVID	all	119,627	0,000	2,374	0,080
COVID_STRING	UNEMP	COVID	new	7625,288	0,000	0,771	0,410
COVID_STRING	PROD	COVID	new	625,810	0,000	2,627	0,104
COVID_STRING	RETAIL	COVID	new	68,707	0,000	1,386	0,198
COVID_STRING	TB_5Y	COVID	new	4,890	0,180	1,402	0,124
COVID_STRING	TR	COVID	new	921,473	0,000	2,019	0,078
COVID_STRING	UNEMP	COVID	old	80,007	0,000	1,270	0,129
COVID_STRING	PROD	COVID	old	192,681	0,000	2,627	0,054
COVID_STRING	RETAIL	COVID	old	16,835	0,001	−0,356	0,744
COVID_STRING	TB_5Y	COVID	old	248,399	0,000	1,180	0,211
COVID_STRING	TR	COVID	old	49,438	0,000	1,364	0,232
PROD	TB_5Y	COVID	all	99,920	0,000	6,498	0,008
PROD	TR	COVID	all	494,102	0,000	65,386	0,005
PROD	TB_5Y	COVID	new	54,783	0,000	1,462	0,146
PROD	TR	COVID	new	225,469	0,000	55,404	0,004
PROD	TB_5Y	COVID	old	57,704	0,000	7,195	0,007
PROD	TR	COVID	old	318,093	0,000	37,756	0,012
RETAIL	TB_5Y	COVID	all	30,524	0,000	3,325	0,057
RETAIL	TR	COVID	all	303,013	0,000	34,060	0,005
RETAIL	TB_5Y	COVID	new	16,252	0,001	1,681	0,117
RETAIL	TR	COVID	new	126,988	0,000	30,919	0,001
RETAIL	TB_5Y	COVID	old	13,359	0,004	2,904	0,063
RETAIL	TR	COVID	old	279,238	0,000	17,984	0,012
TB_5Y	UNEMP	COVID	all	5,108	0,024	0,173	0,901

(continued)

Dependent variable	*Independent variable*	*Crisis*	*Group of countries*	*Granger statistic*	*Granger p-value*	*DH statistic*	*DH p-value*
TB_5Y	PROD	COVID	all	110,559	0,000	0,861	0,572
TB_5Y	RETAIL	COVID	all	16,148	0,000	2,877	0,077
TB_5Y	UNEMP	COVID	new	0,094	0,760	1,200	0,183
TB_5Y	PROD	COVID	new	58,311	0,000	0,150	0,901
TB_5Y	RETAIL	COVID	new	0,445	0,505	0,455	0,655
TB_5Y	UNEMP	COVID	old	6,109	0,013	−0,756	0,484
TB_5Y	PROD	COVID	old	48,104	0,000	0,989	0,438
TB_5Y	RETAIL	COVID	old	77,331	0,000	3,287	0,054
TR	UNEMP	COVID	all	1,017	0,797	−1,711	0,274
TR	PROD	COVID	all	27,334	0,000	0,960	0,722
TR	RETAIL	COVID	all	36,361	0,000	−0,069	0,978
TR	UNEMP	COVID	new	5,377	0,146	−0,758	0,502
TR	PROD	COVID	new	51,001	0,000	1,393	0,388
TR	RETAIL	COVID	new	17,191	0,001	1,264	0,327
TR	UNEMP	COVID	old	1,704	0,636	−1,620	0,264
TR	PROD	COVID	old	7,662	0,054	0,015	0,995
TR	RETAIL	COVID	old	31,110	0,000	−1,232	0,488
UNEMP	TB_5Y	COVID	all	0,338	0,561	4,528	0,010
UNEMP	TR	COVID	all	6,526	0,011	9,281	0,010
UNEMP	TB_5Y	COVID	new	0,101	0,751	0,397	0,712
UNEMP	TR	COVID	new	2,814	0,093	11,982	0,004
UNEMP	TB_5Y	COVID	old	0,798	0,372	5,521	0,006
UNEMP	TR	COVID	old	4,737	0,030	8,857	0,002

6 Challenges ahead

In this monograph we addressed four research hypotheses. Our conclusions presented in this chapter refer to these hypotheses and explain the challenges for the future.

Having analyzed the recent anti-crisis responses of safety net institutions, it is clear that they have learned their lessons from the GFC. In contrast to the GFC, at the onset of the pandemic, the financial system was in a much better situation (e.g. in terms of capital and liquidity), which was due to regulatory and supervisory overhaul post-GFC. This led to higher loss-absorbing capacity and allowed financial stability to be maintained in the post-COVID-19 era, as opposed to the full-blown financial crisis that erupted in 2007. In Europe, the banking sector weathered the pandemic crisis well and rather than being part of the problem (as in the GFC), it can currently be seen as part of the solution. Early 2020 economies faced a huge drop in retail trade and production, but the banking system did not amplify the economic disruptions. This allows us to confirm the first hypothesis (H1). Consequently, a regulatory overhaul of financial system regulations after the COVID-19 crisis is unlikely, as opposed to the regulatory tsunami post-GFC. Still, some fine-tuning of regulations should be expected in the coming years.

While the origins and reasons behind the GFC, PIIGS and COVID-19 pandemic could not be more different, the policy responses in all crises were essentially the same. In early 2020, central banks were quick to implement monetary easing (including lower interest rates, expansion of QE) and fiscal authorities introduced ample support schemes. The difference is in the prudential response, in the case of which prudential authorities eased bank requirements. As explained in Chapter 2, there were no "typical" macroprudential tools in the pre-GFC era. This shows that initial policy easing in response to the COVID-19 outbreak was coordinated and is an example of an effective policy mix. However, as the economies recovered from the pandemic at a different pace in Europe, tightening of economic policies ("normalization") will likely occur at divergent speeds in the face of re-emerging systemic risks. Additionally, given the unprecedented size and scale of policy support, understanding its impact and effectiveness is essential to assess any side effects for financial stability that it might create over the medium term.

DOI: 10.4324/9781003225539-6

The massive pandemic fiscal support, although justified given the scale of economic damage caused by mandatory lockdowns, has side effects. In many European countries the increases of the pandemic public debt were in fact financed through renewed asset purchases by central banks. Thus, one of the legacies of the COVID-19 outbreak is the accumulation of risks to the stability of public finances. Costs of servicing public debt were low given the prevalence of low-interest environment post-GFC. The steep decline in output in 2020, combined with the ample fiscal policy response to the COVID-19 pandemic, led to a substantial deterioration of fiscal balances and higher accumulation of government debt than in the case of the GFC, and at a faster speed. Excessive debt stock, along with gradual withdrawal of monetary (e.g. possibility of interest rate hikes) and of fiscal support, create challenges for the sustainability of high levels of both private and public debt. Currently, the debt overhang weighs on investment and economic growth prospects in the medium term. Such trends fuel the risk of a "debt trap," in which it would be increasingly difficult to raise interest rates without causing economic damage to overindebted economies at the same time. Another challenge is the cyclical vulnerabilities in residential real estate markets, which despite pandemic shock continue to exacerbate in many European countries, leading to overvaluation of property prices. This trend was driven by both demand and supply factors (strong lending growth, gradual relaxation of credit scoring standards, low interest on mortgage loans and the post-pandemic economic rebound). As a result, risks related to the procyclicality and household indebtedness continue to mount. The effects of government interventions in response to the pandemic crisis may also have more long-term consequences on public finances. Part of the support was implemented through measures having a direct impact on the public revenues and expenditure, and such measures directly affect budget balance and, consequently, the stock of public debt. Nevertheless, a large bulk of the liquidity support (mainly in the form of guarantees) did not deteriorate fiscal balances. Moreover, through guarantee fees – the budget result improved. The magnitude of such support raises concerns, however, about the fiscal position in the future. If the guarantees are called upon, additional public spending will be required.

Another medium-term challenge is the need to replenish the policy buffers, in particular monetary, fiscal, and prudential, which were depleted in response to pandemic shock. Low interest rates, inflated central bank balance sheets, record levels of public and private debt, and released capital buffers, all severely limit the available policy space in the case of future unexpected shocks (like new COVID-19 variants) and expose the European economy to vulnerabilities. The pandemic shock clearly underlined the need to have policy buffers for adverse developments, even those not envisaged in stress tests (the "unknown unknown" factors). Therefore, as the European economy slowly recovers, rebuilding policy space has to be a priority. Although elevated uncertainty calls for a cautious approach when implementing the "exit strategy" from stimuli, this should not justify policy inaction or continuation of support for "zombie" entities leading to the ineffective allocation of resources in the economy. Further, as central banks and other authorities have taken extraordinary measures to support the economy and financial markets both during the GFC and in the COVID-19 era, it creates the impression that there will always be a backstop to support financial institutions and limit their losses. This unhealthy market perception could lead to more risk-taking among investors, foster moral hazard and ultimately undermine financial stability. A timely reversal of support measures would partly mitigate this issue. In the case of monetary policy, it would include tapering, i.e. slowing the pace of purchases and eventually stopping them completely, followed by gradual reduction of the stock of purchased securities and ultimately deflating the central bank balance sheet, retrenching from its market-making role. Phasing-out QE could be accompanied by increases in policy interest rates. As for prudential policies, announcing buffer requirements increases in advance would be advised, which in fact has already started to take place in some EU countries. Additionally, central banks, after a long period of low inflation, accompanied by low interest rates, in the post-pandemic period have begun to face the problem of high negative real interest rates in the environment of increasing inflation. This is another challenge, the policy response to which would impact the quality of bank assets in the coming years.

The immediate deterioration of asset quality in the EU banking sector in reaction to pandemic shock was averted due to the massive policy support. The aggregate macroeconomic risks have (so far) not fully translated into corporate losses and the overall level of corporate insolvencies in the EU remains low. However, historically, bank losses lag severe recessions by a couple of years. Consequently, the question arises of how to manage economies, which are slowly transitioning from experiencing an acute illiquidity phase to the solvency phase of the pandemic crisis. As the pandemic-induced stimuli are to expire or are gradually being withdrawn, the worsening of the bank loan portfolio is likely to be expected (already observed increase in the share of Stage 2 and Stage 3 loans in EU banks), especially in exposures to sectors most vulnerable to the pandemic shock (e.g. accommodation and entertainment). This calls for regular monitoring and addressing emerging asset quality problems early. Moreover, any judicial and procedural impediments to effective resolution of NPLs, both on national and European levels, should be pre-emptively reduced. Due to the fact that the legal framework for financial institutions is very broad and complex, it is worth considering developing a simpler regulatory framework for small- and medium-sized banks and other financial institutions to reduce the compliance costs. Although some changes in line with proportionality principle may be observed, they do not seem to be sufficient.

This allows us to confirm our second hypothesis (H2) in the case of monetary and regulatory measures, as well as in the case of the fiscal policy. The GFC hit primarily advanced economies, and although its subsequent effects were felt throughout Europe, the impact was very different in individual countries, and the needs in terms of the scale and directions of government intervention also varied. The pandemic crisis hit almost all countries in Europe at the same time, and the imposed restrictions forced the immediate launch of stimulus packages. Despite the swift response of individual countries, supported by measures at the EU level (such as temporary state aid rules, activation of the general escape clause), the strong decline in economic activity was not contained. Nevertheless, government interventions enabled a very quick rebound in GDP, but – due to the further waves of the disease, the pandemic affected the economy also in the following year, and an extension of interventions turned out to be necessary.

After the GFC, which forced a significant involvement of public funds to support financial institutions, many measures were taken to reduce the dependence of banks on the government in crisis situations. It was necessary due to the significant impact of the aid granted to banks on the fiscal position of individual countries, which in extreme cases could lead to government default (sovereign-bank nexus). The GFC showed the weakness of the fiscal framework and thus led to far-reaching changes to strengthen fiscal surveillance. Numerical fiscal rules were given great importance, but in the face of the pandemic, they also turned out to be problematic. Escape clauses (if provided) may be too strict to respond to such large shocks. However, the suspension or ongoing amendments of the rules may seriously undermine fiscal sustainability in the long run. Therefore, it seems that some flexibility would be advisable here, allowing for an adequate fiscal reaction, but the conditions under which it would be applied should be strictly defined and monitored on an ongoing basis by independent bodies. The applicable fiscal rules often turned out to be additionally very complicated, which made their independent surveillance difficult. They also did not introduce any incentives to create fiscal buffers in times of better economic conditions. The pandemic crisis showed that the value of implemented fiscal packages was largely dependent on the fiscal space of individual countries, which was often insufficient. Failure to adjust interventions to actual needs may result in deepening economic divergences between European countries.

Last but not least, two new systemic risks gained prominence during the pandemic – cyber and climate risks. The challenge is the development of the prudential framework and tools to mitigate them. New responsibilities need to be divided among safety net institutions, without a negative impact on their hitherto mandates.

First, the increase in digitalization of financial services and the switch to remote work during the pandemic led to higher exposure of financial institutions to operational risk, specifically cyber risk. The incidence of cyber-attacks has surged since the onset of the pandemic and the occurrence of a major cyber incident might trigger contagion, cause erosion of confidence in the financial system, and ultimately impair the provision of critical economic functions. Rising cyber risk vulnerabilities are not sufficiently monitored, nor covered by the safety net in its current state, while cyber resilience remains largely untested. Thus, there are gaps in cyber risk regulations and mitigation procedures, both on the national and EU levels. Additionally, crypto assets based on advanced technologies may pose an additional threat to the stability of the financial system. So far, their regulation is at a very early stage and focused mostly on anti-money laundering aspects.

Second, the looming climate change with the increased frequency of extreme weather-related disasters is a source of risk to the financial system. Both the exposures to physical climate hazards and to emissions-intensive firms are leading to higher credit risk, especially when financial markets would abruptly reprice the risk associated with climate change and ongoing transition to the green economy. Still, financial safety net response to climate risks remains muted so far. Further, financial institutions need to incorporate ESG risk-related considerations into their business strategies, governance structures and risk management frameworks to increase their resilience against ESG factors and risks, which is required by new EU regulations, including taxonomy and disclosures. This direction, however, may be slowed down due to increasing energy prices ("green inflation") and the need to normalize economic policies in the post-pandemic period. In other words, *too many cooks spoil the broth*, which means that prioritization of necessary policy steps is needed to return to normal.

Financial markets experienced a series of crises of various origins but of similar effect: volatility rises and liquidity drops. The reason for this behaviour of market prices is straightforward: a rise in uncertainty limits the market credibility, enhancing risk aversion and worsening market sentiment. These effects are especially visible in emerging markets that are more sensitive to contagion. Based on a literature review and case studies, we verified these phenomena in line with our third hypothesis (H3). Furthermore, we focused on the impact of monetary, fiscal and regulatory tools implemented in the aftermath of the crises, which had significant implications on markets in terms of prices, volatility and liquidity.

The anti-crisis tools, on the one hand, have stabilizing effects, decreasing cost of funds and augmenting market transparency. Moreover, stemmed volatility of prices underpins our hypothesis that the mixture of central bank activities and new regulations can have a positive effect on limiting the scope of uncertainty and eventually stabilizing the market. On the other hand, we witness some side effects. First, the over-liquidity caused by the QE can create some bubbles on the equity markets that are sensitive to tampering announcements. Second, negative interest rates in developed countries fuel speculative investments in high-yield emerging markets, which can have detrimental effects on their long-term stability. Third, regulatory constraints limiting leverage and proprietary trading assisted by the price transparency can hamper market liquidity, curbing market makers' motivation to quote competitive prices.

From the viewpoint of the financial market, the GFC and PIIGS crises were similar due to strong linkages between economic slowdown and market instrument liquidity. This affected the markets with more developed financial instruments that were transmitters of the adverse shocks. However, contagion processes affected the sentiment also in emerging markets. The pandemic crisis was different due to its non-economic origin and profound impact on the real economy. Nonetheless, the shock to the financial market was short-lived due to immediate expectation of fiscal stimulus.

While exploring the connection between finance (the tail) and growth (real economy, the dog), we found that the PIIGS crisis was not relevant from a causality perspective, but two other crisis events showed the link between finance and the real economy. For the GFC, our findings confirmed that causality exists, and its direction varies between "new" and "old" European countries. In "old" countries, it was the financial sphere that impacted the real sector, while in "new" countries, the situation in the real economy impacted the financial sphere. This may be attributed mostly to the difference in the levels of financial development, which is far lower in "new" European countries, and almost no involvement in the "toxic" financial instruments. However, these are probably not the only reasons. These differences may be explained also by the role foreign capital plays in "new" European markets. As "new" countries did not suffer directly from the default of "toxic" financial instruments, they suffered indirectly via ownership links because the capital providers from "old" countries had to reduce their investments. The international investors were involved not only in the financial sector but also in the industry and services sector.

As the COVID-19 crisis hit all countries, such differences between "old" and "new" countries were not detected for the pandemic crisis. During this period, it was the "tail" that wagged the "dog," keeping in mind that the financial sphere reacted first with a sharp decline of asset prices, but then recovered promptly. As already underlined, the banking sector remained safe during the COVID-19 crisis and the problems originated mostly in the real economy, supported by fiscal packages and relaxed monetary policy. As confirmed by our analysis, the response to the pandemic impacted the "dog" and the "tail."

Therefore, we provide support for our last research hypothesis (H4), however, partly also for (H2), as the response measures to the COVID-19 pandemic were confirmed by our analysis to impact the real economy and the financial sphere. The interplay between finance and the real economy requires further analysis for various phases of the economic cycle. Our focus was on the periods around episodes of crisis to show the differences between them. One of the key challenges is the selection of measures of finance and the real economy that may embrace all important aspects. This is due to the fact that the structure and the role especially of finance have been evolving over recent decades. For example, the role of crypto assets is not reflected in typical measures of financial spheres, but their importance has been growing. The same applies to shadow banking activities. Moreover, as central bank digital currencies would develop in the future, they might substantially reshape the financial landscape. All of this may require revision of the way the finance-growth nexus is analyzed.

6.1 Epilogue

On 24 February 2022, Russia attacked Ukraine and started military conflict which triggered a new crisis wave, this time of a geopolitical nature. This military conflict has direct consequences for the societies involved, but may also have consequences for other nations, facing new economic challenges and another immigration crisis. Additionally, a wide range of measures and sanctions were undertaken by different countries and allies, and the consequences are in many cases far-reaching.

In the first week of the war, financial markets witnessed a severe rise in risk aversion. Firstly, this affected the Russian markets, which were hit by economic sanctions. The Moscow stock exchange was suspended, and the ruble lost most of its value. The rise of the global uncertainty had a strong impact also on the neighbouring CEE countries: on the first day of the war, the Warsaw stock exchange lost 15%, Hungarian 10% and Romanian 5%. Also, local currencies lost ground against the euro. However, developed economies were also affected: the German DAX lost 4% and the euro was 2% weaker against the US dollar. The price gainers are obvious: gold, the Swiss franc and bitcoin, which rose immediately in value. However, the US economy reacted positively, with S&P500 over 5% higher than before the Russian invasion. Long-term bond yields are 30bp lower, as the market expects more expansionary monetary policy to help market liquidity and credibility. The key global economic risk is related to inflation, as energy prices (crude oil and gas) skyrocketed compared to the period before the outbreak of the conflict.

In the European banking sector, on the country level, the exposures to Russia and Ukraine mostly comprise of loans and are overall limited, thus direct contagion is expected to be low. Subsidiaries of Russian banks were not wide-spread in Europe and their presence is limited mostly to a couple of post-communist countries covered by our analysis (e.g. Hungary, Croatia, the Czech Republic) and other countries such as Austria, Cyprus, Germany, Italy, Switzerland and the UK. Although the stakes on the markets are rather low, soon after the outbreak of the war, Sberbank Europe (Austrian entity owned by Sberbank of Russia, which is a state-owned entity) and its subsidiaries faced liquidity problems, which led them to collapse. Sberbank entered the Central European market in 2011 by purchasing a stake in Austria's Volksbank, which experienced serious financial problems as a result of too aggressive a business policy. As Volksbank owned some banks in CESEE countries, Russian capital entered their markets in this way. On 1 March 2022, the Single Resolution Board decided that the resolution would be applied to Sberbank Europe's subsidiaries in Croatia and Slovenia. In both cases, they were acquired by the key institutions in the respective countries. The purpose of these decisions was to maintain stability in the banking markets of the two countries. In the case of Sberbank Europe, no public interest was identified and therefore this entity was subjected to a regular insolvency procedure, based on national legislation, providing protection to depositors. In other countries outside the banking union, where subsidiaries of Sberbank Europe operated, they were resolved with applicable tools.

These are the first consequences of this geopolitical crisis; however, many others may be observed in the future depending on how long this conflict lasts and how severe it is. Potential medium-term consequences of the war might include the risk of stagflation, resulting from higher energy prices and increased global uncertainty leading to – along with a return to restrictive monetary policy – a drop in consumer confidence, ultimately dimming economic growth prospects in Europe.

Index

Note: Page numbers in *italics* indicate figures and in **bold** indicate tables on the corresponding pages.

For Product Safety Concerns and Information please contact our EU representative GPSR@taylorandfrancis.com
Taylor & Francis Verlag GmbH, Kaufingerstraße 24, 80331 München, Germany

www.ingramcontent.com/pod-product-compliance
Ingram Content Group UK Ltd.
Pitfield, Milton Keynes, MK11 3LW, UK
UKHW020002200926
475702UK00015B/2441

9781032126425